Praise for *Rebel Heart: Against the Wind*

"I liked the details that show the author's confidence building . . . Rising from the ashes of betrayal is a journey that strengthens. With a passion for justice, and a will to speak for her truth, the author inspires these traits in all of us."

Margalee Pilkington Wright, former mayor, Wichita, Kansas

"From the red-brick streets of Russell, Kansas, to the steps of the Supreme Court of the United States, this rebel heart leads us through her many life-changing experiences. A gifted and insightful writer, she presents her story—rich in high hopes, intelligence, and compassion. I was particularly drawn in by her portrayals of the modern complexities surrounding gender, race, age, and religion—not to mention her deeply personal involvements with frightened university administrators and a flawed legal system. A great read. I loved it!"

Yvette Leerskov Ehrlich, Attorney at Law

"Marietta Anderson's language is filled with action, moving through a life complete with grit, moxie, courage, and persistence. The writing is bold, agile, and lyrical, highlighting a time perhaps undervalued. *Rebel Heart* is rich in historical detail of a life peopled with vivid scenes and situations. An independent heart seeking and revealing the truth of an American life."

Jack Wright, professor, musician

"An intimate story of courage, conviction, and sheer energy against a tide of prevailing injustices . . . riveting accounts of activism, offering a private archive of social movement history and the '60's . . . inspiring resilience in the face of personal betrayal, Anderson seeks her horizon and finds it."

Anna Spradlin, PhD, Equal Opportunity Specialist/Mediator (ret.), Office for Civil Rights, USDHH

"True to the essential purpose of memoirs, *Rebel Heart* chronicles the author's discovery and development as an advocate for justice and equality. Those endeavors, set in the tumultuous turmoil of the 1960s and '70s, are important not only for their own intrinsic worth but also as a powerful reminder of the need to stand up for justice and equality now. Inevitably, the *Rebel Heart* challenges us to ponder our own potential rebel stance in the present moment."

L. Keith Williamson, Associate Professor Emeritus, Elliott School of Communication, WSU, Wichita, Kansas

". . . A compelling story . . . As a student in the 1960s, she distributed pamphlets the university judged seditious, which resulted in a lawsuit that went all the way to the Supreme Court. In a clear, understandable style, Ms. Anderson describes her clash with East Tennessee State University over free speech. Continuing her commitment to stand up for the poor and disenfranchised, she joined the first voting rights march in Selma that saw such appalling police violence that it became known as Bloody Sunday."

Charli Frederick, Director of Media Services, Media Resources Center, Wichita State University (ret.)

"This small-town Kansas native won me over when, upon the loss of her high school debate partner to cheerleading, she declared, 'I couldn't understand why anyone would give up a chance to argue.' She describes her frightening 1965 trip to Selma and sees Bloody Sunday up close. When the university administration accuses her of seditious activity, she sues the university in a case that would land at the Supreme Court. She confirms the FBI recorded her conversations when she requests and receives a copy of her FBI file. This Boomer recommends this refresher course in the 1960s and '70s to fellow Boomers, as well as following generations."

Nancy Robinson, Owner (ret.) Best of Times Card & Gift Shop, Wichita, Kansas

REBEL HEART

REBEL
HEART

Against the Wind

MARIETTA ANDERSON

POST ROCK PRESS
KNOXVILLE, TN

ISBN: 979-8-9875793-4-3
Library of Congress Control Number: 2025907602

Post Rock Press
P.O. Box 24314
Knoxville, TN 37933
postrockpress.org

Do what you feel in your heart to be right—for you'll be criticized anyway.

—*Eleanor Roosevelt*

Kites and airplanes take off into the wind.

—*Anonymous*

Contents

1. THE EARLY YEARS

Origins

Born with a smile on my face and big black eyes welcoming the world, I quickly learned to speak the words read to me. Fairy tales were easy. I liked the dictionary, the encyclopedia, the newspaper.

Teachers called me precocious, imaginative, inventive, and outspoken. I fiercely protected others from mockery, as I had learned to defend myself from bullies. Recognizing injustice seemed to be second nature. Since I first learned to put my shoes on by myself, I alternated between feet. One day, I put the left shoe on first; the next day, the right. It was only fair.

Sometimes my words offended others, and I learned people don't appreciate a youngster who scolds them, satirizes their beliefs, or seems to know more than they do. But words hurt me when they expressed prejudice or lies.

By the time I was 20 years old, I had learned the power, the sting, and the value of words. Words could lift a protest into a movement, could turn a student into a threat, could bring a burning cross to a front yard in the middle of the day. Words could shatter a marriage before it had found its footing.

Words could make a woman stand alone when she had spent years learning to fight for others.

This is the story of how I found my voice—and what it cost me.

———————

My family is a mixture of WASPs, with ties to indigenous peoples and African-Americans. One characteristic flowing through this diverse family tree is a strong sense of independence and the will to survive.

Family is central to our survival. Education is the path to quality of life, career, and fulfillment. Hard work is necessary to become successful, but it is also its own reward.

I was born in Hutchinson, Kansas, in 1943 to hard-working parents who knew each other in their McPherson, Kansas, high school.

Mother did not know her father, because he left her and her mother not long after she was born. Her mother remarried, and the new family came with older stepbrothers and a stepsister. The family grew to include two half-brothers and a half-sister.

Mother's stepfather was part of a crew that built grain elevators in western Kansas in the 1920s and 1930s. The families sometimes lived near the railroads and elevators in ramshackle dwellings. Mother's adult siblings were carpenters, painters, and gardeners. People grew their own food and housed chickens.

Dad had eight siblings, five sisters and three brothers. To do this, his mother had to be pregnant for twenty years. Everybody worked. Kids ran errands and held part-time jobs at grocery or hardware stores. Dad's father was a janitor, had a coffee stand at city hall in McPherson, and in his earlier years played semipro baseball.

The Andersons had two gardens where they grew potatoes, turnips, rutabagas, cucumbers, tomatoes, peppers, herbs, strawberries, apricots, pears, and apples. Root vegetables went to the cellar, and Grandma canned vegetables and fruits.

The only time fruit preserves were absent from the kitchen or dining room tables was when as many as eight people gathered to throw cards on the table in the frenzied card game "Oh, Hell," a chaotic match where everyone plays solitaire on each other's cards.

Hutchinson, with a population of about 30,000, was an agricultural community but also supported a Heinz pickle and apple butter factory and the Rainbo Bread bakery. Wheat farms, which refugees from Russia and Germany planted after they settled, surrounded the city. The aroma of bread baking and the act of smearing it with apple butter made my mouth water, but the straw board factory broadcast very stinky odors.

At 18 months of age, I faced an event that left an indelible impression—not just for the pain it caused, but for the way my family helped me recover and thrive.

Our house in Hutchinson had hardwood floors. In the hallway off the living room, a giant hole with a grate over it blew hot air into the rooms of the house. I frequently lay on the floor nearby with my crayons and paper.

My sister was a year and a half older and very smart. One day I was lying on the floor coloring on paper and most likely on the floor, too.

Wearing no shoes and only a diaper, I got up from the floor to find more crayons. The edge of the floor furnace caught my toe and sent me sprawling. My hand and the side of my right leg hit the grate. I couldn't get up.

Mother was pregnant and taking a well-deserved soak in the bathtub.

"Mom, Marietta fell on the floor furnace and she can't get up. I can smell her cooking," my three-year-old sister said.

Mother got out of the tub, wrapped her robe around herself, and picked me up. On that day, I thought only about the pain in my burning hands and legs.

I remember rubbing one burned leg on my mother's robe. I saw the blood running down my leg and soaking into her robe. Mother made a paste of baking soda to put on the burns. A doctor came to the house and Mother and I left for the hospital. My right hand burned, and the lines on it did not return for 30 years.

The scars on my leg would stay well into my forties. Friends were curious about the scars, and I retold the floor furnace story several times. My parents rarely commented on the scars, other than to say they would go away.

I wasn't self-conscious about the scars until I started swimming frequently. After a stranger told me he thought my skin looked like an alligator, I decided he was rude and I was brave for having survived the burn. My badges of courage.

Figure 1. From left: Charlotte 5, Michael 18 months, and Marietta, 3 1/2, fit on a piano bench in a Hutchinson photo studio, 1946.

Dad had joined the US Navy and trained in Storekeepers School at the Great Lakes Naval Training Station near Chicago. He spent only a few months in Harrisburg, Pennsylvania, as a storekeeper because two of his brothers already were serving, and the war ended not long after he joined.

Dad came home shortly after my brother Mike was born and began working as a cashier in his uncle's grocery store, C. O. Mammel and Company, in Hutchinson.

At age two, a bout with scarlet fever left me weak. My thick black hair came out in handfuls. When it came back in, it was wavy but sparse. I remember Charlotte was also quite ill, she nearly died. We could not take penicillin because the government saved it for the servicemen. The sulfa drug we took turned both of us yellow.

After I recovered, I found many ways to get into trouble.

Sometimes I rode to the store with Mother in our 1939 Ford coupe. There, I met Lizzie, an eccentric woman who lived poorly. She frequently peeked into the store windows to see what was happening.

She was sort of scary, because she was missing some teeth and had messy hair and torn clothing. Dad sometimes gave her produce trimmings and free promotional samples left by sales people. He told the employees who threatened to tell the boss that they should mind their own business.

Figure 2. My parents gave me a harmonica after I recovered from scarlet fever, 1946.

At three years old, following Dad's example, I told customers to mind their own business. They didn't appreciate my comments and tattled on me, for which Dad gave me a mini-lecture about not talking back to my elders.

————————

One day, the sky began turning gray, then black, then green. Fascinated by the changing colors, I stood in the living room staring at the sky. Mother cautioned me to move away from the window because lightning was striking.

"When I was a child, I watched a rainstorm from the front door and was knocked on my rear end by a lightning strike," she said.

The radio announcer was delivering tornado warnings, and Mother and Dad were anxiously gathering up us kids and moving to an interior room.

I stood frozen to my spot in the living room. The wind was whipping up tumbleweeds, sheets of paper, and pieces of trash.

Mother was hollering at me to get away from the window and into the safe space in the utility room.

"I want to watch the trees," I said.

The wind was churning violently when our two large catalpas snapped, creating a deafening noise as they fell to the ground.

"Get in here or you are going to get snapped, too."

Dad came into the living room and scooped me up, casting a brief glance to the front yard at the downed trees.

"Let's get out of the way of the storm," he said.

"Okay, Daddy, that was kind of scary," I said.

When we reached the safe area, Mother said, "I told you to get away from the window."

I giggled and said, "Those trees were pretty. I hope they grow back."

The storm dissipated, and our house did not suffer serious damage. I had a large dose of wind and came away unscathed except for the scolding I received.

———————

The Carey Park merry-go-round was my favorite entertainment because it had a horse made just for me. The red bucking bronco with flared nostrils let me ride him every time we went to the park. While riding the horse, I could see the nearby lighted fountain with red, blue, and green water spurting out of the ground.

A brick wall supporting part of the gardens beckoned me to crawl up and walk as far as I could before Mother ordered me down. Sometimes Dad walked beside me so I could go as far as possible. Fall off? It never occurred to me. We got ice cream afterwards.

———————

Dad wanted to use what he had learned in Storekeepers School in the US Navy and the business classes he had taken at the local junior college. He and Mother set a goal to open their own store in Lakin, Kansas. Dad's brother owned a store in Syracuse, about 28 miles away, and the dream of creating the Anderson chain of Mammel stores began to develop.

Mother cautioned me against playing with my new neighborhood friend, Mary, because "her mother is divorced," she whispered. I didn't know what that meant, so I ignored the warning.

Mary taught me how to pee in the alley, after checking for spies, of course. When my friend started breaking flower pots on a neighbor's patio and challenging me to do the same, I went along. She said no one was watching, but she was wrong.

The gardening neighbor saw us and reported the damage to my parents. Part of my punishment was to apologize to the owner, clean up the mess, and help the owner in her garden every day for a week.

For additional punishment, my parents forbade me to play with my other friend across the street. He and I sat across from each other on our respective curbs and sang out in our three-year-old voices, "Hey, kid, can you come over?" until the week was over.

Opportunities for getting into trouble diminished when I started kindergarten in the fall of 1948, but I attended only nine weeks because we moved to Lakin.

Mother and Dad opened their C. O. Mammel Grocery store under the name Anderson Grocery and Market in Lakin. Going barefoot risked bodily injury because of the abundance of devil's claws, tumbleweeds, and sandburs. Our family rented a house, complete with the barefoot hazards, until we built a house in a new subdivision.

Charlotte started the second grade in Lakin. I wanted to go back to school, but Lakin did not offer kindergarten, so my sister, brother, and I played school at home when Charlotte was available to lead us.

In the fall of 1949, I started first grade. Because I could read well, school officials promoted me to second grade. Charlotte was in third grade.

Here Come the Bullies

The administration reassigned me to Mrs. K's second grade class. I found my classroom, walked in, and sat at an empty desk. Mrs. K frowned at me and said, "You sort of brought our cart to a standstill, didn't you? We will have to back up to get you."

Everyone stopped talking. I didn't know what she meant. Her yellowish-gray hair was curled up on the sides and front and rolled up in a big "U" in the back. She wore rimless glasses and a gray dress with tiny brown buttons down the front.

Her face looked like it hurt from all the frowning. Tissues peeked out of her dress pockets, and her tightly laced black shoes clicked when she walked.

I fixed my eyes on the big brown mole on the side of her forehead because it wiggled when she talked. I tried not to laugh.

She walked to my seat and said, "Stand up, please. Class, this is Mare-ee-et-ta. It's a long name and hard for you to pronounce, but try to say it."

The class repeated in unison, "Mare-ee-et-ta."

"She is joining our class and may be behind. She will move to the front because her last name starts with 'A.' Everyone will move down one space. Make room for her in the first seat. Marietta, you will learn their names on your own."

A week later, Mrs. K. introduced our first art project. I needed a bathroom break. Mrs. K said to hurry because she wouldn't wait for me. When I returned to a busy class, she gave me a picture of a landscape and said, "Turn over your tablet and paste it on the back." I thought that was odd, but did exactly what she said. I turned over my tablet and pasted it onto the back of the tablet.

Figure 3. Aunt Charlene created curls for my second-grade school picture, 1949.

She walked around the room and held up a few of the scenes to show the class. I knew immediately I had done it wrong, but I didn't have another thing to paste the picture on. So, when the teacher stopped at my desk, she held up the incorrectly pasted print and said to the class, "Now, you see, this is an example of what you should not do. She did not follow instructions."

The air filled with giggling and whispering and continued until Mrs. K quieted the class. Turning to me, she said, "You should have stayed in the room. You might have learned something."

Then I really wanted to run to the bathroom, but I stuck it out until the end of the day and kept my mistake to myself.

After school, Dwayne, the overgrown kid who sat a few seats away from me, started taunting me as I walked home. "You dummy. You can't even paste a picture." Hitting me on the arm with a chubby fist, he chanted, "Dum, dum, de dum, dum." He finally stopped when his mother pulled the car up to the curb and told him to get in.

Dwayne continued to bother me at school, so I told my folks. They called Dwayne's parents. Dwayne's dad said, "We know he's kind of a brat, but we hoped that going to school would help him grow out of it."

The parents eventually decided the kids should work it out in a game that had rules. Their solution was to hold a boxing match. Both dads had served in the military and picked boxing as a harmless way to settle a score.

Dad told me I was a tough girl and could take care of myself. I saw an ad in a magazine for Charles Atlas, the bodybuilder, and I tried to flare out my shoulders and flex my muscles like he did.

Besides, if a girl could beat Dwayne, maybe he would learn a lesson. Everyone agreed, kids included, and they set the match for the end of the following week.

Dad gave me a few pointers about how to hold my feet and protect my face. He said, "You have big, broad shoulders. Stand up straight, and you will look tough. Even if he is bigger than you are, you are smarter."

I practiced with a pair of borrowed kid-sized boxing gloves, but I didn't want to punch my Raggedy Ann doll, so I just jumped around punching the air.

At school Dwayne continued poking at me and taunting me about how he was going to smack me in the face and knock me down. "I've got real gloves, and my uncle has been training me. You better be ready."

Then the big day came. Before heading for the boxing ring—a space in the back room of our grocery store—I put on a pair of blue shorts and carefully tucked in a white T-shirt. I put on brown oxfords, and Mother said she hoped Dwayne would not scuff them up. I certainly would not wear my red sandals or my other pair of shoes, black patent leather Mary Janes. Dad wrapped my hands with gauze and helped me pull on the gloves.

The store employees created a boxing ring in the back room of the store by turning over wooden banana boxes and placing them in a square. The spectators—employees, parents, and brother Mike, after he crawled out of a banana box—sat there to watch the match.

When everyone was ready, Bill, one of the store's cashiers, directed us to our corners. He rang a bell and said to come out swinging. I straightened up to my full height, flared out my shoulders to look bigger, and walked into the ring. Dwayne left his corner and came out toward me. I looked Dwayne in the eye, swung my right arm out, and punched him smack in the mouth.

He dropped to his knees, crying, "No fair. I wasn't ready." He was too embarrassed to get up, so his mother got into the ring to help him up.

She said, "Okay, you're not bleeding. You'll be okay. I hope you've learned your lesson. Don't pick on people or make fun. It's not nice, and besides, they could knock you down a notch or two."

All the parents walked to the center of the ring. Everyone agreed we should shake hands. I hoped that was the end of it.

After we got into the car to go home, Dad said, "You might never have to defend yourself again, but if you do, you will know what to do. Just remember, we never start fights; we only defend ourselves." That outlook has stayed with me.

I wondered what I might do if Mrs. K continued to make fun of me. When school resumed on Monday, the class was buzzing with stories about a fight. Someone said they used a big bell just like in a real boxing match. Mrs. K, her mole quivering, tried to make an example of me by asking me to stand and explain why I challenged Dwayne. I told her I didn't challenge him, but she didn't believe me.

Dwayne finally stood to say, "She's right. She didn't pick a fight with me. And our parents say it's all over." Mrs. K's mouth dropped open; she collected herself and resumed class activities.

I sat down at my desk and said to Dwayne, "Thanks, we don't need the gloves anymore. I sure hope Mrs. K doesn't start poking me. I might have to borrow them again."

Rain, Rain, Go Away

The next year flew by. On May 20, temperatures had reached the 90s, and the wind was nonexistent. The white lacy clouds embedded in the pale blue canopy hadn't moved for hours. Flags hung withering on their poles, and tumbleweeds lay trapped in storm drains, huddled in alley corners, and nestled near fire hydrants. As the two o'clock freight whistle blew in the distance, complacent drivers and straying livestock cleared the railroad tracks.

The Andersons and store employees were sitting in the back room, finishing lunch, and listening to the farm report. At that time of day, work in the grocery store had slowed while would-be customers finished their after-lunch snoozes.

Without warning, the sky turned black as a nightmare and unleashed a pounding rain that pelted windows, car roofs, and awnings. Puddles grew in the middle of the streets in a matter of minutes. Strong winds and surging water ripped tumbleweeds from their resting places, and before anyone could help old Mrs. Cavanaugh and her cocker spaniel to shelter, they got drenched.

"Was it supposed to hail?" Dad said, as he listened to the rain assault the roof. He stepped to the back door to see what was happening.

He opened the back door to a cascade of water. "It's raining to beat hell," he said. "We'd better see if the kids are okay."

The radio crackled as the announcer abruptly interrupted the farm report to say there was a powerful storm on the way to Kansas.

Mother left to check on us kids at home. Driving the six blocks to the house was usually easy, but on that day, cars became dangerous foreign objects in the hands of frightened drivers. People were speeding through standing water to get home or pick up kids from the park. A few children were playing in the gutters, splashing each other, oblivious to the dangers of the storm.

A shocking crash of thunder rocked the earth, and everyone came to an abrupt standstill. Drivers squinted through windshield wipers looking for signs of a letup. When double saw-toothed lightning struck nearby, the wading children scrambled for shelter.

The school year was over, so Mike, Charlotte, and I were at home watching the rain from the living room window. Mike hung over the back of the sofa and dropped right to the floor as a shard of lightning struck nearby.

Mother pulled into the driveway, hurried inside, and told us to stay in the house until it stopped raining. "Stay out of the windows when lightning strikes, or you might get electrocuted," she said.

She checked the crawl space and said she was returning to the store as soon as she looked things over. We had already closed the window over the kitchen sink, but some rain had run over the top of the counter and dripped to the floor.

"We should be okay since this is a new house," she said.

The weather reporter speculated the Arkansas River could reach flood stage. Charlotte, who had just finished fourth grade, said to Mike and me, "The Arkansas River comes into Kansas from Colorado and goes through Syracuse, where our cousins live, to Garden City, and a lot of other towns in Kansas."

We watched the rain as Mother checked the house. "Can we go outside and play, Mom?" Mike asked.

"We'll see," Mother said. "I have to go back to the store."

"That means, 'No'," Charlotte said.

Mother carefully drove back to the store across the railroad tracks, which were fast disappearing into the water. As she opened the back door of the store, she found Dad and the employees looking for leaks in the back room. They were moving boxes away from the wall as best they could.

Lightning had hit a transformer on the other side of the street, and some people were already without power. Someone reported that natural gas meters were being knocked over in places where the river was gushing and the ground was shaking. Weather reports speculated the

Arkansas River had reached flood stage at the Colorado border and soon would overflow its banks.

Several business leaders, teachers, and farmers were in the store's backroom discussing what to do in case of an emergency. They said others were gathering in the pool hall, and they would all meet to compare notes. How would they handle a flood? Should they evacuate? What about old people? What about the hospital? The water ruined people's property. People had no Plan B.

The mayor and Sheriff McCray were trying to calm people, saying it would not flood in Lakin, that the radio people knew no more than they did. McCray said the ground was flat and the water would just run off into the fields.

Some farmers said it had rained so much, they were afraid the ground was already saturated. The store telephone started ringing, and everyone stopped talking so Dad could answer it.

Charlotte called to report about the house.

"How's the crawl space? There are some blankets and odds and ends stored there," Dad said.

"I can see a lot of water," Charlotte said.

Mother came home to check on things. The water was rising in the streets and driving was very slow, even though the rain seemed to have let up. When she arrived home, we three kids were standing under the porch roof waiting for her.

Mother directed us to a neighbor's house. I went first. Mother carried Mike, and Charlotte walked behind her. The mud sucked at our feet on the way. Our crawl space flooded and we lost everything in it. The next day, we used pumps to siphon the water from the crawl space.

Mother returned to the store. The temperature was cooling, and the sky had darkened. When she got there about five o'clock, one employee remained. The others had gone home to their families or to the school.

Mother and Dad tried to block the doors from what looked like whitecaps on the rising floodwaters. They stacked cases of canned goods first, then loaded two-wheeled dollies and the long four-wheelers with 100-pound bags of flour, salt, and sugar to stack on top of the cases. They used up most of their inventory, and the surge of water overwhelmed their efforts.

Sewers backed up and emptied into the streets. Sirens sounded. Telephones stopped working. The electricity went out all over town. Cars and pets stood alone without their owners, and furniture and trash were floating down the street. There was nothing anyone could do.

Figure 4. Mother stood in the water in front of the grocery store after the flood. Cases of canned goods and sacks of sugar and flour did not stop the water from flowing into the store, 1951.

Three years of hard work were literally going down the drain. The IGA grocery store four doors up the street received minimal damage.

As the rain subsided, Dad and Mother drove home. They were tired and emotionally wrung out from the devastation, but they did not share the extent of the destruction with us kids. Mike and Charlotte had the checkerboard out and were playing keep away. I was pretty sure we would not have a cake today, even though it was my eighth birthday.

Dad said, "Well, not exactly a happy birthday this year. You know we'd make a cake, but we have no flour, eggs, sugar, or much of anything else. How about a big hug today and I'll write you an IOU for a party next year."

"That's okay, Daddy."

Mother had scooted off to the bedroom and shut the door. After about half an hour, she came out, but we could tell she had been crying. We stayed in our house for several days while Mother and Dad made plans.

A test of the front yard revealed a spongy mess, with little grass in sight. Mud clogged the storm drains. Two lost dogs were sitting on our front porch. The flooding flattened shrubbery and left a thick layer of sludge on the driveway.

"Put your overshoes on and don't touch any of the mud," Mother said. "You're likely to get a handful of sewage, if you do. You'll get typhoid fever. And leave those dogs alone."

As we all piled into the car to go survey the damage, Dad pretended the streets were just another obstacle course. He tried to see how well he could dodge the trash, the orphaned furniture, and the rivers of mud.

The mud challenged even the best of drivers because it was so slick, and you couldn't tell how deep it was. I said I hoped it wasn't quicksand, or we would have to call Tarzan or Wonder Woman to pull us out.

After about 20 minutes, a trip that ordinarily took five, we reached the store and parked out front. Some people were out hosing down sidewalks, but there was water still standing in several low places in the street.

Dad tried to open the front door of the store, but mud oozed from the seams around the door. He pulled a crowbar from the car and jacked the door up enough to open it halfway. The inside was unrecognizable. Sugar, flour, potatoes, lettuce, bananas, green beans, dry beans, rice, and cornmeal lay in wet piles.

Two check stands had crashed into each other and tipped over, their contents spilling into the muck. Pencils, rolls of receipt paper, charge slips, paper clips, and staples were stuck in the mud.

Soggy boxes of cherry-flavored Smith Brothers cough drops, Butterfinger candy bars, rolls of Life Savers, and packs of Black Jack gum floated in the remaining pool of water near the front of the store.

The contents of the ice cream freezer had merged into a sloppy stew. Mired in the sludge were two cash registers.

"Don't open the freezer door, and don't touch anything," Dad said.

The sliding glass doors on one of the closed produce cases had cracked, and a mixture of oil, silt, and rotted fruit clogged the compressors. Cleaning tools and supplies blocked the aisles, forced there during the race to stem the rush of water. The odor was powerful, and I said, "It smells like dead cabbage."

After everyone started to cry, Dad said, "I guess we have our work cut out for us, don't we?"

Not long after that, Mother and Dad took us kids to Mother's folks' house in McPherson while they cleaned up the store and determined if they could salvage anything. They cleaned up what they could and salvaged some of the canned goods which they gave to Dad's brother in Syracuse.

Another disaster was in the making. Mother and Dad discovered their insurance did not cover floods. The county had no flood control measure in place.

Our family had no other choice. We had to abandon the store and sell our new home at a loss, declaring bankruptcy. Dad's brother in Syracuse rode out the storm unharmed.

A heavy pall settled over our family. Money and shelter issues dominated the conversation, but the biggest issue for Mother seemed to be the embarrassment: "What will people think of us? How will we ever live this down?"

2. No Fixed Address

Chores at Grandma's

The horrible mess in the grocery store haunted my dreams. Ours was the only store that flooded. It didn't seem fair to our parents that theirs was the only one. They worked hard, the community accepted them, and they treated employees fairly. The questions emanating from these thoughts were very difficult for this eight-year-old.

Mother was sure she was being punished for something and for many years, she lashed out at her children and family for the harm done to her.

Dad was eventually philosophical about the flood. Shit happens. Mostly, people are not to blame. Certainly not for a flood. We would get through this. He would get another job. His optimistic attitude carried the day.

Both sets of grandparents, Andersons and Kings, lived in McPherson. One of Dad's sisters still lived at the Anderson home. Mother preferred living in her parents' home, so we moved in with the Kings.

Grandma and Grandpa King, Mother's mother and stepfather, lived in a house with two good-sized bedrooms, a small sewing room, and an enclosed porch off the kitchen. There was a large living and dining area, a small eat-in kitchen, and one bathroom. Charlotte and I slept on the porch, Mike in the sewing room, and Mother and Dad used the spare bedroom.

Dad started working in Canton, 15 miles east of McPherson. His sister Claudine and brother-in-law Myron Fisher managed the grain elevator. The wheat harvest started not long after we arrived.

They worked long hours weighing, analyzing, and dumping grain. Dad stayed at the Fishers' house during the week when he had to work late and came to McPherson when he could.

Our grandparents and Gladwyn, Grandpa's son who lived next door, shared the large garage and driveway. Gladwyn, or Jack, as friends called him, his wife Norma, and son Jay Dee were in and out of the house frequently.

Grandpa and Jack were carpenters, and Jack had an enormous garden and heated greenhouse in his backyard. Grandpa and Grandma kept chickens in a coop in their backyard.

Grandma King did alterations and tailoring in her home and later designed and made custom drapes for a local furniture store. Scraps of white satin wedding dresses, gold satin tap dance costumes, shoulder pads, and gabardine suit remnants poked out of drawers and shelves in the sewing room. An adjustable body form stood at attention in the corner by the closet.

When we arrived at the King house and brought in our belongings, Mike asked, "Can we call you by your first name, Grandma Flora?" Mike asked. "We have a Grandma Edith."

"Flora is a horrible name," Grandma insisted. "I don't care if it is supposed to stand for 'flower.' My mother had no business naming me that. Call me Grandma or Grandma King."

Everyone but her children and grandchildren called her Charlotte, her middle name, because she said otherwise, they would break out in hives and only she had the cure.

"We'll put your things where they fit," Grandma said. "Today is Thursday, so we will have to clean house today, because, if we do it on Friday, someone will die before Monday."

"Mother said you were born in Kansas," Charlotte said. "How did your family get here?"

Even though we visited the Kings when possible, we knew few details about their upbringing.

"They came from Wisconsin and eventually settled in the Hill City area where my brother John and I were born. I was born in 1900, easy to remember how old I am. You've had enough of that for now," she said. "Let's get you settled and line out your chores. You have to earn your keep around here."

And that is how we settled into life in McPherson.

"I'll show you how to gather eggs and bring them into the house. You'll have to get up early."

Gathering eggs became my early morning duty. Grandpa and Grandma ate breakfast before they started anything. Sometimes Uncle Jack and Aunt Norma came over, and they all ate together.

I awoke the next day to singing, birds chirping, and the rich aroma of coffee. Patti Page sang "On Mockingbird Hill," and Grandma chanted, "It's time to get up in the morning." I wondered how long I could wait until I got a poke in the arm, reminding me to go to the henhouse to collect eggs for breakfast. About 30 seconds.

Charlotte was still asleep, so I slipped out of bed, yanked off my pajamas, and pulled on a pair of blue and white striped seersucker shorts and a pink T-shirt. I ran to the bathroom, so nobody would see me, through the dining room and living room to put on clean underwear and brush my teeth.

The rooster frequently strutted around the yard, but the hens were in the coop. When I entered the henhouse, eight hens were sitting on their nests. Four of the hens fluttered off.

I had to move the others to see what they had laid. Three offered no resistance, but the last one, "Mrs. Grouch," honked at me in such a way, I laughed at her impersonation of a duck.

While I was laughing, I tried to pick her up, but she pecked my hand and looked me right in the eye, as if to say, "Oh, no you don't. That's mine." Well, that did it for me. She could just keep her egg.

Dad rigged up a candling box like the one we had at the store so we could tell if the eggs were okay. The rig comprised a light bulb and a box with a hole in the top just big enough for the egg. We placed the egg in the hole, and the light underneath showed whether the egg had already started to grow.

I candled seven eggs in the lightbox to make sure they were okay. Grandma pronounced them ready to cook—no fingers or toes sticking out of the shells.

All of us kids wanted the air conditioner job. We had to keep the water-cooled air conditioner wet. It lived in the dining room window and did well at keeping the entire house cool.

To keep it wet, we had to go outside, hook up the hose, turn on the water faucet, and run the water over the back of the cooler to keep the padding wet. Sometimes it spit into the dining room if we soaked it too much, creating a round of giggles from us kids.

The Neighborhood

Kids came running when they saw a sprinkler and a garden hose in operation. Everyone pretended to dodge the spray, but few succeeded.

Donna, the girl who lived across the street, usually ran over at the sight of one of us kids in the yard. Her mother came out onto their porch in her baggy tan shorts, red halter top, sandals, and socks, dangling a cigarette from her lips. She shouted at Donna not to run across the street. I wondered how she could yell at Donna and smoke a cigarette at the same time.

We always knew when Bobby Hapgood was home, because he played his drum set loud enough to hear it all the way down the street. Bobby was a classmate of cousin Jay Dee.

After a good soaking of the air conditioner and a run through the spray, we all formed a band and marched down the street to the sound of Bobby's drum. Bobby grew up to form the band King Midas and the Mufflers, and played rock 'n roll dance music until his death in 2007.

Jay Dee was three years older than Charlotte and had lots of tricks up his sleeve. He often gathered us kids around to show off his vial of mercury, his pocket container of cinnamon toothpicks, or his *Mad* and Superman magazines.

When Charlotte wasn't reading Superman comics, the two of them devised several ways to tease me. For example, they assured me that if I let green flies sit on my skin long enough, they would eat the flesh right off. Jay Dee captured lightning bugs, pulled off the "lights" and stuck them to me. And one of their favorites was convincing me they had something new to show me. Then they would produce a firecracker, a dead bug, a garter snake, or something else to scare me.

Jay Dee got a kick out of the hogtie. First, the victim had to lie face down on the ground, then he produced a rope. I thought it would be a fun game, but I soon learned it wasn't fun at all.

Jay tied my hands together behind my back, bent back my legs, and then tied my wrists to my ankles. He said, "Okay, now you're hogtied. See if you can get loose." I could not move.

I hollered long enough, and someone would come to untie me. Jay Dee had run off to hide and claimed he had no idea I couldn't get out of the tie-up. My sister claims she was not involved in hogtying; it must have been one of Jay's friends.

I was determined to get loose if he tried it again. And he did. About a week later, after he accused me of being a crybaby, he bet me two cinnamon toothpicks I couldn't get out of the tie-up. I took up the challenge.

While he was tying me up, I resisted bending my legs back very far and didn't cross my wrists or ankles. That meant the ropes were not tight enough to hold me.

After he ran off to hide, I loosened the knots enough to escape. I ran into the house and acted as though nothing had happened. He never tried to tie me up again. But I never collected the cinnamon toothpicks.

One of my uncles said I had acquired a crap detector. On the Fourth of July, he let me light my firecrackers from his lighted cigarette.

Uncle Jack often tended his garden near the henhouse, talking to his tomatoes while hoeing and watering. They must have liked what he was saying, because they always produced bushels of red and dark mahogany beauties.

Friends in town came by the house when they thought the tomatoes were ready.

When the tomatoes started ripening, Uncle Jack and Aunt Norma covered the counters in their kitchen and back porch with newspapers. They placed the tomatoes on the papers in various stages of "doneness," Uncle Jack said. They cut the green tomatoes into half-inch slices, dipped them in egg and cornmeal, and fried them in bacon fat they had saved in a coffee can on the stove.

Mike was up and outside, following Jack around the garden. Jack didn't want anyone stepping on the plants or packing down the soil. Soon he was hollering for Mother, saying, "Peggy, come and get this young'un before I have to take a pitchfork to him."

Mother came out of her bedroom and into the dining room, brushing her long black hair. She should brush it 100 times, Grandma said. Mother went outside to corral Mike and make sure he hadn't stepped on anything important.

Every year, the garden produced green beans, peas, corn, tomatoes, lettuce, turnips, potatoes, cucumbers, peppers, and strawberries. Sometimes he added a few exotic products, like eggplant, rutabaga, or celery.

––––––––––––––

Aunt Claudine often called Jack to buy his vegetables. Once a week she came to McPherson, picked me up, and took me back to Canton to play with cousin Myra, two weeks younger than I.

The Fishers always seemed to have the latest thing at their house, including a television set and a restaurant booth in the kitchen corner. Turquoise vinyl upholstered the booth with a matching Formica tabletop. Later, they were one of the first in the county to have a color television set, according to cousin Myra.

Besides managing the Canton grain elevator, the Fishers had cattle, some horses, wheat, maize, and sunflowers. Myra always put on her fringed buckskin suede jacket when we pretended to ride horses. Claudine bought Myra and me each a red and white striped T-shirt to go with our jeans, as well as a holster, cap gun, and real caps.

Mother made me leave these gifts in Canton, however. She said she didn't need anyone else to buy clothes for her kids. And she didn't want me watching television because it would ruin my eyes.

Figure 5. Cousin Myra Fisher and I play at her house in Canton. Aunt Claudine gave us matching shirts, 1950.

I asked Mother if Claudine was still coming to pick me up to go to Canton. "She will, whether I want her to or not. And I don't want you shooting off any caps." She didn't say I couldn't go, so I got ready.

Charlotte and Mike would not be going to Canton. Charlotte was staying home to read, and Mike wanted to wait to play with Freddy, who was visiting his cousin across the street. About 9:30 that morning, Claudine and Myra showed up in a pale blue Lincoln Continental. Mother had her mouth set in what I called her "lemon face." Her jaw was hard, her lips had disappeared, and she was standing at the front door with her hands on her hips.

Myra was skipping up to the house, wearing her buckskin jacket. She was the only fair-haired, blue-eyed kid in the entire group of Anderson cousins. She favored the Fisher and Dole sides of the family, who were parents of Uncle Myron, her dad.

"I suppose you're going to want one of those now," Mother said. "Well, don't even ask." I wasn't sure what she meant. I knew I couldn't have a buckskin jacket, even if I wanted one, and I couldn't drive yet, so I didn't say anything.

Claudine got out of the car as Jack came from the garden with a basket of vegetables. He tipped his hat to her, and she asked, "Are those some of your famous peas?"

"Yes, ma'am. How many do you want?"

She pulled out two dollars. "I'm fixing lunch for five hungry people."

He put a big pile of peas into her empty bag but told her one dollar was enough.

Mother said, "How do you get away with taking some of Jack's peas? Not everybody gets to sample those."

"She called me yesterday and asked if I had any for sale," Jack said.

"Were you going to share them with anyone else?" Mother asked.

"We'll see," Jack said.

Canton was 15 miles east of McPherson on Highway 56. As we approached Canton, I saw two water towers identifying the name of the town. Sure enough, there they were, "Hot" and "Cold." Myra said her mother had a hand in that. She was a member of the city council and suggested they paint them as a tourist attraction. The council went for it.

"Fisher (Claudine always called her husband Myron by his last name) and your dad are coming home for lunch. We can stop by the elevator to see how they check the wheat. A few truckloads have pulled in already, even though some of the wheat is a little green."

The Canton grain elevator was on Min Street (that's what the sign says). Located in the parking lot were two gas pumps. One for white gas (additive-free gasoline) and one for diesel. We pulled into the parking area and went inside the office.

A farmer pulled his loaded truck up next to the window of the office onto the weighing platform at just the right place. The person at the weigh station window slid open the glass door while another elevator worker climbed onto the truck to scoop out a load of wheat.

Moisture content of the wheat was important, so the person working in the office took the full scoop, tested it, and recorded the measurement. Claudine let me weigh and calculate the next load of wheat just as Dad was walking into the office.

"Hey," he said, "don't get too good at that, or I'll be out of a job."

I ran to Dad to give him a hug. He stooped down on one knee to hug me back. Dad asked, "Are you two staying out of trouble?" Myra and I shook our heads yes. "See you later for lunch."

Meanwhile, Back at the Ranch

We returned to the house. Myra was ready to play. She pulled two holster belts off the hooks hanging by the back door and got out two cap pistols.

We outfitted ourselves and went into the tack room off the back of the house so we could look at Fisher's saddles. Uncle Myron was in the tack room, came over and patted each of us on the head. He told us a local Mennonite farmer had made the saddle and the wooden stand by hand.

"Isn't this a beautiful saddle! We use a western saddle around here. They are sturdier and heavier than English saddles that riders of show horses use." The Fishers' farm had two saddle horses and two quarter horses, reputed to be too wild for us girls to ride.

Myra and I usually played "Cowboys and Outlaws," because she liked being Jesse James.

With my feet apart and hands on hips, I prepared to draw my gun, just like Wyatt Earp did. "I'm ready," I said.

Myra had a gun on each hip, but my holster had room for only one gun. Over my objection, she gave me caps for my gun, in case we ran into a rattlesnake.

We mounted our imaginary horses and galloped off toward the pasture, careening around the cow patties. Bright sun lighted up the bluestem and Indian grasses, milkweed, and sunflowers. A breeze amplified the sounds of the prairie, sending a playful melody to soothe the cattle who were grazing in the pasture.

I always thought the cattle slobbered a lot. I wasn't exactly afraid of them, but I kept my distance. A group of four or five who were quite close to me milled about as though they heard or saw something threatening.

"I'm riding off to Missouri. See if you can catch me," Myra said.

As I stopped to pick some sunflowers, Myra ducked behind a hill, and when I turned around, I couldn't see her.

Crouching down to make myself look smaller, I crept to the hill where I thought she was hiding. I popped up over the hill with the sunflowers in my left hand and my right hand on the gun. She wasn't there. The cattle were all bunched up and moved toward me.

Twisting away from the herd, I looked for Myra. She darted from behind a cedar tree, saying, "There's a rattler by your foot."

I dropped the sunflowers, backed away, drew my pistol, and fired. "Uh oh. Am I in trouble now!" No rattler appeared. I shook my head and walked far away from the cattle.

"Let's do something else. Wyatt Earp isn't for me. How about Annie Oakley?"

We skipped and dodged our way back. I was careful to look for snakes as I avoided the rocks and cow pies. Myra had her guns drawn, just in case, but mine was safely in its holster. We made it back to the house as Dad and Myron pulled into the driveway.

"Go wash your hands. We're almost ready to eat lunch. Your dad is here." Claudine said.

"Have you girls been staying out of trouble?" Dad asked as we took off our holsters and pistols.

"Marietta shot a snake," Myra said.

"You did?" Dad asked.

"Marietta got scared when she thought she saw a snake and tried to shoot it with her cap pistol."

We settled down to a lunch of baked round steak, fried potatoes, sliced tomatoes, Jack's fresh peas, and bread. I wasn't much of a steak eater, and I was still suffering from total humiliation, so as soon as I could, I asked to be excused and left for the living room. When everyone finished, I returned to the kitchen to help pick up the dishes. Claudine said we didn't have to help, so I followed Dad into the living room and sat on the floor beside his chair.

"Am I in trouble?"

"You know your mother doesn't want you shooting caps."

"It was an accident."

"You and Myra better finish up what you were doing, because I think Claudine is going to take you back to McPherson pretty soon."

After we left Canton, Claudine kicked the cobs out of the Lincoln to return to McPherson, and Mother was waiting at the door. She thanked Claudine and asked Myra if we had fun.

Swat Fest

"Marietta almost killed a snake. She'll tell you all about it," Myra said.

"What did you do? Did you get into trouble?" Mother asked.

"I accidentally shot a cap pistol."

"How do you accidentally shoot a gun? Were there caps in it? I specifically told you not to use caps in that gun, didn't I?" She grabbed my hand, jerked me out onto the porch and down the steps to the spirea bushes.

"Break off a branch and make it a long one. In fact, make it two and hand them to me." I tried to break one off, but it was too tough and my hands were raw from running them up and down the branches.

"Don't move. I'm getting a knife."

Now's my chance to escape. Where can I hide?

She came back out before I could escape. I knew I could outrun her, but should I try? She cut off two long branches and stripped off most of the leaves. She grabbed my hand and said I was going to stand still until she thought I had had enough. I pulled away from her and started running toward the backyard. I tripped and fell, and just as I started up, she caught me by the foot and started whipping me on the arms and legs.

"Hey, that hurts."

"It's supposed to. Now stay still."

I rolled over and over, but she still got in quite a few licks. Finally, she stopped and dropped the switches. "I hope you've learned your lesson." She turned and went back into the house.

I stayed outside until grandma called me to come inside for a cookie. I waited awhile and then went inside. Mike and Charlotte were in the kitchen with Grandma having milk and cookies—the pink, brown, and white kind that looked like flat ice cream cones with frosting in the middle.

I plunked down at the table but guessed I didn't deserve a cookie, so I declined the offer. I thought I didn't deserve a whipping for having an accident with the cap gun, either.

The sting of unjust punishments stayed with me.

———————————

Tomorrow promised to be a good day. Grandma said Aunt Charlene would take me out of Mother's hair for the day. Charlene was Mother's younger half-sister by 11 years.

A 20-year-old beautiful, sociable blonde who played the piano, Charlene had married high school sweetheart Bob the previous year. He worked at the National Cooperative Refinery Association (NCRA) until the US Navy called him to the Korean war. Bob and Charlene lived in a small house in McPherson.

Charlene and Bob took all three of us kids to Kanopolis Lake and to the drive-in movie several times. At the drive-in, we sat in the backseat giggling because we thought they were going to kiss each other.

Charlene generously hauled us to the drugstore to treat us to a Coke and sit in the ice cream chairs. Sometimes we could spend a nickel on the Wurlitzer jukebox, the one with the lights that changed colors.

"I'm ready to go," I said, as I sat down at the breakfast table.

I get to run around with Charlene and her friends.

"Lois and Beverly will come to pick you up about ten," Grandma said. "After that, you're on your own. You'll probably miss the chocolate cake."

I didn't mind missing cake, because if we went to Lois and Beverly's house, I might get to put on Charlene's Carmen Miranda outfit she used in tap dance recitals. Grandma made the costume out of orange and red taffeta. The skirt buttoned in the front, was split up the middle to the drop waist, and had four tiers of cascading ruffles falling all the way to the floor. I was sure I would start my movie career wearing this costume.

After we arrived at the Lupfers' house, Beverly and Charlene were deciding which costumes to try when the phone rang. Lois answered, and after a few minutes of conversation, she said that we needed to go over to Ann's house—soon, if we could. They were talking in that "don't let the kids hear this" way.

I wasn't ready to go back to the Kings' house. I hoped they would take me with them. We left to go to Ann and Gary Robinson's house.

We drove Lois to the furniture store and went to the Robinson house. Ann had dark eyebrows, curly hair, and very brown skin. She and I compared tans by holding our arms up side by side to see who was the darkest. I was pretty sure she was from an exotic country.

Before we got to the house, Charlene said, "Ann isn't feeling well. Their kids have gone to their grandma's house. You can entertain yourself with games and puzzles. We'll do some tap dancing later."

"That's okay, I'd like to get out their Lincoln Logs if that's okay."

"Of course. Gary won't mind," Charlene said.

I loved looking at other people's houses. The Robinsons' frame house was white with dark green shutters. The porch was as wide as the house, and the railing was painted white with fancy cutouts in the wood. Gary and Bob built the white picket fence in front of the house by the sidewalk.

The living room extended across the whole house. A dining room and kitchen lay behind the living room on one side, and two bedrooms separated by a bathroom were on the other side. A hallway divided the bedrooms from the living areas. Painted bookcases with shelves and drawers lined the hallway. I would find games and toys in one of the drawers.

We walked into the house after Ann answered the door in her robe and slippers. Her straggly hair hung over her forehead on one side, and dark circles made hollows under her eyes.

Charlene spoke to Ann, who went with Beverly to the dining room. Charlene brought me a box of Lincoln Logs, an Erector Set, and another box containing farm animals, buildings, and farm machinery.

"Wow, I can really build a mansion now. We'll have to move it to a city, though. I don't want to live in the country."

I imagined the mansion with a wooden dance floor and stage for performances. A secret passage connected the library and conservatory, like the ones in the Clue game. I would tell only special people about the secret passage. I built an indoor swimming pool and a boathouse and a wharf next to the lake. I hoped Uncle Bob could bring his boat to my mansion and help me polish my waterskiing skills.

I had to reimagine the Lincoln Logs as some other building material, like "Fallingwater," a house Frank Lloyd Wright designed. My waterfall would cascade into the lake, near the wharf and boathouse. For now, I could use the Erector Set to build the wharf and a bird statue for the yard.

As I lay on the floor creating my idea of a mansion, I heard Charlene say, "Oh, gee, a D and C sounds dangerous. What is that exactly?" Beverly got up from the table and closed the pocket doors between the dining and living rooms. They were whispering, so I knew they were talking about something I wasn't supposed to hear.

I heard things like, ". . . just got home from Wichita . . . lots of cramps . . . bad headache."

I walked down the hallway from the living room to the bathroom, where the metallic smell grew intense. When I reached the bathroom and closed the door, I saw an overflowing wastebasket. Thick white, blood-soaked pads filled the wastebasket; the smell was overwhelming. I finished fast and washed my hands twice.

What did I see?

Someone had been bleeding, and it must have been Ann, since it was her house. Gosh, no wonder she didn't look very good.

The Erector Set captured my attention again, and I grabbed a couple of pillows from the couch to create rocks for a waterfall and building platform. I stacked the logs to represent building levels that would overlook the waterfall. I turned the farm animals into deer, peacocks, and rabbits for my version of a park in the city.

Then Beverly and Charlene came into the living room to tell me Charlene was going to take me back to Grandma's.

I put away the toys and was ready to go.

She and Beverly were going to prepare some food Ann could reheat for dinner when Gary got home from work.

"If you want to know more about Ann, ask your mother," she said. "Just don't tell her I told you to ask her."

The Diary

Charlene dropped me at Grandma's house, where Mike and Charlotte were playing a game of keep-away on the checkerboard. I wasn't interested in checkers or backgammon that day, so I went outside.

I walked down the street toward the tennis courts, about three blocks away, and sat down on one of the spectators' benches.

Under the bench next to me lay a silvery object protruding from a mound of grass. A handsome soft leather book bulged with paper, leaves, and ribbons. The front had a silver heart stamped on it, and a push-button attached to a leather strap held the book together.

I pressed the button and the book popped open. Inside were pages of writing, dried flowers, a pair of ticket stubs for the movie "The Third Man," and a list of books called "Must Read." The list included *The Wizard of Oz*, *The Invisible Man*, and *The Grapes of Wrath*. I didn't know any of these books but the *Wizard*, so I thought I would ask Charlotte. We could go to the library and check them out.

Water had stained the ink, so some of the writing was hard to read. A very clear page read something like, "Dear Diary, it seems like ages since I last saw you in the drugstore. I have been babysitting my cousins in Lyons, and haven't been in for a while.

"I need to earn some more money before I can afford a banana split. They must be up to 35 cents by now. Well, I must go now, so don't take any wooden nickels."

Farther into the book, the writer noted something about a man beating up someone in her kitchen. The person was bleeding and bruised. The writer ran to a neighbor's house to get help. Several blank pages followed. The next page said, "I have to go now."

I dropped the book and looked around to see if anyone had seen me. I started walking fast back to the Kings' house. About a block from the house, an old car pulled up by the curb. A young woman with a long brown pageboy and bangs rolled down her window and asked me to come near the car. She looked okay, so I moved closer to the curb.

"Did you find something in the park? I saw you leaving it a few minutes ago."

"I saw a little book, that's all. It's under the second park bench. I tried to find a name in it, but some pages are hard to read. I put it back."

"Thank you. I need it." She made a U-turn in the middle of the street and drove quickly back to the tennis courts. I saw her park the car, go pick up the book, and hurry back to the car.

I had reached Grandma's house but waited to see if the woman came back. She drove on in the other direction. Three days later, when Charlene and Beverly took us to the drugstore, the mystery lady was sitting at the soda fountain talking to the soda jerk. She saw us come in and sit down.

Charlene whispered to Beverly, "Isn't that Gracie, that girl who had to drop out of school a few years ago?"

"Yeah, we were freshmen, and I think she was a senior. It was right after her mother died. I think she lives in Lyons now."

While they were yakking, I looked Mystery Woman right in the eye and did the tick-a-lock sign on the side of my lips to indicate my silence. She did the same, and I never saw her again.

———————

Several aunts and uncles came to the Kings' house one Sunday to eat dinner. After everyone had finished eating, Dad got our attention.

"Now, before you get too comfy and can't hear what I'm saying, I want to make an announcement," Dad said.

"Uh oh," Aunt Dorothy said. "Get out the cards."

"This is even better," he said. "We're moving to Russell."

"What? Who wants to live there?" Uncle Kenny asked.

"We do. I am going to work for Betts Baking Company as a bread truck driver. It's a sales job and I'll be opening new territory."

"Oh, boy, Little Miss Sunbeam, Holsum, and Old Home bread won't know what hit 'em," Uncle Norwood said.

"We need to move before school starts, so wherever we light may not be our first choice in houses," Dad said.

Then everyone started talking at once about the new job, where we would live and go to school. "We'll just have to see," Mother said. "I don't know anyone out there." The adults started a game of pinochle while Charlotte, Mike, and I had a noisy game of canasta.

3. FINDING OUR FEET

Russell, Here We Come

In about a month, Dad and Mother had found a place to live in Russell, a town in the middle of the oil boom where housing was scarce. First, Mother, Mike, Charlotte, and I lived in a rooming house while Dad was in Hutchinson training for his job.

Then, we moved to a house carved out of the ground—a basement house—for a few months until we found a bigger place. The basement house windows didn't let in much light, so Mother painted the kitchen turquoise and the living room chartreuse.

The house was two blocks from the swimming pool; I soon learned I am closely related to dolphins.

Our neighbors to the east were the Fields, and to the west, the Schmidts. All the kids on the block were about the same age. Bea Schmidt showed me how to play her accordion, and I tried to show her how to swim.

Every day the Fields boys challenged Mike to "King of the Mountain," at the dirt pile created from digging out the basement house. Charlotte maintained her post inside, reading whatever book, magazine, or comic she could get from the library or trade with friends. We had survived the flood and acquired our second set of pets: a deodorized skunk and a duck. When we lived in Hutchinson, we had a puppy that bit me in the face when I picked it up. *What's one more scar?*

The skunk turned out to be mean, so Dad took it away. Someone stole our duck and although we were sad, Dad said whoever did it was probably hungry, so they should have it instead.

Our Russell adventure had begun.

We moved into a real two-story house with hardwood floors leaving behind the basement house, the monster pile of dirt, the rabbit, skunk cages, and those nasty boys next door.

"No more chartreuse cinderblocks! No more basement houses! No more Fields boys or pet skunks," we three kids cheered in unison.

In our new place, Charlotte and I shared a bedroom, and Mike had his own room on the second level. The single bathroom was on the ground floor where Mother and Dad slept. There was a piano in the living room, and the kitchen had eating space. The house was a long way from the swimming pool and I would have to figure out how to get there.

Let's Put on a Show!

Mike and I were sitting at the kitchen table playing two-handed canasta when Charlotte came in and plopped down at the table with a stack of papers in her hand.

"That's pretty, all tied up with bows," I said.

"I have written three plays, *Lo-Su, the Girl Pirate*, *The Adventures of Mike the Goblin*, and *The Pranks of Mary the Demon*," Charlotte said. "I've been working on them for almost two weeks now. I used a paper punch on the pages and then stuck ribbon through the holes and tied them up. I'll tell you about the one I think we should perform, and then we can decide who will play the parts," Charlotte said.

"We could sell tickets and charge admission," I said.

"I will be directing the play, so I won't be playing any of the parts. We'll have to get some other kids in the neighborhood to help."

As Mother took a casserole of ham and scalloped potatoes out of the oven, she said, "Your dad will be home soon. What is it you are charging admission for? I see you didn't get the piano dusted, Marietta."

"Whoops," I said. "I was at violin practice—for hours and hours, and I forgot."

Dad came home, and when he was ready, we all sat down to dinner.

Everyone started talking—telling stories about their day. Mike lost his baseball some place. I left my violin at my instructor's house and had to go back after it, and Charlotte told us about her play.

"Lo-Su, the Girl Pirate is the name of it. The queen commissioned the pirate Lo-Su, who is of some obscure Asian descent with legendary sword-brandishing skills, to return her treasure excavated in the Himalayan Mountains.

"Lo-Su will sail her ship with this precious cargo back to the queen's palace. On the way back to the palace, she must defend her ship and crew when thieves try to board and steal the treasure. She and the crew successfully defend the ship, and nobody gets killed. They all sail back to the palace to claim their reward."

Mike jumped up from the table and claimed the right to play Lo-Su. He said he knows someone with a sword and one of those things you stick it into. All he needs is an eye patch.

Charlotte said, "You don't want to play a girl's part, remember? I think Marietta will play the part of Lo-Su."

"Oh, yeah, I forgot. How about Mike the Goblin? Can I play him?" he asked.

"We won't have time to do both plays." Charlotte said. "You can help set up the stage, pull the curtains, and sell tickets."

After we cleaned up the dishes and took out the trash, we sat at the table to decide the particulars of the play: when, where, how, who, and, of course, costumes. Dad produced a movie ticket to use as a guide, and we made up about 25 tickets. Admission was five cents.

A challenge went up to see who could sell the most tickets. Charlotte would be too busy working on stage directions to sell tickets, so Mike and I collaborated. I still had to memorize my part, but there would be plenty of time. Everyone started naming people they thought might buy tickets, and we came up with 20 names.

"What about that guy who walks all over town with the suitcase?" I asked. "Does he live around here?"

"He's too scary," Mike said. "He won't buy one."

"You mean that man who wears a suit and tie and a hat?" Mother asked.

Dad said, "I don't know—he might toss you into his oven and cook you for dinner."

The next day, we got together with neighborhood kids. We decided to perform the play in the Browns' yard across the street. Their swing set could serve as the front of the stage. We could wind the swings around the posts to give more room. Nancy and Freddy did not want to perform, but would help set up chairs and take tickets.

I practiced memorizing lines by asking a friend to work with me. She lived in a different neighborhood, so she wasn't performing in *Lo-Su*. Other neighborhood kids didn't want to perform, so Charlotte decided to read the other parts. Mike acted the part of the thief who tried to board the ship. He didn't want to get knocked off, but Charlotte assured him it was a part that only he could play.

As I was walking home from Carol's house after practicing, I saw Suitcase Man go into the Conoco service station. After a few minutes, he walked out of the office, went around the corner, down the street to the first house where he went inside.

I ran across the street into the gas station. Dad parked his Rainbo Bread company truck there so the owner could service it. I asked him who the Suitcase Man was, and he said, "Oh, he lives down the street there, right around the corner. Sells greeting cards. I think his name is Finley. He's a recluse."

I ran home and checked the dictionary for the definition of "recluse." Hermit was a word I knew, because a friend said her uncle was one. He stayed in his house out in the country all the time and only stepped out to go to the barn.

Charlotte gathered up the actors and stagehands to rehearse. We practiced three times in three days. After the third day, Charlotte thought we were about as ready as we would ever be. We had sold twenty tickets, but Mike and I hadn't talked to Mr. Finley yet.

"I'm going to sell one to Mr. Finley," I said, as I made another ticket. "I'm leaving. Anybody else?"

Charlotte declined because she was busy reading. Nancy and Freddy said they had to go home. Margery told us we were crazy because he was too odd. Mike decided he would come, if I would go first.

"We'll go together," I said.

As we walked down the street toward Mr. Finley's, the wind began to whistle and make little dirt funnels in the dusty street. Mike and I looked at each other and wondered if we should go back. A siren screamed, and we saw an ambulance flash by on the highway up the street.

"Uh oh," Mike said. "Let's go back."

"It's not for us, silly. Besides, we've come this far. Let's run."

We reached Mr. Finley's house and rang the doorbell. We waited and waited. I didn't want to leave without seeing him. Then we heard footsteps, and the door creaked open.

A man appeared. Through the screen door, I could see he was wearing a beige suit and a wide blue tie pulled away from his skinny neck. His pale blue eyes faintly smiled, but the lids drooped at the corners. He wore a wrinkled tan shirt, and his brownish, wiry hair stuck out on the left side, like he just got up from a nap.

A faint, watery voice said, "Yes?"

"Are you Mr. Finley? This is my brother Mike, and my name is Marietta, and we live down the street. We're selling tickets to the play my sister wrote. It's called *Lo-Su, the Girl Pirate*. And it's an outdoor play. Would you like to buy one? It's a play and it's not very long. They're only a nickel," I said.

Mr. Finley straightened up to his full height, only slightly taller than me. Then his shoulders sagged, and his hand quivered as he pressed it to the screen door. Mike and I took a step backward.

"Well, I don't know. When is it?" Mr. Finley said.

"It's Saturday," Mike said.

"I'll see if I can find a nickel," he said. "You can come in."

Mike and I exchanged glances as Mr. Finley walked back into the house. We opened the scraping screen door and stepped inside. Squinting to adjust my vision, I saw stacks and stacks of boxes and magazines, piled so high I couldn't see over them.

There was no furniture in sight and no lights were on. I wondered if Mr. Finley had a nickel to spend. I looked at Mike, whose eyes were bigger than Raggedy Andy's. A narrow path wound into the house, but I couldn't see the end of it. Mr. Finley had disappeared, so we stopped walking and stood still.

"Come on back."

We looked at each other again and nodded yes. Mike wanted me to go first. We crept single-file through the dusky warehouse in search of Mr. Finley. When we went as far as we could, we saw him standing stock still, clutching a coin purse.

Behind him were boxes spilling with greeting cards. A large yellow cat sat in an open box. Mr. Finley asked me to hold out my hand. I thrust out my open palm. His long, skinny fingers unzipped the coin purse, and one by one, he counted five pennies into my hand.

"There, that should do it," said Mr. Finley.

"Wow! Thanks," we said in unison.

"I guess we better go," I said as I gave him his ticket. "See you at the play."

We ran all the way home, laughing about our success with Mr. Finley, bragging to each other about how brave we were to have met the hermit. When we got home, it had started to sprinkle, so the other kids were starting to go home. I said, "We sold a ticket to Mr. Finley."

Margery said, "Sure you did, uh huh. That guy is weird."

"You'll see, you'll see," Mike shouted.

With everyone seated at the kitchen table the next day, Mike and I stumbled over each other, trying to tell the story about our sale. Charlotte was skeptical about whether he would show up and said he bought the ticket just to be nice. Mike and I protested, explaining that he obviously didn't have much money and wouldn't want to waste it.

Show time! The cast and stage hands assembled to set up the stage, props, and tables. No one had practiced hanging the curtains, so we delayed the start of the play to wrangle them. The curtains didn't want to stay up, and no one was tall enough to hold it. We finally decided the audience would just have to use their imaginations and pretend a curtain was there.

As the audience gathered, I looked around for Mr. Finley. "He's not here yet," I told Charlotte. "We can't start until he gets here."

Most of the audience sat on blankets or stood to watch the play. In a rare moment, for the sake of the theater, someone brought card table chairs and placed them in the yard.

"The audience is ready," Charlotte said.

"There he is," said Mike, as he waved to Mr. Finley, decked out in his suit, tie, and hat. "We can start now."

The play started off well. Charlotte, the narrator, thanked the audience for attending and introduced the play, saying the setting was a remote Asian country with a reigning queen.

Lo-Su wore cowboy boots, a T-shirt, and shorts adorned with a scarf tied around her waist. Mike, the thief who tried to board the boat, wore an eye patch, black pants, a long-sleeved white shirt, and a rubber dagger hanging from a belt loop. The stage hands stood at the ready in case they needed to change a prop.

The queen called Lo-Su in to negotiate the terms of the venture. Lo-Su would share in the proceeds of the treasure as long as no one got hurt.

Freddy and Nancy provided sound effects for the ship sailing away into the sea by stirring water in a big tub off stage and using their mouths in a whooshing sound to enhance the sound of the waves.

Soon, Mike, the thief, climbed into a tree (the ship's ladder), to the narrator's words. "Oh, no, here comes another pirate looking to profit from our venture. Someone needs to stop him."

Lo-Su stepped close to the "tree" to thwart the thief, who lost his balance and fell, stopping the play. I looked for Mr. Finley, but he had already started to walk toward his home.

As if he knew we were watching, he stopped, turned around and tipped his hat. Mike and I poked each other and giggled. Mike went to the doctor's office to have his collarbone examined, and the doctor fitted him with an apparatus that kept his bone in place until the break healed.

For many years afterward, we retold the story of the day the hermit came out of his cave to watch our sister's play. I believed I had done something special, including someone in our event whom other people had ignored and mocked. It was only fair. I liked this part as much as—maybe even more than—pretending to be Lo-Su. I thought our family was one of the good ones. My sister and brother were smart, my parents seemed happy, and everyone was well. Then fear struck our community when the polio epidemic raced around the world.

Mother Falls Ill

Polio is a virus of the nerve endings that can cause paralysis. Other symptoms include difficulty breathing, headache, and nausea. Mother had been feeling sick, and as fate would have it, she had contracted a limited case of the horrid disease.

Her treatment consisted of hot packs, physical therapy, and pain medication. She did not have to endure the torture of the iron lung that many children did, nor did she experience permanent paralysis. Mother improved and eventually recovered, but post-polio syndrome affected her in later years. One of her legs was weakened, and when she was tired, the leg dragged a bit.

Polio is highly contagious, and Charlotte, Mike, and I took gamma globulin shots to prevent our catching it. Each shot took a long time for the serum to enter the bloodstream, and it hurt going in.

The nurses calculated one's weight and then determined the amount of the dosage. I was nine years old and weighed 89 pounds, a bit on the chubby side, someone said.

One of Dad's sisters came from McPherson to help with household tasks, but each of us kids had chores to do every day. Everyone was worried about Mother's health, and Dad was meeting himself coming and going, as he tried to do his job and get home as much as possible.

I Am Healthy

I had survived the usual and unusual childhood accidents and illnesses. Running barefoot at full speed when I was four years old, I stepped on a broken mayonnaise jar in the yard and sliced open my foot. After circling the living room at full speed, when I was five, I fell and hit my head on the corner of the radio console.

A couple of years later, wearing shoes, I stepped on a nail, piercing my shoe and foot. The nail stuck out the top. It looked so funny; I started laughing, but decided I should probably do something about it. I hobbled to my parents' store. Mother took one look and nearly fainted.

And then, there was the nail sticking out of a board that scraped the side of my leg, producing a six-inch gash in my skin. I also skinned my knees several times while roller skating.

When I jumped out of a swing at the highest point off the ground, I sprained an ankle. A klutzy, but normal childhood. And there was the unforgettable incident when my sister slammed my hand in the car door.

Walking on the tops of high walls, swimming in Kanopolis Lake at night, and playing dodge ball were among my favorites. But why not? Shit happens, and then the pain goes away. I could find humor in most situations. The one situation I didn't find funny happened in the front yard of our house.

Pocket Knives Are Handy

Dad had come home for lunch—unusual for him—because his bread route took him all over the region, from 3:30 in the morning to late afternoon or early evening. I heard him talking to Mother while she was fixing lunch.

"I heard that S.O.B. who's been molesting kids has been seen around town," he said. "If people know who he is, why don't they report it to the police? I heard someone in Martha's Cafe saying that people just don't want their names in the paper along with the pervert."

"You mean they know who it is, but nobody will tell the police?" Mother asked.

"That's what I heard," Dad said. "They think if their kid is involved, they're going to get their names in the paper."

"Well, I don't know," Mother said. "I have seen no one like that around here, but we'll be on the lookout."

After lunch, Mike and I were sitting on the front steps of our house fiddling with a pocket knife. Mike dug it up from under a piece of sandstone beside the front stoop of the house.

Mother came outside, said she was going next door for a little while, and told us to be sure to stay in the yard close to the house.

Kids played in each other's yards in those days, and since there were three kids in our family, neighborhood kids frequently ended up in our yard.

When the other kids came over to find out what Mike and I were doing, I said, "we're making gold." We jumped down from the step and crouched beside the sandstone brick.

"Wow," Freddy said. "Can I do it?"

"Yeah, but first I'll show you how," I said. "See, you take this gold rock and this pocket knife and you run the knife blade across it with a little water, and you've got gold!"

Sure enough, a bit of gold dust scraped off the sandstone and mixed with the water.

Everyone took a turn at gold making while we figured out how to save it. We thought we should be able to take it to the bank. Just like the gold rush days. And we agreed to split up the money even-steven at the bank.

As I took back the knife and stone to take my turn, we saw a car pull up to the curb at the house to the south. I continued scraping for gold, and the other kids were watching me. Somebody said we could probably get a hundred dollars for what we had right there beside the porch.

The man at the curb hollered at us from his car, asking if someone named Dennis lived there. We all said no, giggling because we said it altogether. "Jinx, you owe me a coke."

Unnoticed by us prospectors, the man got out of the car and walked into the yard. As he walked, he asked what we were doing. Someone bragged, "We're making gold."

"Oh, really, how do you do that?" he asked.

"We're just playing," I said, beginning to feel very uncomfortable.

We don't know you.

In the next instant, he had picked me up by grabbing my crotch and said, "You're kind of a strong little girl, aren't you?"

"Put me down, put me down," I hollered and kicked my legs as he started toward his car.

Donny started flapping his hands. "Go away, go away," he hollered.

Mike ran next door, yelling, "Mom, Mom, somebody's trying to steal Marietta! Mom, Mom."

I kicked and screamed, telling the man to put me down. But that didn't work. He was getting close to his car. I still had the pocketknife, so I started stabbing him in the leg until he let me go. He finally dropped me on the ground and ran to his car. When he got into the car, he tore off, squealing tires as he sped away.

Mother and the other neighbors came running into our yard. They wanted to know what happened. Everyone was talking at once. I walked off to the side and told my neighbor he had picked me up and tried to carry me away to his car.

The other kids said it was a good thing I was the one making gold, because I had the knife and could stab him when he picked me up. After we all calmed down a little, Mike and I went inside with Mother. She contacted the police and said it would probably be in the newspapers.

The police came to the house, and we had to go through the whole thing again. I described the man, including his hair color, height, plaid shirt, and bowling shoes.

When Dad came home about 5:30 that evening, I thought he was going to croak. He turned red and started cussing. He called the police, too, and asked around the station to find out why they hadn't caught the guy. After all, they had a description, a potential suspect, and a complaint.

About an hour later, Dad and I went to the police station. Two officers handcuffed to a man brought him into an open area about 15 feet from us. There was a large desk separating us. They asked me if this was the man who had picked me up and tried to put me in his car.

"That's him, but he's wearing a different shirt," I said. "He changed his shirt. He was wearing a tan plaid shirt. This one is blue plaid."

Dad started out after him. I had never seen him so angry. "You sonofabitch, you will never hurt another child if I have anything to do with it," he yelled.

It took three officers to hold Dad back. He was ready to do serious damage. The officers handcuffed to the suspect shoved him out of the room and down the hallway. I found out later he was booked and put in jail. He apparently served a lengthy sentence, because he had molested several children in Kansas.

In a couple of days, both *The Russell Daily News* and *The Russell Record* newspapers reported an incident of child molestation. Short story. No names.

The man attacked me; I defended myself and identified the creep. He went to jail, and I was happy. I wasn't embarrassed, because it wasn't my fault. No one tried to blame me for the incident.

Dad read the newspaper stories at the dinner table. "See, no names," he said. "He got what was coming to him. Anybody want ice cream?"

We Have a New House

Several months later, our parents purchased a home in a new housing addition close to where we had been living. The house had three bedrooms, one of which Charlotte and I would share.

Not only did we have a new house, but I got to attend fifth grade in a new school building.

My fifth-grade teacher was a gentle man who read aloud from *The Adventures of Tom Sawyer* after lunch. Every day we begged him to read just one more chapter to know what happened to Tom and Becky.

After school, all three of us kids had chores to keep the house up to snuff. We pulled weeds, kept our bedrooms picked up, helped cook meals, washed and dried dishes, hung clothes on the line, sprinkled and ironed clothes, vacuumed the living room, emptied the trash, and fed the dog. Sometimes we burned the trash. Weeding the yard was my least favorite thing to do.

Whenever we dragged our feet after dinner to avoid starting the kitchen chores, Dad challenged us to see how fast we could wash and dry dishes, take out the trash, and sweep the floor.

Every day after that, he challenged us to see if we could beat our previous record. The challenge worked. We took the bait every time. The record for completing the chores was two and one-half minutes. Occasionally we had to redo a glass or plate, but we laughed the whole time, the best part of the chore.

We practiced our violins, did our homework, and played games with kids in the neighborhood. Kick the can, dodge ball, Annie, Annie Over, and marching up and down the street to imaginary tunes were some of my favorites.

The three of us listened to the radio, and the commercial messages got stuck in our brains. We practiced singing the commercials together. Ipana toothpaste, Dash dog food, and other commercials were our favorites to sing. Each of us had a part. Charlotte sang soprano, I sang alto, and Mike sang bass. One of our favorites was from a popular television and radio Ajax jingle: *"Use Ajax, the foaming cleanser. Floats the dirt right down the drain, bubba, bubba, bubba, bub."*

Charlotte and I memorized a song we had heard called, "We Gotta Put the Shoes on Willie," and performed it for anyone who would sit still. Props were a broom and slouchy hats. When the part about Willie milking a cow came along, we mimicked the action. The whole show was silly, and we had a tough time getting through it without laughing, which added to the absurdity of the song and our performance.

We entertained ourselves; we did not own a television set until about 1957. According to Mother, we would not have had one then if Dad hadn't won one in a raffle organized by the priests at the Cathedral of the Plains in Victoria. Dad bought three one-dollar tickets on a day when he was delivering bread to the monastery. Lo-and-behold, he won. Mother wasn't sure we should accept the TV set.

"That TV set will ruin your eyes. We don't need one just because everyone else has one." She relented, because he had already brought it into the house, along with his other winnings, a red and black lamp. The base of the lamp was a sculpture of a reclining woman.

Our parents ordered us to watch TV sparingly. I wasn't interested in any of the shows until a few years later when we received the show "American Bandstand" and a local dance band show broadcast from Great Bend.

I was busy taking ballet lessons and wanted to dance pointe—dancing on one's toes. The requirements in the 1950s were not as strict as they are now. I started pointe when I was

11 years old. My legs, ankles, and feet were strong, and I had mastered the basic ballet techniques: five positions of feet and arms, *tour jeté*, and *plie*, for example.

Toe shoes have satin uppers and ribbons to tie around one's ankles. For the ballerina to dance on her toes, the toes of the shoes have a steel plate in them. The dancer wears a "bunny" over her toes to protect the toes from the hard steel. A bunny is a rabbit-lined leather cup that fits snugly over the toes, inside the shoe.

The ballet class picked the colors for the costumes we would wear for our first public performance: red and pink. My grandmother made my outfit, the top of which was pink. One side of the skirt was pink, and the other side was red. Our class practiced often until the teacher set the date for our performance.

Figure 6. Taking ballet lessons was my attempt to improve my balance to prevent falling while roller skating, 1953.

While visiting Dad's parents in McPherson one Sunday, I started showing off my part of the dance recital, doing tour jete around the dining room and out onto the front porch. Dancing wasn't enough for me, though. I started mimicking the junior high cheerleaders I had seen at ball games.

I should have known better, but no, I was getting a lot of laughs. Anyway, I fell and hollered because my foot hurt. Not long after, we all headed for home.

The next day, my foot still hurt, so Mother took me to the doctor. He discovered a hairline fracture in my foot. My ballet career was over before it started. Mother pointed out how I could avoid this kind of trouble: stop showing off.

In Trouble Again

When we lived in Hutchinson, we made friends with a family that had six children—all girls. We had visited each other's homes, camped out, and played together. After we moved to Russell, our parents planned a picnic along the Saline River with our Hutchinson friends.

On the second day of the campout, Cheryl, one sister and I explored the river bed. I was Huck Finn, and she was Tom Sawyer.

Cheryl and I started on our trek to discover river treasure. Catfish were jumping out of the deep pools. Fallen cottonwoods littered the overgrown banks of the river. Rocks and minerals had worked their way through the soil, revealing flint, mica, and sandstone. We found one arrowhead.

Every find was a treasure, but the weight of our treasures proved too much to carry, so we went back. Neither one of us had a wristwatch., but our family surely had missed us by now. I crawled up to the riverbank to see where we were.

My friend was getting scared because clouds were forming, and the sun had dropped in the sky. Not long after both of us made it up the riverbank, Mother came walking up toward us. She grabbed my shoulders, shook me, and demanded, "Where in the world have you been? We have been looking all over for you. You have been gone for over an hour."

"I wasn't worried," I said.

"Cheryl, are you all right?" Mother asked. Cheryl nodded.

I got another tongue-lashing in the car after we loaded camp gear, but Dad said, "They had an adventure, and they are okay. Let's forget about it."

School Sparks Action

One ordinary sixth-grade day, our teacher struck a student in the head with a book. His glasses went flying across the room and crashed to the floor, broken. He was hurt and stunned. His face was very red, and he started to cry. The teacher left the room.

I immediately said we should get a petition together asking the principal to fire her. I wrote a sentence saying the teacher hit a student for no reason. Many students signed the paper. We gave it to the principal. They fired our teacher, probably before we turned in our petition, but we thought we had done something important.

For the rest of the school year, the wife of the principal led our class. She was a soft-spoken person who didn't hit anyone.

Figure 7. Sixth grade school picture, 1953-1954.

Until I was nine or 10, events took their time, stretching on and on. After I turned 10, time flew by. I had passed sixth grade and qualified to advance to seventh grade, but was I ready? I was eleven years old.

In junior high, students changed classrooms and teachers for each subject and waved to friends in the hallways. We had lockers for coats and books. At the semester break in seventh grade, those who had made As in English did not have to take the midterm final.

My friend Judy and I were exempt from the final, so we went outside to play in the snow close to the nearby high school.

The high school had a long, steep walkway from the door of the gymnasium to the street. Ice coated the walkway in winter, because the sand meant to eliminate slipperiness didn't cover the entire walk. Judy and I flung each other down the icy walk, making sure we stopped at the curb to avoid flying into the street.

Judy launched me first, and I went sliding down the icy path. I came to the curb, dropped off the curb to avoid an oncoming car and slammed my hand down in the street. I got up off the street with a dangling wrist. It didn't hurt, but it certainly looked funny. My friend was shrieking and hollering for help.

We went inside the gym to find a teacher. One of the high school coaches was standing at the doorway and opened the door for us. "What are you girls doing here?" He looked at my wrist. His face turned red as he said, "Oh my god."

He contacted Mother, and she took me to a local physician who set my arm and put it into a cast. Mother wanted to know why I was playing in the street. "If you had been in class, your arm would not be broken."

Our family doctor sawed the cast off in a few weeks. My explanation of "playing in the street" did not impress Mother.

Going from classroom to classroom was fun, sneaking a whisper to classmates in between classes, but I was ready to advance to eighth grade.

My eighth-grade English teacher was a gem. She wore her gray hair in a bun adorned with a pencil she pulled out to point to a student to go to the board. We diagrammed sentences on the chalkboard and recited poems from memory.

She encouraged me to join debate class and try out for the team when I reached high school. High school debaters came to Russell for tournaments, and she and the debate coach asked me to be a timekeeper for that year's tournament.

A team from Hoisington High School made quite an impression, because one of the two boys was so articulate. He had a deep beautiful voice, had a "Princeton" haircut—not a flattop—and wore a tan suit, white shirt, blue and red tie, and white sneakers with white socks. He looked me right in the eyes when he sat on the edge of the desk to deliver his speech. I thought he was the coolest. Uh oh. Butterflies.

The National Forensic League topic for 1955-56 was *Resolved: That governmental subsidies should be granted according to need to high school graduates who qualify for additional training.* Some arguments centered on fairness, to wit: Does poverty qualify a person to receive a subsidy? Does academic achievement qualify a person for a subsidy? How would the government pay for these subsidies? Who picks the recipients?

The questions and arguments probably were the first serious discussions I thought I had heard, and I was impressed that high school students were making them—especially the boy in the tan suit.

I selected a debate class as an elective in my freshman year. We received one credit hour toward graduation if we took it all year. Course content included how to read and retain material, how to organize thoughts, and how to create an outline and express opinions.

We learned to project our voices and speak in front of an audience. A training manual for National Forensic League events contained rules for debate and included the debate question and sample arguments for the negative and affirmative sides of the question.

All schools that belonged to the National Forensic League debated the same question. Freshmen could not participate in debate tournaments.

My partner and I won third place in our first tournament as sophomores, debating the question: *Resolved: That United States foreign aid should be substantially increased.* My partner dropped debate after she won a spot on the cheerleading team. I couldn't understand why anyone would give up a chance to argue.

I was hoping the next year's resolution would revolve around space exploration. Sputnik, the Soviet satellite launched in October 1957, had crashed to earth after three months.

President Dwight D. Eisenhower signed the National Aeronautics and Space Act into law, creating the National Aeronautics and Space Administration (NASA). America launched its first satellite from Cape Canaveral. My dream to debate a resolution about space travel did not develop. The resolution for the 1958-59 school year was: *Resolved: That the United States should adopt the essential features of the British system of education.* I was disappointed.

Russell High School was a member of the Kansas State High School Activities Association (KAY clubs). Boys joined KAY club, and girls joined Kayettes (yes, a diminutive KAY). The goal of the clubs was to teach leadership skills and participate in community service projects.

I joined the Russell club and selected the recreation committee. The committee created recreational opportunities for the club and children in the community. Kayettes participated in day camp for children in Russell. Craft projects were always on the agenda at day camp. I made four lanyards one year.

Girls across the state gathered in a park near Junction City in the summer of 1958 for the Kayette Leadership camp. Wanda Mae Vinson, administrator of Kansas Kay clubs, was on hand to greet us and explain the activities. We received an assignment that included a group name and examples of kinds of projects we could plan for our communities.

I was excited to be going, in part because I had perfected my Elvis Presley impersonation, and attendees would display their talents on the last day of camp.

Participants ate meals together in a large dining hall, and the sound of voices singing round-robin songs filled the hall during meal time.

The last day of camp featured the talent show. Each group of girls had stayed together throughout the three days of camp. The last day, each group was supposed to perform an original skit featuring a memorable event.

One thing our group learned for sure was, "don't leave your hairs in the sink." Ms. Vinson had impressed this act of good hygiene on us many times during our stay.

Our skit consisted of snippets of the three-day event, with singing, eating, and conversing. As a finale, we pulled a shrunken head (brought by one of our group) out of a large bowl, meant to parody Ms. Vinson's caution about keeping the sink bowl free of hair.

Since it was my idea, I got the honor of "cleaning the bowl." Our skit got a laugh, but we weren't sure how Ms. Vinson viewed it.

Girls Are Jocks Too

I had joined the Brownies after we moved to Russell and enjoyed summer day camp, weaving lanyards, and meeting new people my age. I moved on to the Girl Scouts, and I stayed with the same troop of girls all the way through high school.

Camping out, setting up tents, cooking outdoors, playing outdoor sports, and working on education projects were activities I enjoyed. One summer, our troop traveled to Camp Crowder in Missouri to test our camping mettle.

I paired up with someone in our troop for the week. We set up our tent, trenched around the perimeter, and used a camp stove and charcoal to cook our meals. One night, a storm struck with no warning, and rain deluged our campsite.

When my tent partner and I woke up the next day, we discovered others in our troop cleaning up their campsites, but we had trenched around our tent, secured our belongings well, and slept so soundly that we did not even know there had been a storm.

My tent partner and I were strong, healthy girls, so we helped the others clean up and reset their sites. I enjoyed the friendship and helping others that were central themes to the credo of the Girl Scouts.

Our troop completed hundreds of badges, attended many outings and singalongs, and in our senior year of high school earned the silver wings award.

Figure 8. The Girl Scout troop that stayed together through high school. I am in the top row, first on the left, 1956.

In addition to scouts and debate, one of my favorite activities was sports. Girls' intramural high school sports comprised badminton; tumbling; trampoline jumping; tennis; tenniquoit; and six-person, half-court basketball. I participated in all of them.

The coach called me down a couple of times for slamming the quoit or shuttlecock across the net too hard, but I thought I had to give it my all.

Girls did not play sports with teams from other schools as the boys did.

The high school girls' physical education teacher, a woman, coached all the girls' sports. I wanted to try weightlifting to strengthen my upper body for tennis because I had to use two hands to hit a backhand stroke.

The coach trained me to lift free weights. When the men's wrestling coach saw what we were doing, he said I would overdevelop my muscles, an unattractive quality on a girl. My coach and he had a heated discussion as I looked on.

Later, my coach said we could work out something if I still wanted to strengthen my upper body. I eventually dropped the issue because I didn't have enough time to do all the sports, go to school, play in the orchestra, travel with the debate team, and perform as a twirler with the marching band.

In my junior year, the Girls Athletic Association (GAA) elected me president. Duties consisted of conducting meetings and organizing teams for special projects.

The national GAA had divided the members into committees. Committees discussed their plans for implementing their goals.

The shop class created a frame to hold a large banner. Members of the GAA painted an image of the mascot, the bucking Russell Bronco, from a template and attached it to the frame. The basketball team broke through the banner and onto the court to start the game.

A special task I enjoyed included organizing the contest to elect sophomores to be servers for the Junior-Senior prom. The sophomore class elected the servers who picked costumes appropriate to the theme of the prom and then served food and water to the attendees at the banquet preceding the dance. This was a big deal in our school because the sophomores got to hang out with the upperclassmen.

Friction at Home

Due to time constraints, I had dropped the weightlifting issue, but I seemed to have enough time to get under my mother's skin. I became infatuated with Jimmy, a boy two years ahead of me in school. Mother firmly believed he was a juvenile delinquent, that his father was an adulterer, and that I was too young to hang out with or date the boy.

She consistently referred to him as a "hood" and a delinquent because he drove a black 1949 Ford convertible with dual exhaust pipes that roared. "He's a member of that gang that Fred heads up. You know, the one with a juvenile record. You are going to turn out just like them."

Jimmy had a reputation for driving too fast and drag racing with other such "hoods." However, he was very nice to me, he was smart, and I thought he differed from the other boys I knew who were sort of squirrely.

He had read about Jack Kerouac and the Beat Generation. When Kerouac published *On the Road* in 1957, this boy got a copy of it and read a few parts of it aloud to me. I thought Kerouac and his friends were brave, but also a little odd for taking off across the country just for the experience of it.

I felt very grown-up at ages 13 and 14. My mother thought otherwise and forbade me to date this boy. I ignored her and went riding around with him when I thought I could get away with it. Twice I went to his house to dance to records. Mother thought his mother was a nice person and decided the dancing activity was acceptable if the boy's mother was at home and there were other people there.

When Mother thought I had been in a car with this boy, she grilled me about where I had gone, at what time, with whom, demanding proof. The relationship between Mother and me deteriorated further when she started calling me names.

"You are turning into a juvenile delinquent. If you lie to me one more time, I'll knock you into next week. You go to hell for lying the same as you do for stealing."

When she was angry to the point of yelling, "Go ahead, tell me you hate me, I know you do," I ignored her, which made her even angrier.

She started beating me with a yardstick when I ignored her. I took the beatings until one day I lost my temper. I took the yardstick away from her and hit her with it. I said, "Don't you ever hit me again." She was dumbfounded, and I felt better. My triumph didn't last long.

When my father came home, Mother told him about the incident. For the first time in my life, Dad turned me over his knee and swatted me on the butt once. I was embarrassed beyond tears and ran to my room, slamming the door. The solid core door cracked, and I had to pay to have it replaced out of my babysitting money and money I made as a carhop at the A&W drive-in.

Mother stopped using the yardstick to punish me, but continued yelling horrible threats toward me. "I'll tear your arm off and beat you over the head with the bloody end of it," was one of her favorites, as was, "I'll slap you so hard you won't know what hit you, if you don't answer me."

The threats came so frequently, I started laughing at them. After my sophomore year in high school, the juvenile delinquent joined the US Marine Corps, and I rarely saw him again. My feelings about how Mother had tried to degrade me did not fade.

My friends had parties in their homes, but I was not allowed to attend them. Mother was certain that alcohol would be served, or that boys would attend, or that parents would not be at home.

I avoided hosting parties in our home. Mother had told me she would stand at the front door and smell everyone's breath to make sure they had not been drinking before she let them in. Despite my reluctance, I eventually held a small party at our home and invited both boys and girls.

Mother did exactly what she said she would: she stood at the door and asked guests if they had been drinking. If they said no, she tried to smell their breath. I was mortified.

Figure 9. Charlotte (top row, third from right) and I (center of middle row), belonged to a girls' social club. Mother's pizza created quite a stir at a meeting at our house, because no one had tried it before, 1959.

Charlotte and I belonged to a girls' club not affiliated with the school system, and every month, a different member held a meeting at her home. The hostess provided a snack for attendees.

When it was our turn, Mother made pizza, unknown to most people in Russell. She worked hard making the dough. She added cheese, hamburger, spices, and tomato sauce and baked the pies. We liked the pizza so much; we gobbled it down.

Mother got mad because she was running out of food. She asked a neighbor to fetch the missing ingredients so she could make more pizza. After everyone was gone, Charlotte and I told her how impressed everyone was, and all she could say was, "Don't their parents ever feed them?"

Mother seemed angry all the time. I asked if I could have a lightweight jacket to wear instead of my heavy coat. Mother said, "What makes you think you deserve a new jacket? I never had anything like that. No, you may not have it." This was the standard response if I asked for a new item of clothing.

Prejudice Outs Itself

In the summer of 1958, a friend and I landed jobs teaching at the city swimming pool under the auspices of the American Red Cross. We had qualified to teach lessons through the water safety program held by the Red Cross.

I acquired a very dark suntan each year. One day, this friend and I were teaching when a local resident called the manager of the program and wanted to know why two "N-----" girls were teaching at the pool.

The manager, my friend's mother, pacified the caller by telling her we were not Black. Using the N-word offended my friend and me, but not by being mistaken for Black. We thought the caller was wrong, and so did my friend's mother.

I wonder why I see no Black people in the pool.

I asked the manager why no Black people were in the pool, and she said she would let them come in, but that she would probably lose her job. A Black friend on the debate team had told me she did not know how to swim. If she did not know how to swim, it would be hard to learn if she couldn't go into the pool.

Here was a prime example of "damned if you do, and damned if you don't." Catch-22 in today's parlance.

Besides swimming, debate and forensics were still two of my favorite activities. In 1958, when I was a junior, the debate coach suggested I enter the original oratory event in addition to debate rounds to deliver at tournaments.

Rules for this event required a student to write their own oration and deliver it orally in front of judges. The goal of the oration was to offer a solution to a problem the orator defined, and to use persuasion and compelling language to present the solution.

Schools all over Kansas held forensic events. The coach of the host school enlisted drama coaches, attorneys, teachers, and ministers to judge the events.

The US Supreme Court had decided in *Brown v. Board of Education,* 347 US 483 (1954), that segregation in public schools violated the Fourteenth Amendment. I naively thought this would cure prejudice.

I wrote an oration that dealt with bias toward Black and Brown people. I defined prejudice, gave a historical review of slavery and racism, and advocated allowing interracial marriage. The thrust of my argument was that if interracial marriage were the norm, we could eliminate prejudice and bias. People would become a mixture of all the colors of the world.

Mostly, I received high marks for adhering to the guidelines of oratory. However, among my critics, ministers were the harshest. One of them demanded I leave the tournament and told my coach he should not allow me to deliver the oration again. He indicated that my delivery was very good, but he could not give me a high mark because of the content.

My coach protected my right to deliver the oration, but it surprised some of the other presenters that I stayed in the tournament. A girl from Meade and a boy from Hays told me I should leave. I simply told them they were prejudiced, and I did not care what they thought.

The coach took as many debaters and speakers to compete in tournaments as his budget allowed. If we spent the night, the boys stayed together, and the girls stayed together. At one motel in southwestern Kansas, the coach asked us five girls to stay in the car while he checked us in.

A member of our debate squad who was Black turned her back and tried to hide when the coach told us to wait in the car.

We had a room with two double beds and a rollaway. Discussion ensued about who would sleep where. Everyone in our room agreed that I had to sleep on the rollaway because I tossed around too much, stole covers, and walked in my sleep.

It was months later that I realized why my friend had tried to hide. The coach was afraid she might not be able to stay in the motel if the owner saw her. No one talked about this.

I wanted to propose this girl for acceptance in the International Order of the Rainbow for Girls, a youth club that teaches leadership, confidence, Christian values, and citizenship.[1] Secrecy was also part of the ritual, and was supposed to be discussed only in the presence of other Rainbow Girls.

I approached the Mother Advisor, the adult sponsor of the local organization. She told me not to propose my friend because they did not allow Negroes into the organization. This girl was smart, friendly, did well in school, and was planning to go to college.

"Gwen goes to church. She is smart, and she is an excellent speaker. Why wouldn't the organization want a girl like this? She would make a very good Worthy Advisor," I said.

"It is the policy of the organization. There is nothing I can do," said the Mother Advisor.

"I'm not sure I want to belong to an organization like this."

"You knew what it was like when you joined."

"No, I didn't."

"We are not the only group that does not allow Negroes in."

I felt angry much of the time toward such attitudes and picked arguments with friends and family for using racial slurs and for trying to justify their prejudice with such statements as, "It's always been that way."

Our parents raised us to be nice to everyone, no matter what color they were.

I experienced a similar offensive event in Hays, Kansas, when two friends and I went to a boys' basketball game between the Russell Broncos and the Hays High Indians.

One of my friends could drive, and her parents let her take one of the family cars. After the game, we went to a popular restaurant, Dan's Drive-In, to get a soda and see our friends.

There was a sign in the window saying, "N-----, don't let the sun set on you." My friends and I entered the restaurant and were looking for a place to sit. The owner/manager approached us and demanded to see my driver's license. He did not want to admit me because he thought I was Black. This restaurant was one of many stores that barred Black people from their establishments.

Here we go. Not again. This idiot is trying to keep Black people from eating his crappy hamburgers. Should I let him think I am Black and make a big issue out of this?

My friends did not know what to do. All three of us were confused.

"I think it might be illegal to keep me from coming in," I said.

"I own this restaurant, you little n-----. I can decide who comes in here and who doesn't. Show me your driver's license."

"I don't have one."

"What's the matter? Can't you read?"

I couldn't fathom how a Black person could deal with this kind of behavior every day. Instead of flying off the handle and yelling at him, I turned to my friends.

"Let's leave. I can't talk to this moron."

My friends agreed, and we left. After we got into the car, Bette and Cheryl let out big sighs of relief.

"I thought for a minute you might hit him," Cheryl said.

"It's over now. Thanks for sticking up for me. Imagine what it must feel like to deal with this every day."

"Well, fortunately, we don't have to," Bette said.

"That is not the point," I said. End of discussion for now.

When I reported the incident to my parents, they were extremely upset. Especially my father. In his job as a supervisor at Betts Baking Company, he oversaw the delivery of Rainbo bread, buns, and rolls to the restaurant in question.

He was angry enough to confront the owner. He threatened to discontinue bread delivery if the owner ever refused, based on race, to seat someone in his restaurant. The owner backed down and said he would take down the signs.

Figure 10. Dan's Drive-In, Hays, Kansas, denied me entrance because the owner swore I was Black. Here's the evidence, 1958.

How do people come to be so hateful of someone whose skin is a different color? Kansas entered the Union in 1861 as a free state. *Brown v. Board of Education of Topeka*, 347 US 483 (1954), was a landmark US Supreme Court decision in which the Court ruled that state laws establishing racial segregation in public schools are unconstitutional, even if the segregated schools are otherwise equal in quality.[2] Private businesses did not stop discriminating against people of color, however.

School Activities

Figure 11. During my junior year in high school, I refused to wear the glasses meant to correct my astigmatism because they messed up my hair, 1959.

Research into governmental actions, legislation, and argumentation sparked my interest in politics. Another friend, also a debater, asked me to help her campaign for secretary of her class. She put me in charge of the campaign. *Yikes!*

I had to think of something to set her apart from the other campaigners. With permission from the school administration, I arranged for the high school dance band to march into the auditorium after I introduced her at the candidates' forum.

After her introduction, I closed with, "She is the best choice for Secretary. Let's strike up the band for Annie!" The band marched into the auditorium from the rear entrances up to the stage playing "Happy Days Are Here Again."

Annie marched in front of the band and walked to the podium, where she raised her arms in salute to the packed auditorium. She gave a rousing speech after the band finished. When the principal announced Annie won the election, the campaigners whooped and hollered.

The band played to support a high school candidate for office for the first time. The event had a positive effect on the voters, because the high school grapevine had favored the other candidate. Seeing a friend win the office she wanted made me happy.

I got to branch out into radio production when the debate coach offered to teach a radio speech class during the 1958-1959 school year. KRSL, the AM station in Russell, agreed to carry the 30-minute program every Monday evening at 5 p.m.

Five people signed up for the class, and the coach appointed me the producer. Everyone had a role as a reporter and/or announcer. Students used class time to gather material for the program and to practice vocalizing with a microphone. I determined the order of the items in the program and communicated with the radio station.

We had permission to leave class to interview three students in each grade to name their favorite song that week. I selected two of the most popular to air during the program. I notified the sound engineer at the studio so he could queue a tape of them. Our student announcers introduced each one during the program.

Other members of the team selected news about academic achievements, athletic games, and upcoming events. I edited these items, and we took turns reading them on the air. I introduced the program and signed off every week.

The choir director at my church worked at the radio station. She warned me that the disc jockey/engineer was ornery and might try to make us laugh while we were in the studio. He tried by making faces or nonverbal gestures, but we all managed, just barely, to make it through the programs without cracking up.

I came to believe that radio messages affected the listener because the message did not need to be complicated, so it was easy to remember.

To further use radio as a tool for encouraging students to become involved in politics, I suggested broadcasting student debates, speeches, and other forensic events on the radio or through the intercom system. This idea didn't go anywhere, but I developed a reputation for speaking my mind when others remained silent.

My friends and I discussed current local and global issues. Wearing proper clothing to school, the dangers of rock and roll music, gangs, drag racing, ducktail haircuts, and the Beat Generation occupied parents and teachers.

In a more serious vein, racism, the threat of communism, poverty, and the role of girls and women in the home, workplace, college, and politics were subjects of interest to me.

Senator Margaret Chase Smith (R-Maine) was the first woman elected to a full term as a US Senator from Maine. She supported the expansion of the military and defense budgets, and like most Republicans of the time, she was staunchly anti-communist.

I thought she demonstrated courage during the McCarthy hearings when she took to the Senate floor to condemn the tactics of the House Un-American Activities Committee (HUAC) and Wisconsin Senator Joseph McCarthy.

I initiated discussions in history class and with the debate team about what HUAC had done, as well as what kind of system communism was. Some class members roundly condemned me for bringing up the subject of that evil system, even if they didn't know what it was.

Debaters were more likely to talk about communism because they could argue. How did one define it? Was it a political system or was it an economic system? Was it good or bad for the people of the Union of Soviet Socialist Republics (USSR)? What was socialism?

I didn't favor the systems, even though I admitted I knew little about the subjects. I thought if everyone contributed resources to the community and took out only what they needed, then everyone would have something.

Theoretically, no one would be left without. Those who had more would contribute more, and those with less would contribute less. I thought it was worth talking about.

One student "accused" me of being too altruistic, another said my remarks were treasonous, someone else said I would go to hell for talking against the US. I had managed to offend someone's free market, their patriotism, and their religion. Wow!

Very few students wanted to discover the answers to these questions. They thought even talking about it was wrong in the United States. I became known as a sympathizer who would rather be Red than dead.

No Satire, Please

As Christmas approached that year, the high school principal asked my debate partner Don and me to conduct the program for the senior Christmas dance in the high school gym. This event was traditionally a casual event. No one was concerned about celebrating this holiday in a high school facility. Don and I introduced the program as "A new look at the meaning of Christmas."

Don began the discussion. "Is Christmas a religious holiday? Is it a time to decorate the house? Is it a time for giving presents?"

No one in the audience offered to speak, so I took my copy of the Christmas edition of *Mad* magazine and read from it. Don and I wanted to show that the commercialization of Christmas was a distortion of the Christmas message. We took turns reading from the magazine and apparently offended a couple of students.

Two of the offended students ran to the principal, who came to the gym and took Don and me to his office for a lecture on making fun of Christmas. We returned to the gym, ceased our parody, and enlisted glee club students to sing a few popular tunes and a couple of Christmas songs. This seemed to offend no one. One singer told me I should stop trying to make trouble.

"I was not mocking the birth of the Christ child, but I was pointing out that turning Christmas into an opportunity to make money was a far cry from the original message," I said.

Don and I learned we do not all share the same sense of humor.

Athletic activities continued to occupy some of my free time. I had noticed for some time that two girls, Martha and Vicky, were being mercilessly teased or shunned.

I asked an acquaintance why. She said "Have you seen Vicky's tail? That is the strangest thing I have ever seen."

"Why are you making fun of her? She can't help it."

I talked to the health and physical education teacher about it. "Vicky has some extra cartilage at the end of her tailbone. It is unusual, but there is nothing wrong with her. Why do you ask?"

"Some girls are making fun of her," I said. "Can you do something about it?"

"I can talk about body anomalies in health class," Mrs. Wright said.

"What about Martha? Girls talk about Martha behind her back. They say she looks like a man instead of a girl."

"What do you think you should do about it?"

"I've told a couple of people I've seen men who look like girls, too. I think we should remember the Golden Rule and treat others as we want to be treated."

This sort of approach had a positive impact on some of my acquaintances, but for some, it solidified their opinions of me as odd or goody two-shoes.

Other Students Organize

While Don and I were researching a debate topic, I came across Students for a Democratic Society (SDS). Interested students held their first meeting in early 1960 on the University of Michigan campus at Ann Arbor.

Later, I found out the first convention participants adopted the SDS manifesto, known as the Port Huron Statement, in

June 1962, based on an earlier draft by staff member Tom Hayden.

SDS developed from the youth branch of a socialist educational organization known as the League for Industrial Democracy (LID). LID itself descended from an older student organization, the Intercollegiate Socialist Society, founded in 1905 by Upton Sinclair, Walter Lippmann, Clarence Darrow, and Jack London.

The Port Huron Statement captivated me because of my growing interest in politics and because students and labor organizers had composed most of it.

While researching debate topics, I found a large quantity of subject matter that was new to me. Kansas was a right-to-work state, and few workers were members of a union. However, most railroad workers, gas workers, and semi-truck drivers were members of unions, even in Kansas, but union organizing activity was rare. Attempts to unionize workers usually made the newspapers, and not without controversy.

When the time came in my senior year to select an elective, I hesitated. My counselor recommended home economics for girls so that we could prepare ourselves for marriage. I asked what he recommended for boys so they would be prepared for marriage. He tried not to laugh, but told me not to be such a smart aleck.

Sewing was my enemy in eighth grade. I would never master the sewing art. The pocket on the apron I made never looked right, even after ripping it out four times. I didn't mind cooking, but I just was not interested in the subject of homemaking.

I wanted to take mechanical drawing instead. Mechanical drawing could be a precursor to architecture. If I earned a degree in architecture, I could design my own home one day.

I talked to the teacher, but he refused because he said my presence would disrupt the rest of the class, consisting of all boys. I expressed my anger by marching into the principal's office to demand entry into the class. The principal said he thought it would be okay, but I would still need permission from the teacher, who was the football coach.

My father pleaded my case to the principal and the coach. "I'll take her out of this school and send her to another high school if you don't admit her," he said.

Finally, the coach relented. I attended class. When I entered class on the first day, there was another girl already there. We each earned an "A" in the class—with no disruptions other than the moaning and groaning of some boys who did not do as well as we did, despite my having contracted hepatitis and missing some classes. The other girl in the class told me the principal had recruited her to join the class, which she willingly did.

Hoopla at the National Convention

Hepatitis quarantined me to the hospital in Salina, and I missed many of my senior classes. Teachers made sure I received my assignments, and I graduated with the rest of my class in 1960.

I became more interested in politics when I learned that Aunt Claudine was an elector for the Republican Party in McPherson County.

Figure 12. I was ill and got out of bed to take my senior class photo. The photographer applied the makeup for the color shot, as I had never worn makeup before, 1960.

She made it known that the national party was organizing busloads of people to attend the convention. She offered my cousin and me two of her tickets to travel with Kansas Youth for Nixon to Chicago to participate in demonstrations at the convention. I thought I was probably a Republican. Grandmother Anderson told me the Andersons were all Abraham Lincoln Republicans because he had freed the slaves. Some of her relatives had served in the Union Army.

My parents decided I was well enough to go to the convention in July if I would go to bed early and behave myself. Grandma King, an accomplished tailor, told me she would make a suit for me to wear.

I selected a Vogue pattern and a black and white houndstooth lightweight wool. Despite the Vogue pattern's glut of pieces, she agreed to make it. I loved it, thought it was appropriate for the event, and felt very grown up wearing it with a pink linen sleeveless top she made.

Twelve busloads of Kansas Youth for Nixon arrived in Chicago on July 27, our day to create spontaneous demonstrations. I thought calling a planned demonstration "spontaneous" made little sense.

Before going to our hotel, our buses traveled through some of the poor neighborhoods of the city.

Our chaperones informed us that people in these parts of town were strong John F. Kennedy supporters and we should open the windows and shout "Kansas Youth for Nixon" at people on the street. Some passengers on the bus were mocking the people on the streets, most of whom were Black.

We arrived at our hotel and later re-boarded buses to go to the convention site, the International Amphitheater. The convention nominated Vice-President Richard M. Nixon for President and Connecticut Senator Henry Cabot Lodge for Vice-President.

Our chaperones told us we should be able to reach the convention floor, but many did not. I pushed my way in, and a man wearing a metal engraved name tag, Assistant

Secretary of Defense, helped me weave through the crowd. He said anyone who looked as sharp as I did should get to the floor.

Delegates were talking with each other. They wore replicas of their state flower and straw hats beribboned with the names of their states or choices for president. Many wore large campaign pins with photos of their senators or governors.

Delegates shoved campaign pamphlets for Nixon (California), Lodge (Massachusetts), Rockefeller (New York), and Underwood (West Virginia) at me, and dense smoke hovered above the crowd. People jostled each other as they tried to get farther into the convention center.

"Experience Counts," and "Nation Needs Nixon," said the Nixon posters. Not very catchy slogans, but they suited the person.

I caught glimpses of the stage. Red, white, and blue bunting hung from the rafters behind the speakers, as did hundreds of flags and banners with mottos. Demonstrators far behind me were waiting with their signs to get to the floor.

I was holding a "Kansas Youth for Nixon" sign, and the Secretary was leading me, elbowing people out of the way. Soon I could not move any farther, and my escort had vanished. The Kansas kids had disappeared. I continued to push forward, getting in far enough to think the people on stage could see my sign bouncing up and down. The crowd was moving me forward, and my feet left the ground.

I was excited but running out of energy. "Here's my sign. I am going back," I said to the guy next to me.

Twenty minutes later, I made it to the exit and found a place to sit outside to wait for the buses to fill up. My cousin had joined a group of kids she knew and we went back to the hotel. I went to bed. They went out to some parties, and I was asleep when they returned.

We boarded buses the next day to return to Kansas. I was not sure I had learned anything about policy, but thought I had learned something about the hoopla around campaigning and communicating the slogans of a political party.

The people on the bus making stereotypical comments about the Black people we saw disappointed me. I thought they were inappropriate and offensive. If Nixon supported this kind of behavior, I did not want to have anything to do with him.

The Republican ticket lost to the Democratic ticket of John F. Kennedy and Lyndon Baynes Johnson. The four televised debates showed Nixon as a sweating, defensive man with a five o'clock shadow and Kennedy as a youthful, attractive man with quick answers.

4. INTO THE WORLD

Breaking Away

I had contacted no colleges about applying for admission. My illness had caused me to miss many days of school, spurring my parents to suggest I wait a year before attending college. Because of the lost school days, my grades had suffered somewhat, but I wanted to graduate with my class and go on to college.

I lobbied my parents to let me attend Fort Hays State College, because it was only 25 miles away, and it had a good academic reputation. I enrolled and moved my belongings into one of the women's residence halls.

The daughter of one of the residence hall faculty advisors lived in our neighborhood, and Mother knew her. She asked her to keep an eye on me to make sure I was getting enough rest and staying in the dorm.

No problem there. Campus rules required women to be in the dorm by 8 p.m. during the week and Sundays, and midnight on Fridays and Saturdays.

Fort Hays was a nineteenth-century military outpost. The school opened as a "normal" school or teacher's college in

1902 in the outpost. Limestone classroom buildings sat on lush grass lawns. Cottonwoods, Osage orange, and elm trees surrounded the buildings.

In the fall of 1960, approximately 3,000 mostly Caucasian students made up the undergraduate and graduate student enrollment.

A student union building in the middle of the campus held the offices of student government, a cafeteria, and activities offices.

The two- and three-story dormitories lined the edges of the main campus. Most rooms were adequate for two students, complete with desks, dressers, beds, and closets.

Orientation leaders instructed all freshmen to wear "beanies," a close-fitting cap worn on the back of the head, to signal their newcomer status to the campus. I thought it was silly and misplaced my beanie most days.

Clothing choices were typical for the times in Kansas. Most male students wore jeans or khaki pants. A few wore suits or sport coats. Many of the girls wore skirts or dresses. Sweaters over oxford cloth button-down collars were a consistent part of the uniform for men and women.

What would I study? Like many freshmen, I didn't know what I would declare as a major. I would have to conquer the requirements for a Bachelor of Arts program first.

Figure 13. I joined the Fort Hays Penguin Club; I am in the top row, third from the left, Hays, 1961.

I wanted to improve my swimming skill, so I joined the Penguin Club to have access to the pool, and to satisfy a physical education requirement.

I enjoyed researching debate topics, studying current events, and interacting with people to find solutions to social problems.

My high school English grades qualified me for the honors program. I didn't want to give up completely on architecture, especially after earning an A in mechanical drawing, but a degree in architecture usually took five years and was expensive.

I scheduled a general curriculum. Politics still intrigued me, and I learned how to run for a seat on the student council. Each class elected a representative from each of the dorms and from groups of students living off campus.

The student activities office held public candidate forums for each class. My debate experience helped me develop an effective platform for my campaign. I advocated for several changes: the inclusion of students on the university Deans' council, the elimination of dorm hours for women, hiring more students to work in dorm cafeterias in exchange for meal tickets, representation in dormitory decisions, and a seat on the Kansas Board of Regents.

In future years, universities incorporated many of these changes in college rules and guidelines. I cannot claim credit for the changes, much as I might want to.

In addition to the speeches the activities center sponsored, I gave a few impromptu speeches at the soapbox site in the outdoor quadrangle near the student union.

I received the most votes in a field of three to represent the freshman class, possibly because many freshman students were Russell High School graduates. I delivered what I thought were humorous, rhetorically rousing speeches, for which I received much applause.

The Student Government Association promoted and protected student rights and welfare to the administration, the state legislature, and the Board of Regents. The council forwarded the minutes of each meeting to those institutions.

If students brought issues to the council, they could state their cases, and the council would include them in the minutes. Sometimes the council published an account of the issues in the campus newspaper or conducted forums for discussion.

One student brought a case to the council of a teacher's alleged discrimination. He explained that the teacher moved him to the back of the room after he had selected a seat in the front row. He believed the teacher forced the change because he was Black, and a White girl wanted the seat. The council appointed a committee to investigate, and the committee resolved the matter in the student's favor.

After the election, the debate coach approached me in the student center. He said he had scouted me as a high school debater and had heard some of my campaign speeches.

I recognized him because he had judged me and my partner at a tournament in Hays. He invited me to join the debate squad.

I knew the two champion debaters from Russell who were part of the Fort Hays squad. They were a team in high school. Now I was going to be on the same crew as these two accomplished women! They invited me to join Pi Kappa Delta, the forensics club.

Two other members of the squad had won the national intercollegiate debate tournament the previous year. In the final debate, they defeated West Point senior cadets, whose teams attempted to intimidate their opponents by wearing full dress uniforms, ready for battle.

I was eager to meet the new champions. Rumor had it that one of them was handsome, had a deep resonant voice, and was a senior.

I liked being on the council, but my class schedule and the debate team soon would leave me little free time. Balancing everything could become a challenge if I wanted to study and go to bed early.

At my first student council meeting, the president introduced me to the rest of the group, because I had missed the first council meeting.

One representative looked very familiar to me. I felt as though I had met him before. He was tall, slender, had blue/green/hazel eyes and wore a Princeton haircut, a style for boys that was not a flattop or a ducktail. He turned the cuffs of his shirt sleeves under, and his black horn-rimmed glasses added an element of intellect, setting him apart from other young men. A dark brown belt threaded the loops of his khaki trousers, and he was wearing white Keds sneakers. All in all, a very cool image.

Why do my eyes keep wandering back to him? Hmm. He is sneaking peeks at me, too.

The student constitution assigned students to a particular district according to their campus residences and their student status. Districts had approximately the same number of students in each one.

Figure 14. Students elected me to represent the freshman class from
Agnew Hall. I am in the front row, second from the right, 1961.

President Leissig recognized two members of the council
who wanted to speak about the voting behavior of students.
"Welcome seniors Warren Norton, a political science major
and championship debater, and Scotty McNeil, a history
major."

The tag team of Norton and McNeil suggested limiting
student council representation only to the students who vote.
As a result, after the election, the council would have to
redraw the districts based on the students who had voted.
Only the students who had voted in the last election would
have representation.

Even though Norton had momentarily mesmerized me, I
came to my senses and challenged him to justify the
ridiculous scheme he and his colleague described.

I was sure the nutty proposal violated the student constitution and the US Constitution. He and Scotty tried to defend their position, and then gave in, saying they were only joking and wanted to see if anyone would counter their assertion. I said that was a cynical stance to take, just to express their opinions of how dumb they thought the electorate was.

President Leissig solicited comments from other representatives, and several expressed their disappointment with the turnout, but thought the revision to the constitution was going too far.

One of the junior class reps suggested the council could expand the publicity about the election to encourage students to vote. She moved to publish the voter turnout in the campus newspaper along with a person and phone number to contact with further suggestions. I thought this was a workable solution.

Warren Norton commented on the recommendations and put the discussion to rest. His debate skills got a good workout.

After I joined the debate squad, I felt very much at home. *Here was an entire team of contentious people.*

I learned that "Star Debater" Warren and his partner Steve were the two who had won the national intercollegiate debate tournament the previous year, an impressive accomplishment for sure. Wow!

Several people called him Abe, not Warren. I asked him why and he said his parents nicknamed him Abe because his birthday was February 12.

I observed some of Abe and Steve's practice debates, and their styles were complementary. Steve spoke quickly with animated gestures and seemed to bounce when he was at his most persuasive.

Abe maintained his cool. He often sat on the edge of the desk and singled out one person at a time to talk to before moving behind the desk to slam home a point.

Figure 15. Pi Kappa Delta forensic fraternity. I am sitting on the left, and chapter president Warren (Abe) Norton is standing on the right, 1961.

Abe and I became acquainted through the debate team. I was a freshman, and he was a senior. He lived in Hoisington, 28 miles from Russell. Our conversations included sharing family backgrounds, names of friends we might have in common, and our somewhat divergent political views. I held moderate political views, and Abe said he was a liberal.

Then, one day, I was fiddling with a box of notecards and I realized we had met before.

The high school junior for whom I kept time in the Russell debate tournament four to five years earlier was the same cool dude I was sharing conversations with.

Five years is a long time to have a lump in your throat and butterflies in your tummy. It's a wonder I could talk at all.

He told me he remembered the debate very well in which I was his timekeeper. "Me too," I said. "That was my first timekeeping job."

"You distracted me from my plan."

"How did I do that?"

"You were just so cute, and you seemed to agree with my arguments."

Tongue-tied, I could only say, "Oh."

Many of the debaters became friends and hung out together when not in class. Favorite hangouts were the student union, outdoors on the quadrangle, or at the debate coach's house. Harold, the coach, and his wife Kitty generously opened their home and their refrigerator to the team.

They had two small boys who were always part of the conversation, ransacking the fridge, and playing games. We developed a community that included lively arguments, satirical speeches, and a good deal of laughter. Everyone helped with cleanup and babysitting.

Harold and Kitty had just bought a new Corvair convertible, the rear-engine model Ralph Nader would criticize in *Unsafe at Any Speed* (1965). Nader exposed the auto industry's resistance to including safety measures in developing cars.

Group gatherings were the norm instead of single dates. Campus rules required girls to be in their dormitories during the week by 8:00 p.m. and by midnight on Saturdays. The boys had no such restrictions.

I was not one of those girls who sneaked out after hours, probably because I was always tired and needed to study. "Modern Civilization," a class scheduled at 7:30 a.m. five days a week almost did me in. I needed more sleep, and frequently I arrived late and out of breath.

The class convened in the farthest building from my dormitory, and I struggled to get there, resulting in the worst grade I had ever received.

Near the end of October, Abe asked me to join him when he met some friends at the Brass Rail, a saloon in Hays. I had never been to a bar before. I entered to the smell of alcohol and damp carpeting.

Underwhelmed by this kind of greeting, I looked around the bar. Bottles in clear, dark brown, amber, green, and red lined the shelves. It was a lineup of liquids designed to take you over the rainbow, or at least to make you giggle.

A long bar lined with stools faced the colorful liquids. Along the wall opposite the bar were a few tables. Several other debaters and the coach stood at the bar or sat on stools. No one was checking IDs. Lucky for me, because I was only 17.

Drinking age in Kansas was 18 for beer and 21 for hard liquor. On this occasion, I sampled a Scotch whiskey and water, recommended by Abe and the coach. It tasted like bandages soaked in iodine smelled. I did not go back for seconds.

As everyone was leaving the bar, Abe asked me if I would like to come to his house to listen to music. He had recorded several pieces at the radio station in Russell, where he worked. We went to his apartment, which he shared with his debate partner.

The carpeted living room was long, skinny, and sparsely furnished. There was a sofa, two side chairs, and a coffee table. Along one wall was a bookcase loaded with stacks of books, a tape recorder, record albums, a turntable, and a set of bongo drums.

The Wollensak reel-to-reel unit sat on the top shelf, about waist high. Next to it were tapes in flat white boxes. Abe pulled out one of his favorites and threaded it onto the machine.

"I think you'll like this one," he said.

Wow, I was impressed. Here was Mort Sahl doing stand-up routines in Abe's living room! Sahl's pointed political humor appealed to me. He slammed prejudice and injustice. My kind of guy!

Before Abe took me back to the dorm, he kissed me, full on the mouth. I was not expecting this, but a wave of electricity surged through me, throwing me off balance.

Abe and I continued to date. We attended campus evening lectures, student plays, and hung out at the Stones house. He was not fond of dancing, so we usually went our separate ways when a special band came to campus. This surprised me because he had played drums in his high school dance band. Because I liked to dance, I went with a group of girls or dragged along a male friend.

Jazz artist and bandleader Stan Kenton, who was born in Wichita, Kansas, was going to play for the homecoming dance. I did not want to miss it. A junior from Larned, Kansas, a skilled dancer, asked me to go. I would have gone by myself if my friend had not asked me to go.

My dorm friends and I had a tradition of sharing our stuff. Many a weekend found us passing around cigarettes, money, or treats sent from home. We hung out in the student union to play cards, gossip, and talk about course work.

Most of my friends and I had meal tickets to eat in the dorm, and I rarely had spending money of my own. When I went for coffee, I filled up the cup as well as the saucer to get a little extra.

Abe had worked at KRSL-AM in Russell as a disc jockey while I was still in high school and at the campus radio station later. The choir director at my church worked at the station, and she became acquainted with Abe when he worked there. I learned of their work relationship after I started college.

Abe's deep voice captivated my attention, and he articulated his descriptions of musicians and their tunes perfectly. I looked forward to the times I could hear his broadcasts. They charmed me while I was still a high school student.

We soon developed a romantic relationship. We spent more time at the debate coach's home and in Abe's apartment, listening to music. Our conversations covered current events, family personalities, religion, politics, and a few dreams.

After several months of dating, laughter, discussions, and necking, we happily told each other we were in love. This feeling was one I had never experienced before. I was enjoying being together and felt at ease with him.

Abe was considering law school or graduate school, and I had not decided on a major field of study.

In February 1961, Abe received notice that he had received a grant from the National Defense Education Act (NDEA) to study government at the University of Massachusetts (UMass) in Amherst. Abe's three-year appointment was ostensibly the time during which he would complete a PhD.

He asked me to marry him and go to Massachusetts with him. Wanting to continue my education was high on my list. The catalog listings for UMass showed interesting offerings in English, speech, and drama.

Politics and government appealed to me, but I could maintain my interest in them without taking classes.

The NDEA grant added a small amount of money for spouses. I hoped we could afford to pay my tuition to UMass so that I could complete my degree.

I liked the idea of moving to New England. It would be an adventure with someone I admired and loved.

We decided to get married and wanted to do it before summer school at Fort Hays started. Abe had a summer job on the campus managing the student union activities. First, we thought we should meet our potential in-laws.

Figure 16. Abe Norton sits in his parents' car, waiting for me to come out of the dormitory at Fort Hays State College, 1961.

Bert and Jack, Abe's parents, were very open and welcoming. Jack was an avid union man who worked for the Missouri-Pacific railroad as a conductor and brakeman. Bert was a stay-at-home mom who opened her home to Abe and his sister's friends for holidays, after athletic events, or just to hang out. I had my second drink of iodine-laced bandages at their house. Quite a few "colorful" jokes accompanied games of pitch, which they taught me to play.

Mother was wary of Abe because he was four plus years older, and I was only 17. She wondered whether I was well enough to leave home. She did not want me to ruin the work they put into getting me well.

Was I old enough to get married? Abe's mother had married at age 18, and Mother was 18. I would turn 18 in May, and we wanted a June wedding.

Dad expressed his concern about the uncertainty that lay ahead. He wanted me to be happy and didn't want me to get lost in the focus on Abe and his award. Later, I learned he had talked to Abe about his concerns.

At the end of my freshman year and Abe's senior year, we married in Russell, Kansas, at the First United Methodist Church. Both sets of parents approved of the union, but my mother didn't want us to move so far from Russell. I was ready to move.

Three days before the wedding, Mother and Dad held a dinner in our backyard. The evening was a pleasant 80 degrees in early June. Mother fixed fried chicken, roasting ears, mashed potatoes, and green beans. Several members of the wedding party attended.

We sat around the picnic table chatting until Reverend Eklund stood, the cue to stop talking and bow our heads for the blessing. Just as he started to pray, I opened my eyes to see my brother across the table.

Greeting me was a huge open-mouthed smile, upper teeth capped with corn kernels. I choked down the water I was drinking to keep from spraying the table. As soon as the prayer ended, I went inside the house to keep from laughing.

———————————

Grandma King made my wedding dress, veil, slip, and a garter. I did not want ruffles or netting. The fittings were a nuisance because I wanted to simplify the whole process. I had to arrange rides back and forth from Hays to Russell and then on to McPherson, where Grandma lived. Grandma had enough patience for both of us, a quality far from my reach.

My parents' friends from Hutchinson filmed parts of the wedding and reception with their 16mm camera, but a technical error ruined the film. Professional photographers were a luxury, so friends took candid photos of me getting dressed, of someone putting Grandma's garter on my leg, and of members of the wedding party. We saved photos of the two of us in wedding clothes.

Abe and I didn't have money for a honeymoon, but we promised each other we would take a nice trip after we had the time and saved some money.

Abe's debate partner was still living in the apartment, but the landlord offered us a basement apartment near the campus for $50 a month. It had a bedroom and living room which were divided by a curtain, a small eating area, a range, sink, refrigerator, a few pieces of furniture, and a bathroom. It was dark and dreary, but we made the best of it.

Figure 17. Abe and I at our wedding, June, 1961.

I took a class in speech and drama. Abe managed the student union on the campus, so we had a tiny income.

We made plans to move to Massachusetts without a place to live and having never seen the campus or the town of Amherst. Our parents were nervous about our moving so far away from home, but Abe and I looked upon the move as the start of an exciting journey.

I adopted Abe's last name, Norton, as my own, after much deliberation. My Auntie Neen, one of Dad's sisters, thought Abe should change his surname to Anderson.

I reluctantly agreed to do what everyone else told me was traditional, but Mrs. Last Name didn't feel like me. I wondered from time to time who I was or would become.

Someone else's name was on all our bank checks, which I rarely wrote, because Abe had taken charge of our checking account. I soon asserted my desire to participate in budgeting and handling money. Abe began to see I was quite capable of participating in the management of our life partnership and was happy that he didn't have to do it alone.

5. Crossing State Lines

New Englanders Are Friendly

In August 1961, we moved with our meager belongings in Abe's British Morris Minor to Amherst, Massachusetts. Abe's father acquired three packing barrels from the Missouri Pacific Railroad in Hoisington for the rest of our things and shipped them by rail to Amherst.

We learned right away that Bostonians considered anything west of Boston to be western Massachusetts. Amherst was right in the middle of the state, beautifully situated amongst lush hardwood and pine trees, flowering shrubbery, and white Cape Cod and colonial style homes.

Driving through Amherst, we encountered our first traffic controller standing in a white box in the middle of an intersection with six converging lanes. He wore a blue uniform with gold epaulets, a step-out cap with a bill, and white gloves. The whistle in his mouth was getting a workout.

To indicate the next driver's turn to proceed, he swung his arm, looked directly at the car, pointed, then motioned for the driver to go. If the driver did not take off immediately, the officer blew the whistle and pointed again. Everyone performed their part beautifully with no accidents.

As we gawked around the town center, we found the stately colonial Lord Jeffrey Inn, the Emily Dickinson Museum, and Amherst College, a four-year private liberal arts college founded in 1821. We were excited to learn more of the history in Amherst as soon as we found a place to live.

We located the university, which had opened as a land grant agricultural college in 1863 and evolved after World War II into a university in 1947.

The main architectural styles were federal, colonial, and Victorian, with modern dormitory buildings and expansive science centers, proof of the constant growth of the university system.

The government department office would become Abe's new daytime home. When we reached the office, the staff welcomed us with open arms. A local real estate agent had made a tentative offer for a graduate student to rent one of her properties. We met with the agent and struck a bargain.

Our new landlady-to-be, Barbara Footit, was a young widow with a teenage daughter, Jean, who showed Morgan horses. The Footits owned four homes in the area. One was in Amherst and three were in Shutesbury, a township nearby where she owned 360 acres of ground.

The Footits lived in Shutesbury in the summer and in Amherst in the winter. Both homes they occupied had horse stables, including the one in Amherst. If Jean attended UMass, she would have her horse close by.

Barbara called the other two Shutesbury houses "camps," local vocabulary for rustic houses in the woods. One house had insulation, while the other did not. She had rented the insulated camp to a couple, Wesley and Leslie Honey, who had graduated from UMass and were working.

The owner had divided her main house into two apartments, and she and her daughter lived in the side closest to the tack room and stables in the summer. We were to live in this portion of the house in the winter and move to the camp in the summer.

Figure 18. We lived in the side of the house in Shutesbury with the screened-in porch. Abe searches for something in the boot of the Morris Minor, November 1961.

I told people we were going to live in the country—outside of Amherst. Then someone reminded me that in Massachusetts, one is always inside a township. Shutesbury township is 11 miles from Amherst.

The house sat on a plot of 10 cleared acres. Down a hill behind the house lay a spring-fed pond. The two-story white frame house with black shutters was typical of many New England farmhouses.

Over the years, owners had added buildings to the main house. An oversized two-car garage, a mudroom, a tack room, and two stables completed the layout of our new winter home. The ground floor consisted of a large living room with a closet, an eat-in kitchen, and a full bath. The second floor had a bedroom and a small room that Abe used as a study. All the rooms had some furniture.

Settlers cleared the land and used the stones they turned over to build fences to define land borders and protect crops. They used the stone to build walls, which now lined the roadway leading to the house. Hardwood and pine trees surrounded our summer home: a cozy cabin with two bedrooms, a bath, a large living room/kitchen combination, a fireplace, and a screened-in porch.

The only issue with living in an uninsulated camp was that teeny critters smaller than mosquitoes, but just as annoying, got into the house in the summer. Locals called these critters "no-see-ums."

The stone fireplace got a workout on cool evenings. Can you imagine using a wood-burning fireplace in Kansas during the summer?

A screened-in porch stretched along one side of the house. The bathroom had a tub but no shower, so Abe added plumbing for an outside shower. We paid $75 a month to live in Shutesbury, winter or summer.

After we had occupied one side of the main house for several months, a couple and their daughter moved into the other side of the main house. It had three bedrooms, a living room, an eat-in kitchen, a dining room, and a study.

Ted, who was from Long Beach, California, designed knives and knife handles for a company in Sturbridge, Massachusetts. June was a stay-at-home mom with a two-year degree from Colby Junior College in New Hampshire.

Abe and I had a washing machine in the basement. Ted and June bought a dryer, and we shared both appliances. This worked well, with no problems.

I had not lived with anyone besides my immediate family, except for the short time I had a roommate at Fort Hays. We soon discovered we each had our own ways of doing things.

When Abe was an undergraduate student, his mother starched and ironed his shirts and laundered his other clothes. When he was at Fort Hays, he took them home to his mother and returned home to pick them up. He always looked very sharp.

Once, his mother bought him a new pair of shoes, but they were not comfortable. She wore them to "break them in" when he complained about them. I thought he was joking, but his mother confirmed this. No way would I have asked, nor would someone have offered, to break in a pair of shoes for me. Ah, well.

Abe wanted to wear a starched white shirt to class every day, and for a while, I starched and ironed them for him. He complained they weren't quite like his mother finished them.

I did not want to compete with his mother, so I turned the task over to him. He said he would do them himself, but before long he did not have time and stopped starching them.

Before I married, my siblings and I washed or dried dishes, cooked, did laundry, cleaned house, and fed the dog. My sister and I shared a bedroom and a closet, but we did not have many clothes, so it worked unless we wore each other's belongings without permission.

Abe wanted to do the cooking, and for the most part, he got his wish. I had a limited repertoire of things I knew how to make and wasn't particularly interested in learning new recipes.

I enrolled at UMass with a speech and drama major. The woman acting as my advisor had a Master of Arts in drama from Smith College in nearby Northampton. She impressed me with her engaging personality, her welcoming attitude, and her willingness to spend time with me discussing my interests.

Abe worked in the small upstairs bedroom. He frequently had the radio on, but I did not read well with the radio on, so I read or studied at the kitchen table. A month later, the hepatitis I had contracted in high school flared up. I felt nauseous, fainted a couple of times, had no energy, and lost my appetite. Exhausted and having missed a week's worth of classes, I tried to stick it out, but finally dropped out in the hope I could save some of the tuition.

Despite feeling a bit like a failure, I concluded the decision was a wise one. I recovered the cost of the tuition. Money was always a concern, though we never wanted for anything. But then we never went anywhere to spend money, either.

On one memorable occasion, we said to hell with the budget. We came across some gorgeous lacquered red Dansk serving bowls in a store in Amherst. We bought two and ordered three more.

Danish modern was our favorite style, but items of this kind were expensive. We both loved the bowls and used them often to serve vegetables, sauces, or potato chips.

Abe selected political theory as an emphasis for his doctorate. The faculty who agreed to sit on his master's and PhD committees would shepherd him through his classes, his thesis, foreign languages, and oral exams.

Felix Oppenheim served as his committee chair. Dr. Oppenheim had earned a Juris Doctor degree from the University of Brussels and a PhD from Princeton. Oppenheim was a stickler for clear, concise writing, which proved to be a challenge because Abe consistently wrote papers using the passive voice.

Other members of his committee specialized in constitutional law and politics. Abe did well in his classes but labored to meet the standard in two required foreign languages (as did many graduate students). He managed German, but he struggled with French. He finally did well enough to meet the language requirements and performed well on his oral examinations.

The literature review for his dissertation required him to spend more time in the library and his home office working on an outline and shaping a thesis.

After a couple of months of rest, recovery, and boredom, I got a part-time job at the alumni office on campus. My boss, Wesley Honey, our neighbor, had recently graduated from UMass with writing credentials. He had been editor of the campus humor magazine, *The Yahoo*, and served as assistant editor of the alumni magazine, which the office published quarterly.

His wife, Leslie, was working in the office part time until she got a job teaching English at Bement School, an independent K-9 school in Deerfield, Massachusetts.

The office staff also published regional alumni newsletters and invitations to alumni events. I hoped to get a chance to proofread or participate in the production of publications.

Political campaign posters and yard signs filled the alumni office, left over from the Collegiate Young Democrats campaign for Chub Peabody, an unsuccessful candidate for governor of Massachusetts.

The *Massachusetts Review*, a quarterly publication of literature, arts, and public affairs, had offices in the building's basement. I felt fortunate to work in the middle of all the creative energy surrounding me.

Figure 19. My boss Wesley Honey and I work on files of university graduates who live in states outside of Massachusetts, 1962.

Wesley's friend Paul Theroux, who was still on the staff of *The Yahoo*, dropped by frequently. I thought Paul and Wes were quite clever; satire was the frame of reference for most conversations. They included me in their repartee, partly out of amusement at what they called my Southern accent.

Because I was so young, they tried to catch me in a mispronounced word or factual error, or certainly a gap in my knowledge (no problem, there). Big teases, they were.

We shared vocabulary differences. A milkshake in Kansas was called a frappe (frap) in Massachusetts. You could make your own in the student union by going through a cafeteria line to make selections of milk, ice cream, and flavorings.

I asked if they drank malts, but they were not familiar with them. "Never heard of them," Wes said.

"You're kidding. Malts contain malted milk powder added to the shake. It adds a toasted flavor to the shake. Better than a shake."

My pronunciation of the names of cities and townships amused Wes and Paul. For example, I said "bar" for Barre. With exaggerated laughter, they said, "No, it's Barry."

Then Paul said, "Pronounce this" (pointing to a city on the map).

"Wor chester shire," I said.

After much laughter and pointing at me, I eventually got it right by arriving at "Wuhstuh."

While I was working on locating UMass alumni in Arizona, they tried to tell me that "Tucson" was pronounced "Tuckson." I didn't fall for that one.

Theroux would later write and publish scores of books, including *The Great Railway Bazaar*, *The Old Patagonian Express*, and *The Mosquito Coast*, a novel adapted to a movie starring Harrison Ford, and a television series with Justin Theroux, nephew of Paul.

The building also served as a frequent venue for student art showings. I was happy to make a nodding acquaintance with writers, painters, and editors, even if only due to proximity.

One day, William Shumway, a student painter, hung some of his work in the building's lounge. During lunch hour, I wandered into the lounge where he was working and admired several of his works. I introduced myself, and he said to call him Bill.

He was graduating at the end of the semester and would soon start a master's degree in fine arts. I asked my bosses if I could help him create a pamphlet with notes about his art to distribute at the show. They thought it was a good idea and the exercise would give me some writing practice.

I did not have an example to use as a guide, so I sketched out in pencil how I thought it should look. Bill said he liked it.

The finished pamphlet consisted of a numbered list of each piece with its name, date of the painting, and a note about the inspiration for the subject. Evan, the alumni association director, let me create a stencil and reproduce the piece for distribution at the showing.

I purchased one of Bill's oil paintings, *Keep Away from the Glass*, and one of his pen and ink drawings, *Chillingworth*, depicting the ominous character in *The Scarlet Letter*. Proud of my acquisitions, I displayed both pieces in our living room in Shutesbury.

Bill gave me a pastel drawing for helping him and let me pay for the artwork over several weeks' time. I had in my possession original artwork by an artist I knew.

My boss, cynic that he was, told me Bill would probably work in a paint store after he graduated, rather than be lucky enough to sell his art, but I disagreed.

Figure 20. *Keep Away from the Glass*, William Shumway, (Strong blues and black), 1962.

As things turned out, William Shumway established a studio and gallery in Corvallis, Oregon, producing many kinds of art pieces for several decades. While I was contacting him to tell him I wanted to include a photo of one of his pieces, his assistant notified me he had died in May 2024. I recognized him from the picture published with his obituary, which praised his work for its appeal to the imagination and his life for his gentleness and kindness.

I Don't Want to Be Sick

Radiators heated the alumni offices, and there was a period one winter when I went home with a headache every day. I developed a severe sinus infection, which led me to the campus infirmary for two days of inhalant therapy and rest during homecoming weekend.

Abe and I were unlikely to have participated in any homecoming events, but he did not come to visit me in the infirmary. Disappointed, I told myself he was busy with classes and studying.

When I returned to work, Wes asked me about the homecoming party. "I was in the infirmary trying to breathe."

He asked if Abe had enjoyed himself, as he had seen him at a party on the campus.

I asked Abe about it, and he said Patricia, a graduate student in government whom I had met, asked him to go and he felt an obligation to attend because most of his colleagues went.

"It was a last-minute thing, and no big deal. It wasn't like it was a date," he said, laughing.

I didn't think any more about it. It sounded like a reasonable scenario.

A few weeks later, I began experiencing vaginal pain and bleeding during intercourse. The campus infirmary gynecologist diagnosed my condition as an inflamed, raw cervix. The doctor cauterized the cervix and ordered no intercourse for a month. Abe doubted the diagnosis and demanded to speak to the doctor. After talking with the doctor, he agreed to abide by his orders.

The doctor asked me why Abe had questioned him. I told him we had not been married long, and he was concerned about my welfare. It did not occur to me to tell the doc to ask

Abe for an explanation. I was 19 or 20 years old and somewhat embarrassed by the whole affair.

Abe and I sometimes talked about our illnesses and how we had dealt with accidents growing up. I shared a bit of Mother's experience with polio, but Abe thought she had recovered well and looked pretty good. I thought about it and decided she had recovered well, though it was a serious illness.

"Mother had help from her immediate and extended family," I said. "I would care for you if you were ill or when we are old. Would you take care of me?"

"I don't think I could do it. I'm not sure why, but I just don't think I could."

I didn't let it concern me because we had many years before we would face such decisions.

Someone Likes to Stay Home

During our three years in Massachusetts, I discovered Abe's dislike of traveling, even of leaving the house unless we were going to campus or to a friend's home.

I was excited about living in New England and wanted to explore the area. The landscape, terrain, and towns were nothing like those in Kansas.

The winding roads and secret gardens captured my attention and I often wanted to veer off the road to see what lay beyond.

Nearby Quabbin Reservoir, for example, was one of the largest unfiltered water supplies in the United States. The reservoir covered 39 square miles with 181 miles of shoreline. Limiting recreational activities protected the drinking water of three million people, but people took picnics, hiked, and watched the birds there.

Lake Wyola, a recreational lake two miles from our home, had a small restaurant and bar. Abe declined to go explore with me, because he was always too busy. I did not like to go alone, but when I did, I found historic homes, small cottages, gardens, great stands of hardwood trees, and some cows, chickens, and horses.

UMass, Mount Holyoke College, Smith College, and Amherst College were all within a 20-mile radius of our home. These four colleges had an agreement that allowed students to share the libraries of all four.

I wanted to explore the libraries, but Abe wasn't interested in going just because I wanted to. He spent hours in the libraries to satisfy his coursework and research. Students or spouses could use the libraries, but he would have to come with me.

I needed more things to keep me occupied. Both of us grew up with pets. Our family had a cocker spaniel and Siamese cats, for which we provided stud service. When I met Abe, he had an all-American dog named Lady, who had a favored position in the household. After we lived in Shutesbury for a while, we decided we wanted a dog, specifically a beagle.

We spotted an ad in the Sunday classified ads for beagle puppies. Fearing we might miss our chance to get one, we drove to New Hampshire to the filling station where baby beagle "aroooos" greeted shoppers.

The owner showed us to the backroom, where four pups and the mother were playing on a blanket inside a fenced-off area. One baby came over to us, curious to see what was happening. She looked like she picked us out, so we had to take her.

She had such a cute face and bubbled with energy. We were sold. We paid the $5.00 and took her home. Her nose was a bit long for a beagle, but we knew there was no guarantee that she was a thoroughbred. She was worth every penny, as any beagle is, no matter the price. We were big fans of the comic strip "Peanuts." Snoopy she was.

Figure 21. Abe plays with our filling station puppy Snoopy, 1962.

Wes and his wife, Leslie, had a Basset hound they named Lord Jeffrey Amherst (1719-1797) after a historic military gentleman of the British army and the namesake of the town.

We compared dogs and pronounced both magnificent. I commented that driving to New Hampshire to purchase Snoopy was the first time we had been very far from home.

Leslie, who was about five months pregnant, chided us for not having seen the ocean. "How could you live in Massachusetts and not visit the shore? We know a place at Cape Ann where you can pick out your own lobsters. We could stop at my parents' home in Lynnfield to take a break and go for a swim in a nearby pool," Leslie said.

When Abe heard we could pick lobsters out of the ocean, he was all in for the trip. The four of us loaded sandwiches and water into our Morris Minor and headed east. We took a break at Leslie's parents' house in Lynnfield.

Their house was a large white colonial with two fireplaces and three bedrooms. Her father was a shipbuilder. In the bin beside one fireplace was a wood I had not seen before. Leslie introduced us to lignum vitae, a very hard wood native to the Caribbean that her father used in shipbuilding.

The builders used lignum vitae to make sheaves of blocks on sailing vessels until the introduction of modern synthetics. The wood was one of the densest woods in the world and had blue, green, and reddish hues running throughout the pieces we saw.

Leslie's parents used the wood in their fireplace because a small log burned for hours.

Next on the agenda was a tour of the Joseph Tapley home, built in 1715. A mammoth central fireplace in the kitchen heated most of the house and retained original cooking and utility objects. The entire atmosphere was cozy and warm, despite the lack of central heat. Original 8- to 12-inch-wide plank pine floors covered the floors.

I had never seen a house this old. It was on the National Register of Historic Places and displayed a brass plaque by the front door.

Next, we headed for the natural swimming pool. Rock lined the sides of the sand bottom pond. I tried out the diving board and, after swimming a few laps, got out of the pool to head to the shore.

From the Anderson home in Lynnfield, we went north along the rocky shoreline of Cape Ann and then drove south along the shore to Provincetown, an artist community. After viewing art installations and open-air galleries, we went back to the car. Leslie was getting tired and thought we should get our lobsters and head home.

We stopped in Barnstable and selected live lobsters "to go." The fishermen weighed our four choices at one to two pounds each. They banded the claws together, bagged them, and put them into the car. In about two hours and forty-five minutes, we would be home.

The return trip from the shore started out well. We found our way back to the highway for home. Not long after we merged onto one of the busiest highways in the country, the car started hiccupping. Jerk . . . and go. Jerk . . . and go.

The car sputtered until Abe could drive onto the shoulder where, as we idled, it stopped sputtering.

Major congestion had already become a problem around Boston. When Abe could merge back onto the highway, the sputtering started up again about 30 miles later.

Abe said it was the carburetor, and he could fix it. He pulled off to the shoulder again and tied a string to a part of the carburetor that was acting up. Then he threaded the string into the car through a window. Everyone in the car started laughing when we realized a hunk of string salvaged from Rainbo bread boxes was going to get us back to Shutesbury.

We squeezed back onto the highway to honking horns and exasperated drivers. Abe pulled on the string when the carburetor noise started again, and it worked, but poorly. We stopped a few more times to adjust the string.

Leslie said her belly was flip-flopping and hoped we got home soon. We made it home with everything and everyone intact and had a delicious dinner. Fresh lobster meat dipped in melted butter and lemon juice was heavenly. Especially when each lobster cost only $.69.

New York, then a Clambake

We had such a pleasant trip to the shore that it did not take too much wheedling on my part to convince Abe we should meet my brother and his friends in New York City. The choir he belonged to was stopping on its way to Germany to entertain army troops.

We connected at Lindy's restaurant and heard stories about their expectations for the trip, including their performance of the musical *Brigadoon*.

After that trip, we stayed home most of the time. Abe's classes kept him busy. I talked to my parents on the phone occasionally, and they encouraged us to travel back to Kansas.

The cost of plane tickets would squeeze our budget, and driving would take too much time. When both sets of parents visited us, we gathered friends and neighbors to our home to help create a clambake.

A day at the beach! We dug a hole in the front yard of our home, placed stones in the bottom and sides, and built a fire in the pit out of kindling and logs we found on the property.

Friends of Leslie and Wes drove from Boston to Shutesbury, loaded with littleneck clams, cherrystone clams, lobsters, and seaweed. Someone else brought roasting ears and baking potatoes. Everyone dived into the food prep.

I washed the clams, checking to see if they were alive, and placed them in a bushel basket with cornmeal. Someone scrubbed the potatoes, and we left the corn in the husks. Our neighbors made clam fritters and placed them in a warming device outside when the other food was nearly ready.

After the New Englanders judged the fire to be just right, we layered everything into the pit: potatoes, seaweed, corn, clams, and lobsters. Someone spritzed each layer with water, then Wes threw a large tarp over the whole shebang to let it steam.

People doused cherrystone clams with hot sauce or lemon juice and ate them raw. I passed on those. Mother's ulcer was bothering her, so she couldn't sample everything.

Dad helped dig the pit and asked many questions of the locals about how it all went together. Some guests brought liquor.

I had camped out many times with family and Girl Scouts, cooking over fire or camp stove, but this event was way over the top. A giant pile of seafood and vegetables in the middle of Massachusetts! Everyone participated in the preparations and everyone helped with the cleanup.

My next trip was an airplane ride to Kansas. Charlotte asked me to serve as matron of honor in her wedding to Kent Crawford. Charlotte and Kent were planning to marry before completing their last semester at Kansas State University.

Grandma King would make Charlotte's dress and headgear, as well as those of the attendants.

Because I was in Massachusetts, I sent my measurements to Grandma. She cut out the dress using my measurements and basted it together.

I flew back to Kansas alone a few days before the wedding. Grandma whipped up my dress after adjusting the seams. I weighed 108 pounds and had very short hair.

Who wanted a January wedding in Kansas? The morning of the wedding, the temperature was 17 degrees below zero. Some cars would not start.

I wasn't sure I wanted to wear the headdress Grandma had made. I looked in the mirror and saw a rabbit. The pale blue satin band had two "petals" sticking up from the top of the band. All the other attendants had long hair, and their entire outfits looked stunning. I threatened to hop into the church, but didn't. Charlotte was distraught enough without my acting up.

After graduation and a stint in Washington, D.C., Kent and Charlotte established residency in New Jersey, where Kent enrolled as a graduate student at Princeton.

For four years, Charlotte taught eighth-grade and freshman algebra. She earned a master's degree in educational and psychological statistics from Rutgers University. Abe and I called them the Brain Trust.

They had invited us to visit them, but I didn't want to drive alone, and Abe was too busy.

For other entertainment, we visited one or two friends' homes, but most of the time, friends came to our house. We once had a party where we served Bronx cocktails. The cocktail consisted of gin, sweet vermouth, dry vermouth, and orange juice, shaken with ice or drunk straight.

We had just given the woodwork in our living room a fresh coat of white paint. Someone set a partially filled cup on the newly painted counter in the entry, and when we picked up the cup during cleanup, we noticed some of the liquid had slopped out onto the cabinet top.

It had taken the paint off the cabinet. Just like Pepsi and Coke. Oops.

Abe thought he needed another project besides his studies, so he found a 1961 Austin-Healey Bugeye Sprite and bought it. The car was missing a top, so he made one.

He created a mold for the top with some plans he found in the library and then fashioned a top out of fiberglass cloth and resin. After sanding and painting it, as well as attaching it to the car with fasteners, the car was drivable and looked very sharp. Constant research and writing created pressure, which he relieved with the car project.

The car was lightweight, so if it got stuck in the snow, we opened the car doors, stuck out our feet, and dug in our heels until we moved the car. We sold our Morris to another student.

1963: The Horrible Year

In 1963, nine years after *Brown v. Board of Education*, my interest in justice for Black people resurfaced. I remembered the discrimination incidents at a restaurant in Hays, in the Russell swimming pool, the motel, and in the Rainbow girls' policy.

Civil rights advocates sought public exposure for their efforts to desegregate lunch counters. Black people demanded their right to vote. Network television covered the violence of police using dogs and fire hoses on protesters.

I wanted to join the Freedom Riders, who traveled south to protest discrimination in schools, restaurants, public toilets, drinking fountains, and transportation. But I didn't.

Bull Connor became internationally notorious as the Commissioner of Public Safety in Birmingham, Alabama. He ordered attacks on the protesters in Birmingham the day after they gathered as part of the "Children's Crusade" May 2, 1963. By May 7, Connor and police had arrested 3,000 protesters, many of whom were children.

The violence saddened me. Unfortunately, it was public exposure of the authorities' treatment of the protesters that brought many skeptics to a realization that the protesters had a point.

Photographs and television images of the violence appeared around the world, revealing the brutality directed at the protesters. The images unmasked the rampant prejudice in the South.[1]

I glued myself to the radio and television to soak up all the news about what was happening in the South.

On June 11, President Kennedy proposed passage of a federal civil rights act. However, Congress would not enact it until after fanatics had killed President Kennedy and many other civil rights workers.

On June 12, 1963, Medgar Evers, a civil rights activist in Jackson, Mississippi, was going home from an NAACP meeting. He reached his driveway and got out of the car carrying NAACP T-shirts.

An assassin shot Evers in the back, and the bullet pierced his heart. He rose and stumbled several yards, falling near the front door of his house. His wife Myrlie found him.[2]

Medgar had told his wife he felt an impending doom that day, because he did not have his FBI and police tail.

I wondered why not.

An ambulance took Evers to the local hospital where hospital staff refused him admittance. Eventually the staff admitted him, but he died less than an hour afterward.

Arlington National Cemetery accepted Evers with full military honors, and over 3,000 mourners attended the funeral. Bob Dylan and Phil Ochs wrote songs about Evers, and Malvina Reynolds mentioned him in her song, "It Isn't Nice."[3]

Police arrested Byron De La Beckwith, a member of the White Citizens Council and the Klan. After three trials, De La Beckwith went to jail for 30 years and died in prison.

I followed the news about the murder, the funeral, and the conviction of the murderer with sorrow and anger. When would people see their treatment of Black people was wrong?

On September 15, 1963, Rev. John H. Cross, Jr. was preparing for church service in the Sixteenth Street Baptist Church in Birmingham, Alabama. Addie Mae Collins and her sister were in the church when a massive explosion shattered windows and sent concrete and debris flying. Four girls, ages

11 to 14, died in the explosion. Another twenty-two people suffered injuries.[4]

The deaths triggered public outrage. The Reverend Dr. Martin Luther King, Jr. spoke at the girls' funeral. Civil rights advocates met at the church to discuss strategy and to demonstrate their sorrow over the murders.

The police brought out the dogs and fire hoses, resulting in shocking scenes of violence.

The police are supposed to protect people, not cause them harm for gathering legally to support civil rights.

Four more deaths, and of children. And there were many others. *This cannot go on.*

The killers were getting away with their murders, but it seemed obvious to me what had happened. The police and the FBI dragged their feet on finding the killers.

An FBI investigation finally revealed that four Ku Klux Klan members had planted dynamite under the concrete steps leading up to the church.

Not until 1977 did a jury convict Robert Edward Chambliss, one of the Klan members, of the bombing and murders of the four girls.

November 22, 1963, started like any other day. I was working in the alumni office at the university. Wesley and I stopped to have our lunches and listen to the radio. We were chatting about the beautiful fall foliage having faded, and that winter was fast approaching.

The tone of the broadcast pivoted from cheery to somber. A man had gunned down President Kennedy, who was riding in an open car in Dallas.

Born in Brookline, Massachusetts, and graduating from Harvard, John Kennedy had been my coworkers' senator and president. He was one of their own.

"What?" Wesley asked. "Did you hear that?"

I turned up the volume on the radio, and several other staff members came into the office, asking what was happening.

We all listened as announcers added more details. One reporter said four or five shots had come from the direction of the Texas School Book Depository. Texas Governor John Connally, riding in the same automobile, had also been shot.

Jackie Kennedy had climbed to the trunk of the car to retrieve something. Reporters said it was part of Kennedy's skull.

Someone had shot a police officer; other officers were holding a witness in a brown and white polka dot dress. People were running for cover from the parade route, and police cordoned off the grassy knoll nearby because witnesses reported activity from that location.

Around 1:30 p.m., Walter Cronkite broke in to report that President Kennedy was dead. He said police had arrested Lee Harvey Oswald, a juvenile delinquent, US Marine court-martialed twice, and defector to Russia, for the murder of our president.

Time and energy ceased to exist. I was dazed. Everyone in the room shook their heads in disbelief, and then came cries.

"Oh, no, not him."

"It can't be."

"Why would anyone do such a thing?"

Wes and I repeated similar comments.

Helplessness washed over the room, and I wanted to connect with Abe. I tried to reach him, but he was unavailable—in class or in the library.

Candidate Kennedy had traveled to Hays, Kansas, to campaign in 1960. Abe, his debate partner, and the debate coach accompanied Kennedy to several speaking venues. Abe was an eager supporter, and I knew he would be devastated.

Secretaries scrambled to answer the phones. Alumni frequently gathered in the lounge to view exhibits, read, or visit. Several alums came running into the offices to confirm what they were hearing.

On the plane from Dallas to the White House, Federal Judge Sarah T. Hughes, a friend of the Johnsons, swore in Vice President Lyndon B. Johnson as the thirty-sixth President of the United States. Newspaper reports worldwide reflected the global community's shock, horror, and profound sorrow.

In Massachusetts, conspiracy theories circulated rapidly from newspapers, disgruntled politicos, and mischief-makers. LBJ did it. The CIA did it. The Mafia did it.

President Johnson established The President's Commission on the Assassination of President Kennedy, November 29, 1963, to investigate the murder. The Warren Commission, chaired by Chief Justice of the United States Earl

Warren, issued an 888-page report on September 24, 1964, to President Johnson and to the public three days later.

The report concluded Lee Harvey Oswald, a lone gunman, fired the fatal bullets from the book depository in Dallas during the President's motorcade advance.

Abe and I watched every bit of news we could. The horror of the events caused everyone to stop what they were doing. People were afraid that more violence would follow.

Before police had transferred Oswald to a county jail, they notified news outlets the transfer would occur at 9:15 a.m. As the officers brought him into the basement of the jail, Jack Ruby, a Dallas nightclub owner, entered the city jail basement. Police knew Ruby, because the courts had convicted him of nine felonies.

I watched as Ruby approached Oswald and shot and killed him on national television. Seventy police officers were present.[5]

Two public murders created an atmosphere of suspicion and fear. Mark Lane, a civil rights activist, spoke at the University of Massachusetts claiming the Warren Commission would be wrong to type Oswald as the lone gunman. In 1966, he published *Rush to Judgment*, in which he maintained the Warren Commission used flawed methodology and came to false conclusions.[6]

In 2012, Lane published *Last Word: My Indictment of the CIA in the Murder of JFK*. I read *Rush to Judgment* with skepticism, but believed Lane had many valid points, particularly with the single-bullet theory.

Though eyewitnesses heard more than one shot, the Commission concluded that one bullet entered Kennedy's back, exited through his throat, and entered Governor Connelly's chest, hand, and leg. Conspiracy theorists called this the "magic bullet."

Two of my coworkers believed LBJ had ordered the murder of Kennedy. They believed he was a power-hungry redneck who would take the country back to the dark ages. I did not like his Texas accent and his skill at bullying allegiance from members of Congress, but I wasn't one who bought the theory that LBJ was a murderer.

How does such a horror happen in a democratic country where elections, not incidents of violence, decide who will hold office? The murders of prominent and vulnerable people sent shockwaves throughout the country. People suffered mental anguish over the deaths and of the police violence directed toward protesters.

I'm Learning

Political theory soaked into my consciousness while I helped Abe with his master's thesis. Examining assertions more carefully, researching propositions, and presenting sound solutions to problems came more easily to me than before I began helping him.

Abe was an excellent student. I sometimes reviewed his papers for clarity and voice, for consistency of arguments, and for support of assertions. Our friends, who were government graduate students, lawyers, and debaters, held conversations that fascinated me for their creativity and intellect. Having never watched television much, I became a fan of programs featuring justice issues.

CBS aired *The Defenders*, with award-winning actor E.G. Marshall, from 1961 to 1965. The show was a courtroom drama usually dealing with important, often contentious issues of the day.

I never missed an episode of *East Side, West Side*, with George C. Scott and Cicely Tyson. The show dealt with issues of interest in urban settings and often were controversial and grim. It aired only one season 1963-1964.

Another favorite of mine was David Susskind's *Open End*. I remember watching programs that covered race relations, the draft, sex change operations, IQ testing, and organized crime.

Discussions about controversial topics enlightened me. The only other venue in which I had heard more than one side to a question was in high school and college debates.

Three years went by quickly, and Abe's grant was ending. He had finished his master's degree long ago, it seemed.

If he did not finish his PhD, he could apply for other forms of assistance, but he wanted to go to work to earn some money. We had saved money, though, despite our limited resources.

I was eager to return to college but was concerned that Abe might not finish his doctorate if he left the campus, as some of his professors warned him. I was willing to look for a better-paying job and to try to secure more funding for his tuition. Abe wanted to teach.

In the spring of 1964, he had completed much of the research and some of the writing for his dissertation. Nevertheless, he applied for teaching jobs at several universities.

The University of Hawaii, his first choice, replied that they did not hire applicants ABD (all but dissertation). They told Abe that once someone moved to Hawaii, they never wanted to leave. Despite the university's decision, Abe continued to subscribe to a Honolulu newspaper, "to keep up," he said.

He accepted a position as assistant professor of political science at East Tennessee State University in Johnson City, Tennessee. The chair of the department, which included history and political science, welcomed him, as did the other faculty.

6. YANKEE GO HOME!

Culture Shock in 1964

Abe's interview with the president of East Tennessee State University (ETSU) in Johnson City was a harbinger of what was to come. President Burgin Dossett welcomed Abe, then rose from his desk to shake hands. He moved his ample figure back behind his mahogany desk which was flanked by an American flag and a Confederate Flag. Brass spittoons stood on each side of the desk.

"Well, Mr. Norton, tell me a little about yourself. You are married. How many children do you have?"

"None, yet, sir."

"Are you planning to have some?"

"After we get on our feet, we hope to."

"Yes, well, we here like our professors and their wives to have a religious foundation to help direct their lives. Do you and your wife go to church?"

"We both grew up going to the Methodist church, sir."

"Um hunh. I see you have a degree from the University of Massatoosets, is that right? That's not one of those liberal schools, is it? Tell me about the political science department."

"The university is a land-grant college, and the government department employs several high-powered professors from universities across the United States," Abe said.

"As you know, history and political science are in the same department. Most of our professors are moderate in their political views, and many are Southerners. They are all older than you are. You can learn from them while you are here."

The questions, inappropriate but not illegal at the time, poured forth from the president in a drawling, nasal voice, accompanied by grammatical errors and occasional lapses of attention.

He got the job, assistant professor of political science, with a professional military draft deferment (2-S). He was 25 years old.

When Abe reported the conversation to me, I was shocked. *We left Massachusetts for this? What would my teachers be like if the president of the university is a Neanderthal?*

We were moving from the pastoral setting of liberal Amherst, Massachusetts, to Johnson City, Tennessee, just west of the Blue Ridge Mountains.

The landscapes of the two states were similar in many respects. Both had lush trees and mountains, hardwood trees and winding roads, but we found profound differences in attitudes toward "outsiders."

Massachusetts residents welcomed us with open arms, but our experiences so far in Tennessee had demonstrated local folks eyed us with suspicion.

Abe and I rented a house from the university librarian and the following year bought a three-bedroom house with a walkout basement in Pine Crest, a neighborhood within Johnson City. The house cost $6,000 and was a Federal Housing Administration (FHA) foreclosure. FHA made the repairs to satisfy code requirements.

We had saved enough money to put down the required amount after only one year! Depriving ourselves of movies, vacations, new furniture, and other goods (except the red bowls) had paid off.

Figure 22. Sitting at our first dinette set, complete with laminated walnut top and swivel chairs, Johnson City, Tennessee, 1964.

The evening was pleasant, too nice to stay inside. On a whim, we decided to treat ourselves to a movie and a leisurely drive. *The Pink Panther* was playing, and off we went, laughing as we got into the car.

We thoroughly enjoyed the movie. The aroma of rhododendrons and pine permeated the air as I drove with the top down on our MG Sprite. It was the kind of evening that stirred one's longing for new beginnings, of desire, of love.

On our way home, I took a shortcut through the campus. Suddenly, flashing red and blue lights behind us shattered the tranquil atmosphere.

The police stopped us as we entered the campus. The officer demanded to know what we were doing there at such a late hour. It was 10:30 p.m.

He reminded me that all girls were supposed to be in their dormitories by 8:00 p.m. on weeknights. Abe explained he was a faculty member, and I was his wife, but the officer wanted proof.

Our Tennessee driver's licenses provided some credibility, but the cop detained us while he called someone to verify Abe's claim. He grudgingly accepted my proof of marriage when I showed him my wedding and engagement rings. I was 21 years old. Skeptical, the officer finally sent us on our way with a reminder that the campus closed at 10 p.m.

A big gray cloud settled over our lovely evening as we looked at each other in disbelief.

"Do you believe what just happened?" I asked. "Well, really, the campus looks closed. I guess nothing happens here after 10 p.m."

The campus was apparently closed, but there was no evidence of that. No locked gates, no signs. One was supposed to know the rules without having been told what they were.

Little did we know it was the beginning of many instances of harassment, discrimination, and skepticism toward us and others.

———————

Getting acclimated to East Tennessee required some research. While we waited to hear about our home loan application, I discovered an interesting fact about Johnson City. The counties of Carter, Sullivan, Unicoi, and Washington claimed parts of the city. The house we purchased was in a neighborhood in Carter County. Washington County claimed the main campus of ETSU.

We soon discovered the inconsistent liquor laws. Each county had enacted its own body of laws, so that within Johnson City, there were four sets of laws. The house we bought was in a county where possession of beer violated the law.

Law enforcement could enter one's home without a warrant and arrest the residents and confiscate the illegal liquid. Moonshiners and bootleggers opposed any notion of liquor by the drink or state-owned liquor stores because it would put them out of business.

Preachers and bootleggers found themselves on the same side of the liquor issue. Lynchings and family feuds accompanied the quest for liquor.

A bizarre incident would soon raise its ugly head. When a friend told us about an elephant lynching by the citizens of nearby Erwin, Tennessee, I wondered if they were giving the New Englanders a hazing. Then someone produced a newspaper clipping with a picture of the lynching. I became convinced. Not only convinced, but disgusted.

The newspaper reported that at a circus event, a child repeatedly poked a sleeping elephant in the trunk with a stick. The elephant broke out of its cage and came close to attacking the child. It frightened the child so badly he fainted.

Drunken townspeople hurriedly produced a winch and a truck to haul the elephant, allegedly overcome by an evil spirit, to the common area in Erwin where they hanged the elephant.

I wondered why people spent so much energy on a wild, mistreated animal that had harmed no one. How quickly they became angry over the incident in which a child was at fault!

Who are these people? Am I going to go to class with folks like this?

Still reeling from the lynching incident, I enrolled as a sophomore at the university. In the mid-1960s, many people still believed communists were trying to infiltrate the US government and the universities. Anti-communists called criticism of the government "un-American."

I listened to students in my classes complaining about "outsiders" taking over their country.

"Whom do you consider an outsider?" I asked a classmate.

"I guess, someone who isn't from here and has different ideas from us," she said.

"That would be many people," I said.

"Yeah, I guess so."

"Do you mean minorities? Black and Brown people?"

"They don't want to be here anyway."

Very few people of color took the same classes I did. In fact, very few people of color had enrolled at the university. Abe and I shared stories with each other about folks we encountered who thought we were crazy for talking about the First Amendment to the Constitution, discrimination, and poverty. I was glad Abe and I were allies in the war of ideas.

I applauded Mario Savio in December 1964 when he led about 3,000 students and faculty in a sit-in at the University of California-Berkeley to show support for the First Amendment to the US Constitution.

The student movement during the 1960s challenged many campus regulations, including those limiting speech and assembly. Later, students would include their opposition to the Vietnam War.

I believed the movement could advance the cause of students, and I initiated a discussion with Abe's colleagues at a social gathering of the department. Many of them also supported the movement in part. They did not, however, express their opinions in public.

Abe loved being in a classroom, and he quickly became a favorite teacher amongst political science, sociology, and philosophy majors. He was young, spoke eloquently, dressed well, was handsome, and enjoyed teaching.

His reputation as a superior debater followed him to Tennessee, and he soon made friends with the university debate coach. They shared many war stories about forensic wins and undeserved losses.

I declared a major in English. Some of my teachers labeled me a Yankee, a derogatory term, I learned, when they heard I had moved to Tennessee from Massachusetts. I apparently had adopted some Massachusetts speech dialect, because students tried to mimic the way I spoke. They also attributed liberalism and aloofness to me, qualities they associated with the New England Yankees. I did not get a chance to reveal I was a Yankee from Kansas.

They told me if I criticized the United States like a lot of Yankees do, I should leave the country. I wondered if, as a college student, I would have to confront similar bullying tactics I had experienced in elementary school. If so, I was ready to put on the gloves.

Communists Are Hiding

English majors took an advanced composition course in their sophomore year. During a discussion of the subject of patriotism, my teacher, Miss Leab, asserted that communists were hiding in the United States.

"How do you know they exist if you can't see them?" I asked.

"They are very hard to find."

"Where do you think they are hiding?"

"They are very sneaky, but you will know them when they emerge from their hiding places. Many are hiding in Washington, where they are extremely difficult to find."

"How will I know a communist when I see one?"

"You'll know them when they sneak out of their hiding places."

Miss Leab demanded to know where I came from, and I told her Massachusetts.

"We've got a Yankee in our midst. How did that happen?"

She instructed the class that during the Revolutionary War, some citizens in Massachusetts sided with the British and painted tar around their chimneys to let the Brits know who sympathized with them.

"Did you know that?"

"Well, yes. They were a small group of rich landowners among the older, more conservative, well-established elite."

"Now most people in Massachusetts are liberal and free-thinking and are very much different from us here in Tennessee, or in much of the rest of the country. Some communists probably live there, too," she said.

Why is she ranting about something no one was discussing? I'm staying out of this for now.

She gave me an F on my first composition, citing some obscure misuse of the subjunctive mood. I built a strong case to counter her grade, but she wouldn't budge. Thereafter, I worked hard not to contradict some of her irrational and racist statements.

I found my classmates' lack of awareness of current events troubling. When three members of the Nation of Islam assassinated Malcolm X in February 1965, no one mentioned the incident in any of my classes.

Though I would have liked to discuss the incidents, I kept my mouth shut rather than risk starting an argument. The murder of public figures whom I admired affected me as though I knew them personally.

About this time, I discovered Dr. Martin Luther King's "Letter from Birmingham Jail." Police arrested Dr. King for demonstrating against segregation.

The letter is mainly a treatise on civil disobedience, peaceful, nonviolent activity, and change. Dr. King was the first president of the Southern Christian Leadership Conference, a civil rights organization formed in 1957 in Atlanta, Georgia.[1]

In a philosophy class, I found a few students who at least had some awareness of current events, including budding cultural changes and baby steps to integration and Black Liberation.

The Bachelor of Arts degree I worked toward required taking courses in science, math, English, and foreign language. I selected geology to satisfy the science requirement.

A student in my English Composition class also took geology. Frequently, we met on our way across campus to class. He was majoring in American Studies, so we shared some of the same courses.

One day, he was struggling with a serious cold and needed a handkerchief. His effort to control coughing and sneezing wasn't working. I was glad I had several tissues in my purse and hastily gave them to him.

We laughed about having avoided the danger of snot flooding the geology building. John suggested we had rescued what might have become a lost artifact—petrified snot. Finally, someone with a sense of humor appeared, even though the joke was sophomoric. Well, we were both sophomores.

We didn't have time to chat more that day, but later we discovered we liked much of the same music and art. He must have been the first friend I made at ETSU. John came over to the house a few times and listened to some of Abe's and my record albums.

In a conversation after class, John invited me to go to the university Methodist Church coffeehouse called Agape. The minister and his wife had located it in the parsonage basement. I had heard other students commenting on the place, and I convinced Abe to come with me to see what was going on.

John sang and accompanied himself on a twelve-string guitar. He sang Woody Guthrie's *Deportee* and *I Don't Want Your Millions, Mister*, Bob Dylan's *Blowin' in the Wind*, and *Don't Think Twice, It's All Right*. Other students sang or read poetry.

In 1964, folk music of all sorts was coming into its own. Radio programs featured protest songs, blues, and current popular folk music.

Not long after my first visit to the coffeehouse, I bought a twelve-string guitar and started learning to play and sing as well. Agape began holding "Happenings," which were spontaneous events during which people could take to the stage and sing, improvise comedy, read poetry, or rant.

I played a set on my guitar with a group on one occasion and helped another group produce a short film about a motorcycle rider. I enjoyed these creative activities, especially the ones with a political message or satirical format.

Performing Again

English majors took public speaking, required for graduation. The speech teacher was also the debate coach. After I had delivered two assigned speeches, Coach Harding invited me to participate in a forensic tournament on the Harvard campus.

He suggested I prepare for the extemporaneous speaking event and join an established four-person team missing a member who was ill. I enjoyed entering extemporaneous events in high school, so I agreed to try it. The debate coach's new friend, Abe Norton, accompanied the team to the tournament.

Extemporaneous speaking events required the entrant to be prepared to give a seven-minute speech with references before an audience. Entrants drew a topic from a pool, then got 30 minutes to prepare their speeches.

Abe and the coach sat on each side of me on the bus, asking me questions about current events. I could answer their questions. When the event was called at the tournament, I prepared my speech and entered the auditorium to deliver my first extemporaneous speech as a student at ETSU.

The auditorium was small but packed with students, judges, and coaches. I did well and received a "I" (the top rating) in each of three rounds I entered. After the day was over, both of my coaches told me to stay away from the other students after the rounds were over, because they would probably go out to get a beer. Abe didn't want me to go without him, and Coach Harding had invited Abe to have a drink with him. I was 21 years old.

I didn't think I needed a chaperone. Abe told me he didn't think it was appropriate for me to go out with the other debaters without him. He and the coach were getting together for a drink, so I crashed their party.

Though the debate team and I did well, I continued to get unsolicited advice from both of my very own personal "coaches." One coach told me to stand behind the podium; the other told me not to stand behind the podium. One coach said I should practice lowering the pitch of my voice, and the other said I sounded too much like a man.

Frustrated by the contradictory coaching team—on and off campus—I stopped entering collegiate forensic events. I solved this problem by avoiding a prolonged confrontation.

"I don't think you're handling criticism very well," Abe said.

"The contrary double-coach routine doesn't work for me," I said. "I have done well in my speech class, and that is enough for me. I earned an A."

The forensic experiences did not deter me from auditioning for a play, however. The neighborhood play, *Lo-Su, Girl Pirate*, my debate experience, and my roles in three high school plays seemed like an adequate resume to audition for a college play.

I read for a role in the Tennessee Williams two-act play, *The Lady of Larkspur Lotion*, and landed the role of Mrs. Hardwicke-Moore, a troublesome tenant in a boarding house.

My friend John knew two of the other actors and came to some rehearsals. He also attended the live production, as did other English, speech, and drama majors.

One evening, the cast took a break. John was in the audience and I went to say hello, taking a seat in the row in front of him. He leaned forward to say something to me. I turned around to see him just as he reached up to touch my face. "Chunky makeup, but we had to make me look a lot older than I am," I said.

"It looks good," he said.

He leaned forward and brushed his lips against my cheek. He surprised me, but the kiss was as gentle as a whisper.

I leaned in and said, "I hardly know what to say."

He leaned toward me and kissed me on the mouth. My feelings confused me. I didn't think I was supposed to like being kissed by someone other than Abe. The cast reassembled, so I left John to return to rehearsal.

Two evenings later, we rehearsed again. The cast members were finding the groove, and the rehearsal went well. I saw John in the audience with a few other students, but I did not leave the stage to talk to him.

As I was leaving the theater, John approached me and asked if he could have a ride to his motorcycle. He had met up with some students at a bar and left his cycle there to ride with them to rehearsal. They were going somewhere else for a party, and he had opted out.

"Sure, I can give you a ride. I'm right over there." I had put the top up on the MG. We got into the car, and John started talking about the play.

"Williams left something out in the second act," he said. "It needs more substance, more oomph."

"I think you're right. I have read that sometimes Williams used his short plays as rough drafts for fleshing out characters. This one is supposed to be a draft of the Glass Menagerie."

"You did a great job, and probably could pull off that characterization, too, but I think you would make a good Maggie in *Cat on a Hot Tin Roof.*"

"It might be fun to try."

John reached over and kissed me. I was wholly in the moment and kissed him back, more passionately than the first time.

I pulled away. "This is a mistake," I said as I turned on the car. "You know I am married, and we can't do this."

"I'm sorry to hear that, but I understand."

The next day, the cast performed a dress rehearsal, and many faculty members attended. I searched for Abe, but later he told me he had not attended because he was sure I wouldn't appreciate his criticism. I told him I was hoping he could come just to enjoy the play, that I wasn't planning to pursue an acting career.

He said it wasn't a good play, and I was too young to play this character. I thought he was entitled to his own opinion, but I was disappointed because he had nothing constructive to say.

John sat in the audience, but I was reluctant to talk to him. I was relieved that his American Studies curriculum diverged from mine somewhat. We were coming and going at different times.

I continued to find my way to the coffeehouse, where John and I laughed and talked about classes, music, and politics. Abe was not a fan of the experimental music and drama, so he opted out.

On one occasion, I excused myself to go to the restroom. John was waiting for me when I came out of the ladies' room.

He took my hand and led me outside to the small, secluded garden.

"I'm leaving soon to return to Florida State to finish my American Studies program."

"Well, good luck. You will do well."

"I'm glad I met you. I wish things could have been different."

"That is a compliment. Thank you and take care." I never talked to him alone again.

My studies consumed most of my time from then until I graduated, but I often thought of John when I picked up my guitar, having absorbed by osmosis how to strum a twelve-string instrument.

7. THE FIGHT FOR JUSTICE

I Get to Vote

The presidential election of 1964 rolled around quickly. Since I had attended the 1960 Republican Party convention, I had switched parties and was ready to vote for Lyndon Johnson.

The values and platform of the northern branch of the Democratic Party aligned more closely with my own values. I hoped that Johnson and Congress would enact the civil rights legislation the Kennedy administration had presented.

Abe and I arrived at our polling place to a disquieting scene. In Kansas, the law required campaign signs and paraphernalia to be at least 200 yards away from entrances.

Apparently not so in Tennessee. Scores of campaign signs lined the pathway to the building, close enough to be illegal in my book. Someone had brought a Sno-Cone cart to the voting party. Another person had brought what he called the "hillbilly" breakfast to sell: RC and a Moon Pie.

"This looks like a circus to me," I said. "It's my first time to vote. Is this right?"

Abe said he didn't like it, but he wasn't surprised.

I decided not to complain.

A gentleman with gnarled hands and white hair greeted me, patted my arm, and asked me if I was sure I was old enough to vote. I showed him my driver's license to prove I was 21, and he commented on how young I looked to be 21.

"Are you married, and is your husband here?"

"Yes, why?" I asked.

"We'll check with him. Most of our ladies like to talk to their husbands to see how they are voting," he said.

"Here is my valid license. I can decide for myself how to vote. May I have a ballot, please?"

He raised his eyebrows, patted my shoulder again, and handed me a paper ballot. He instructed me to sit down at a table draped with a red and white checked tablecloth. If someone else was sitting at the table, voters used a piece of cardboard lying on the table to hide ballots.

I finished voting, took my ballot to a secure box, inserted it, and walked outside, but I hoped my next voting experience would go better. I also thought it inappropriate that the man touched me and patted my shoulder.

My choice for President of the United States won. All the Way with LBJ, as his campaign signs said.

In the next three years, President Johnson and Congress passed into law some of the most far-reaching pieces of legislation since the Franklin D. Roosevelt administration.

I cheered as Congress passed the Civil Rights Act of 1964, the most comprehensive piece of anti-discrimination legislation to date.

The Great Society, as Johnson liked to call his vision, included laws governing public broadcasting, Medicare and Medicaid, the environment, and education. *This looks like progress.*

The War on Poverty became the unofficial name of the programs designed to eliminate poverty, which stood at 19% of the US population in 1963.[1] I liked the fact that Johnson identified the cause of poverty not as the personal moral failings of the poor, but as a societal failure.

As Johnson said in his inaugural address, "The cause may lie deeper in our failure to give our fellow citizens a fair chance to develop their own capacities, in a lack of education and training, in a lack of medical care and housing, in a lack of decent communities in which to live and bring up their children."[2]

Governor of Alabama George Wallace, a member of the Southern Democratic Party, challenged attempts to enforce civil rights legislation in Alabama. In his 1963 inaugural address, he had thundered, "Segregation now, segregation tomorrow, segregation forever."[3]

I hoped the law could take Wallace to task for his segregationist views. *He should be in jail.*

In June 1964, angry segregationists had killed three Congress of Racial Equality (CORE) field workers—Michael Schwerner, Anthony Reed, and Andrew Goodman. Four hundred US Navy sailors and the FBI found the CORE workers' burned-out car near a swamp three days after they disappeared.[12]

The FBI followed a tip and found the civil rights workers' bodies two months later. Their investigation revealed that members of the local White Knights of the Ku Klux Klan, the Neshoba County Sheriff's Office, and the Philadelphia Police Department were involved in the incident.[4]

Legislators in the southern states scorned the War on Poverty programs. Many did not take advantage of funding that would have helped stem the tide of poverty.

But trouble brewed in many states outside the South as well.

Violence and Black Power

Malcolm X, born Malcolm Little (Muslim name el-Hajj Malik el-Shabazz), May 19, 1925, in Omaha, Nebraska, was an American Muslim minister and civil rights leader.

Malcolm excelled in school, but an eighth-grade teacher told him he should take up carpentry instead of the law, as Malcolm had wished.[5]

As a rebellious teenager, he lost interest in school. Petty criminal activities led to more serious crimes, and he served time for robbery from 1946 to 1952. While in prison, he converted to Islam and later became acquainted with Elijah Muhammed.[6]

An eloquent, charismatic speaker, he quickly rose to become a leader of the Black Power movement and changed the lexicon from "Negro" and "colored" to "Black" and "African-American."

In contrast with Dr. King's emphasis on civil disobedience and redemptive suffering, Malcolm asserted the importance of Black identity, freedom, and independence.[7] I liked his positive approach to Black pride.

He was speaking at a gathering in Manhattan when a man rushed forward and shot him once in the chest with a sawed-off shotgun. Two other men charged the stage, firing semi-automatic handguns. Malcolm died on February 21, 1965.[8]

A Memphis jury found three members of the Nation of Islam guilty of murder. New evidence exonerated two of them.[9]

Malcolm holds a great fascination for me because his evolving belief system played out in public, with no apologies. He found peace with his beliefs, which included international unity, not a one-dimensional Blacks-only value system.

Though Malcolm's death is an example of political violence involving only other Black folks, there were plenty of White police officers directing violence toward the Black community.

On August 11, 1965, Los Angeles police stopped Marquette Frye and his brother Ronnie for drunken driving in Watts, a southern neighborhood of Los Angeles, California. Marquette failed a sobriety test but resisted arrest, with the help of his mother.

To arrest him, a police officer struck him in the face with a baton. Rumors circulated about the police having kicked a pregnant woman who was present at the scene.[10]

Allegations of police abuse motivated residents of Watts to continue rioting for six days. Their frustration with living conditions, police brutality, lack of education, and jobs played out in many communities in the country and in other parts of the world.[11]

I thought the police initiated and escalated the violence. They overreacted to Black people who did not trust the police. The following exemplifies incidents of police harassment and violence.

Mr. Frye came home from jail to see his neighborhood turned into a war zone. He said the police had hassled him all his life. They beat him up many times and had delivered a blow to his head that caused epileptic seizures. He had severe depression. He blamed it all on the riots. The lowest point in his life was in 1970, when his 18-month-old child with congenital heart problems died.[12]

While residents of cities expressed their many frustrations with their lives, southern Blacks were still trying to vote. Black people who tried to vote paid a poll tax or took tests to determine whether they qualified to vote.

Voting in the South

The proposed Voting Rights Act of 1965 was a tool to enforce nondiscrimination in voting, but southerners actively opposed it because the legislation would effectively end the literacy test.

The State of Louisiana

Literacy Test (This test is to be given to anyone who cannot prove a fifth grade education.)

Do what you are told to do in each statement, nothing more, nothing less. Be careful as one wrong answer denotes failure of the test. You have 10 minutes to complete the test.

1. Draw a line around the number or letter of this sentence.

2. Draw a line under the last word in this line.

3. Cross out the longest word in this line.

4. Draw a line around the shortest word in this line.

5. Circle the first, first letter of the alphabet in this line.

6. In the space below draw three circles, one inside (engulfed by) the other.

7. Above the letter X make a small cross.

8. Draw a line through the letter below that comes earliest in the alphabet.

        Z V S B D M K I T P H C

9. Draw a line through the two letters below that come last in the alphabet.

        Z V B D M K T P H S Y C

10. In the first circle below write the last letter of the first word beginning with "L".

11. Cross out the number necessary, when making the number below one million.

        10000000000

12. Draw a line from circle 2 to circle 5 that will pass below circle 2 and above circle 4.

13. In the line below cross out each number that is more than 20 but less than 30.

        31 16 48 29 53 47 22 37 98 26 20 25

Figure 23. State of Louisiana Literacy Test. Election registrars used nonsensical questions to test Black people trying to register to vote, 1963.

Many tests asked complicated questions about the US Constitution, and others asked nonsense questions subject to many interpretations.

In fact, anything was fair game to keep Black people from voting. Many southern states after Reconstruction levied a tax on Black people to vote but waived it for White people. Poll workers wielded a lot of power if no one stopped them from questioning answers on the tests. If a person did not produce a receipt for their poll tax, the registrant was denied the vote.

The complete set of 30 questions for this literacy test is available online.[24]

Some northern states instituted poll taxes, but most applied to everyone in lieu of property tax. Most northern states had repealed poll taxes by the beginning of the twentieth century.

I worked with the campus Democratic Party on voter drives, supported or opposed legislation through letter writing, and canvassed neighborhoods for opinions on voting rights.

Students organized campus volunteers with the Southern Student Organizing Committee (SSOC), Students for a Democratic Society (SDS), Congress of Racial Equality (CORE), and Student Nonviolent Coordinating Committee (SNCC).

Organizers set up tables in Black neighborhoods in Johnson City, Erwin, and Kingsport, Tennessee, to register voters. No tests, no poll tax. At first, people were reluctant to approach our tables. After a few people stepped up, we registered several hundred new voters in one day.

Several groups had organizers in the field: The Southern Student Organizing Committee (SSOC), Southern Christian Leadership Conference (SCLC), and the Student Nonviolent Coordinating Committee (SNCC). Student activist and future Congressman John Lewis led SNCC.

I met people affiliated with SNCC at Emory University in Atlanta when I joined a group of volunteers to hear Floyd McKissick's lecture on Black Power.

I hoped to meet Stokely Carmichael, too, as his speaking style was crisp, and his message of Black liberation resonated with me.

The speeches of these two men provided motivation for me to travel to Alabama to support voting rights. Despite Abe's decision not to go with me, I went anyway because I supported the cause and wouldn't miss any classes.

Memories of minor acts of discrimination toward me flooded back, along with recollections of the mistreatment endured by my debate colleague and my swim lessons partner.

The bullying I had faced cultivated my empathy for Black women. I contacted a SNCC organizer in Atlanta to find out how to catch one of the buses.

The march I joined was to be the first of three marches from Selma to Montgomery, the capital. Excitement bubbled up from my new friends and me. The energy on the bus crackled. People were singing and exchanging names, addresses, and their own stories of discrimination.

I was full of righteous purpose. Passengers were students from Emory, the University of North Carolina, and the University of Virginia. We all thought we were helping the cause of justice by doing our part to ensure the protection of voting rights. We slept on the bus, and I don't remember if we stopped to eat.

Two-thirds of the people on my bus were Black. Many Black marchers were already in Selma. Our bus arrived where a group of protesters had stopped to rest.

Almost all the Black people dressed in "Sunday" clothes, and we college students looked shabby compared to them. The marchers welcomed us with open arms. Ministers were blessing people as they emerged from the buses.

Glorious singing rang out with such songs as *Ain't Nobody Goin' to Turn Me 'Round, We Shall Overcome,* and *This Land is Your Land.* Marchers had not yet approached the Edmund Pettus Bridge.

The police were harassing the marchers, trying to provoke us, so they could justify using their nightsticks. Armed mounted police were shouting racial slurs into bullhorns.

"You n-----s are trespassing. Get your Black asses off this property."

"You are in violation of the law."

"You are not qualified to vote."

"God never intended the races to mix."

I took my 35mm Olympus camera from the case. I had already taken one roll of 36 shots and had started on another. A deputy stopped near me, got off his horse, and raised his nightstick.

"Hand over that camera, or I will take it away from you."

"People need to see what is going on here," I said.

He yanked the camera strap from around my neck and took my camera and the case with the extra film cans.

"Let's see how good they are," he said, as he pulled the film out of the camera and exposed it to the light. "See here, looks like they aren't any good."

I tried to grab my camera, but under threat from the nightstick, I gave in. He refused to return the camera. I had taken shots of the bus, some passengers, and several views of the march, including shots of police attacking the marchers. He kept my camera.

Figure 24. This slide carousel represents the presentation I might have made if a deputy sheriff had not confiscated my camera while I was on the Voting Rights March of 1965.

I kept up with the marchers, but the frontliners who started to cross the bridge were almost exclusively Black folks. They took the brunt of the violence, as did many others who did not make it that far.

Tear gas stung my eyes. I had a hard time breathing. SNCC members tended to people who were bleeding from the nightstick's blow. The air was thick with smoke from police gunshots, fired to intimidate marchers.

Figure 25. Bloody Sunday. Police beat back marchers attempting to get to the Edmund Pettus Bridge in Selma, Alabama, March 1965.

Police dragged men away by their coats and the belts on their trousers. They twisted their arms out of their sockets and held bullhorns up to their faces and hollered racial slurs into their ears.

They shoved women to the ground and whacked them behind the knees with nightsticks. The crowd roared with anger and despair as they watched the police deliver blow after blow.

Mounted police pushed their horses into the crowd where I stood, compelling the marchers to disperse. I tumbled to the pavement, injuring my leg and hand, causing them to bleed. Fueled by intense anger, the adrenaline pumping through my veins empowered me to sprint toward one of the mounted officers. Swiftly turning his horse, he saw me coming and stopped dead still.

"You better not come any closer, little lady, if you know what's good for you. You better go on home, or better yet, just go on back to Russia," he said.

I laughed. He was just one of several people who wanted to send me back to Russia. "I've never been there, so I can't go back," I said.

"You little smart ass."

Still angry, I walked toward the Edmund Pettus Bridge, only to discover a nightmare. Alabama state troopers wielding whips, nightsticks, and tear gas canisters rushed the group at the Edmund Pettus Bridge and beat them. TV stations captured the brutal scene, enraging many Americans and drawing civil rights and religious leaders of all faiths to Selma in protest.

I was demonstrating support for thousands of people who had been denied justice for centuries. The police and White segregationists continued to attack the marchers, though I had escaped most of the violence. Several students and I left the area to return to our homes or colleges. We did not want to miss our classes or a ride home.

SNCC buses were gearing up to transport people back to Atlanta, and I quickly got on one of them. A somber mood permeated our bus. We expressed our guilt for not staying to help. People were crying because the police had brutally injured the marchers on the front line.

"I thought this country was founded on the rule of law."

"Did you see those women the cops were striking?"

"I saw one officer walking through the crowd swinging a bullhorn back and forth, hitting marchers on each side."

"The police should protect the marchers."

"Where is the federal government?"

To characterize the event, journalists began using "Bloody Sunday," the designation SNCC marchers used.

I took a bus from Atlanta to Johnson City and arrived Monday morning to clean up and go to class. I found Abe later in the morning and talked through some of my experiences, lamenting the violence and losing my camera and film. He was glad I was home with only a couple of scrapes.

Three marches took place from Selma to Montgomery. The murder of Jimmie Lee Jackson, a 26-year-old deacon in the Baptist church in Marion, Alabama, prompted the first. He tried several times to register to vote, and during a peaceful protest, the police assaulted him. They shot him to death in a Selma café.[13]

The Reverend James Reeb attended the second march and went to dinner after the march with two friends. Four White men started shouting racial slurs at the group. They assaulted Reeb. One of them had a club. He raised the club to strike Reeb, landing the club on his head. Reeb died two days later. The court tried and acquitted three of the four White men indicted for his murder.[14]

Viola Liuzzo, a Unitarian activist from Detroit, thought she could help to make the world a safer place for her five children by protesting in Selma. She drove all the way from Detroit by herself to show her support for the marchers.

Right after the march was over, Ku Klux Klansmen were riding by the protesters and started shooting at them. Liuzzo was driving a Black man home. The Klansmen shot and killed her, but the court acquitted them of her murder. One of the killers was an FBI informant.[15]

After Bloody Sunday, federal troops protected civil rights leaders who led a march of 25,000 people from Selma to Montgomery while Congress deliberated on voting rights legislation.

For the most part, this march from Selma to Montgomery went off peacefully. I believed that many people where I lived supported the White supremacists, and I wondered if things would ever change.

Police violence toward civil rights protesters continued during the middle 1960s. President Johnson and Alabama Governor Wallace met in the Oval Office to negotiate an end to the events. Johnson wanted Wallace to call off the police, and Wallace wanted Johnson to call off the protesters. Eventually, Johnson decided he did not want his legacy to report that he had been on the same side as Wallace.[16]

President Johnson addressed a joint session of Congress after Bloody Sunday, and Congress passed the Voting Rights Act of 1965.[17] I thought the Congress would be the catalyst for calming the violence, but . . .

The legislation did not stop the violence. After Congress passed the voting rights legislation, Jonathan Daniels, a White civil rights activist, and his friend, Ruby Sales, a Black woman, were in jail in Alabama because they had protested White plantation owners' exploitation of Black workers.

On the day of their release, a White policeman pointed his gun at Sales, and Daniels pushed her out of the way and took the bullet instead. The jury acquitted his killer.[18]

The voting rights legislation was cause to celebrate for many, including the ETSU government department. Chairman Richter Moore and his wife, Carolyn Dabbs Moore, held a gathering at their home to discuss the recent events.

Their home was an enormous red brick Victorian in Jonesborough, purported to be the capital of the Lost State of Franklin.

When Abe and I arrived, peacocks, guinea hens, Packlet the Weimaraner, and an orange cat the size of a pumpkin greeted us. Wielding a handful of feathers, Carolyn and

Richter shooed the animals away from the front door so we could enter the house.

Several faculty members and their spouses milled around the sitting room and library. Twelve more people arrived shortly thereafter. Everyone talked about the Selma march and the impact the new Voting Rights Act might make on future elections.

Professor Bob Crawford speculated more liberals would run for office because they could garner Black votes from the newly enfranchised.

One of the history profs thought it would take a few years for segregationists holding public office to enforce the law.

The passage of the voting rights legislation and the Moores' party lifted everyone's spirits.

Carolyn asked me, "Are you enjoying your classes? Did you have time to see the television reports about the march? It was insane."

"I was in Selma for part of it," I said. "Caught one of the SNCC buses from Atlanta. Unfortunately, an armed cop confiscated my camera."

Carolyn announced, "Did you all know that this little lady was in Selma?"

Not one person in the department knew I had attended. Abe, who I thought might mention my trip, neglected to mention my participation.

After answering several questions about my experience, I commented on the shocking brutality of the police. Abe told me later he was too busy to think about what might happen to me, but he and some friends had seen the police violence on television.

Students Continue Their Fight for Justice

Students were awakening all over the country to injustice. Education was unjust for Black and Brown people, women, and poor people.

The University of California, Berkeley had become a hotbed for sit-ins in administration buildings. Students at the University of Michigan took up similar tactics.

President Johnson was passionate about equity in education. Congress passed the Elementary and Secondary Education Act, which focused resources in poor school districts.

National Endowment for the Arts, Head Start, and Food Stamps programs began to operate, but were long-term solutions to help poor folks find a way out of poverty. These programs would not address the impending emergencies brought on by discrimination and the war in Vietnam.

In 1962, the US had about 11,000 special advisors in South Vietnam to train troops in counter-insurgency tactics. In 1964, Johnson ordered combat troops to respond to the Tet offensive, a massive attack by the Viet Cong and the North Vietnamese. By 1965, 25,000 advisors lived in South Vietnam.[19]

Before his assassination, President Kennedy had opposed the military's recommendations to order troops to Vietnam and had ordered the military to desist.

James K. Galbraith wrote in *Who, What, Why*, a non-profit news organization, dated October 11, 1963, that Kennedy articulated his decision in *National Security Action Memorandum 263* to withdraw all US military forces from Vietnam by the end of 1965, completed after the 1964 election. This was the formal policy of the United States government on the day JFK died.

Though I supported peaceful nonviolence to address grievances, Black Power leaders' advocacy of stronger protests and sit-ins made sense to me.

I sympathized with college students Huey P. Newton and Bobby Seale, two prominent Black leaders who established the Black Panther Party in 1966 in Oakland, California.

The Panthers began open carry patrols to watch police activity for threats of violence. Later, the Panthers started social programs, including free breakfast for children, educational programs, and community health clinics. They opposed the war in Vietnam.[20]

The Panthers were one of many organizations that considered themselves to be part of the Black Power movement, whose goal was to achieve self-determination for Black people.

Not everyone looked at the Panthers with kindness. A leather-jacketed Black man wearing a beret nestled into his massive afro with an ammunition belt slung across his body made an imposing figure. An entire row of such young men made a serious statement about their cause. No one could intimidate them any longer.

At first, the NAACP and many in the Black community supported the war in Vietnam, but by 1966, public opinion had shifted. The Black Panthers, Martin Luther King, Jr., Muhammad Ali, Student Nonviolent Coordinating Committee (SNCC), and the Nation of Islam opposed the war.

Newscasters began reporting the demographics of student-draftees who were fighting in Vietnam. In relationship to the percentage of the population, Black people far outnumbered white people. Though comprising 11% of the US population in 1967, Black people were 16.3% of all draftees.

From 1966 to 1967, the reenlistment rate for Black people was 50%, twice what it was for white soldiers.[21] In the US Navy, only 5% of sailors were Black in 1971, with less than 1% of Navy officers who were Black.[22]

It was hard to find humor in violence, unless it was dark.

The hippies who protested in front of armed guards carried flowers which they inserted into the barrels of the rifles the guards shouldered. These actions made me smile, but I also feared for their safety.

Most of my acquaintances opposed sending troops to Vietnam. Senator Eugene McCarthy of Minnesota led the charge to end the war.

Students demonstrated outside military recruiting offices, on college campuses, and near government buildings, chanting "Hey, hey, LBJ, how many kids did you kill today?"

Phil Ochs, a satirical folk singer, released an album in 1965 with "Draft Dodger Rag," a song that became an anthem for Vietnam protesters.

In 1967, in the middle of this chaotic time, Supreme Court Justice Tom C. Clark, a Truman appointee, retired from the Court. President Johnson appointed Thurgood Marshall, the lead attorney in *Brown v. Board of Education, 347 US 483 (1954)*, to replace Clark.

Jimmy Quillen, our congressional representative elected in 1962, was a flag-waving Republican who began a crusade in 1967 to make desecration of the US flag a federal offense. Quillen had voted against the civil rights act of 1964.

He asserted the "radical, left-wing, un-American students" who were dropping the flag on the ground, spitting on it, and burning it should pay a price. Desecration also included letting the flag touch the ground, hanging it upside down, leaving it in the rain, and, of course, cutting it up and sewing it onto clothing.

Most of the alleged flag-burners opposed the war in Vietnam. The so-called flag burners' symbolic activity was their way of expressing their opposition to the war and in favor of justice.

In 1967, while Congress and the public debated the treatment of the flag, Abe composed a letter to the Johnson City, Tennessee, *Press-Chronicle* newspaper. He was a 28-year-old Assistant Professor of Political Science with a professional deferment (2-S) from the military draft and directed the letter toward Congressman Quillen.

The letter appeared over Abe's signature with no reference to the university. The letter stated in part:

> Assuming that our country is strong and cohesive, such demonstrations as flag burning could do no more harm than cause mental anguish to those who object to such treatment of the American flag. Surely, we cannot hope or desire to restrict by federal legislation all or even most actions of which others disapprove. If this were the case, I would have to request that the government silence you, since most of your statements meet with my disapproval and certainly cause me a great deal of mental anguish.[23]

In response, the *Press-Chronicle* published letters to the editor condemning Abe and the flag burners.

"Communists should go back to Russia; the flag is sacred."

"Patriotic Americans know how to deal with you. You'd better watch your back."

"Communists go to jail. We know how to deal with traitors," the letters said.

We received letters at our home address offering to send us "back to Russia in a box with the flags you burn." We reported telephone threats and shared the letters with local law enforcement. They dismissed our complaints, saying no harm had come to us.

Then came the piling on. Someone erected a cross, draped it in a flag, and burned the whole mess in the front yard of our home. We saw the remains when we returned from school. It's enough to piss off a person.

We reported the incident to the police, and one of the county sheriffs came to the house. We hoped they would not search the house, because we had made some home brew (beer) and had quarts of it stored in the basement. The containers looked like a stash of Molotov cocktails.

"It looks like you got quite a mess here, Mr. Norton," he said. "Are you trying to make some kind of political statement?"

"We want to make a complaint about what happened. We did not create this mess, and I think you should try to find out who did. They could have burned down our house," Abe said.

"What do you think happened here? Looks to me like you're trying to tell us something."

"Ask the neighbors, do some detective work. Do your job," I said.

"We'll look into it," the sheriff said.

They dismissed the whole thing after first accusing us of burning the flag ourselves to generate sympathy.

What a joke! We laughed. They were serious.

Finally, they decided it was a prank. The officers interviewed one of our neighbors. He saw nothing. Silly me. I thought the police might do their job and canvass the neighborhood.

The chairman of the political science department assured Abe he would remain employed because he had not identified himself as a faculty member in the letter. He had a right to express himself, just as anyone else did. The president of the university, however, decided otherwise.

This president was the same one who interviewed him for the job, seated at the desk flanked by spittoons and a Confederate flag.

President Dossett acted. He notified Abe's draft board in Great Bend, Kansas, that he was rescinding Abe's professional deferment from the draft (2-S professional classification) and that the draft board should reclassify him 1-A, subject to immediate call-up. I learned of the change when the Barton County, Kansas draft board notified Abe it had changed his status from 2-S to 1-A. We knew this classification meant the board could draft him at any time.

Several faculty members contacted Abe to express their support. We became friends with some of them and got together for dinner or to commiserate. George, Dorothy, and Abe and I hung out together often. George held a position as Associate Professor of Art, and Dorothy, who aspired to working in the library, did not work outside the home. Their three delightful children often joined us when Abe and I visited.

The chair of the history and political science department shared the news with faculty. At a meeting of the local

American Association of University Professors, attendees passed a resolution supporting Abe's right to speak out without fear of reprisal.

The editorial staffs of newspapers across the state printed essays to support him and urged the president to change his position. The *Nashville Tennessean*, the *Knoxville News-Sentinel*, and the *Atlanta Constitution* were among his supporters. Finally, the president relented and the draft board changed Abe's classification to 2-S, the professional deferment he had before the brouhaha.

Meanwhile, radio stations were playing Arlo Guthrie's rendition of his satirical song, "Alice's Restaurant Massacree." Guthrie had performed the song as an impromptu piece, live on radio in New York in 1966 and at the Newport Folk Festival in July 1967.

Guthrie released an album that included the song as an entire side of the album. The song is a deadpan satire about his arrest for littering, which would make him ineligible for the military draft. I instantly became a fan, and on Thanksgiving Day for many years, friends gathered to play the album and curse the draft system.

In 1968, Tennessee Congressman Jimmy Quillen was back in the news with his own sort of Thanksgiving reprise. He sponsored the first federal legislation outlawing the desecration of the flag. It passed. It specified that "[w]hoever knowingly mutilates, defaces, physically defiles, burns, maintains on the floor or ground, or tramples upon any flag of the United States shall be fined under this title or imprisoned for not more than one year."[24]

The many challenges to the federal law consisted primarily of First Amendment arguments. Many states passed their own versions of the law. Challenges to the state laws were many, and the US Supreme Court held in *Texas v. Johnson*, 491 US 397 (1989), that free speech protections applied to a Texas flag-burning law. The Court declared the law unconstitutional.[25]

In response to this ruling, the 101st Congress passed the Flag Protection Act of 1989, giving Congress the right to enact statutes criminalizing the burning or desecration of the flag in public protest. *United States v. Eichman, 496 US 310* (1990), challenged the act.

The Supreme Court struck down the 1989 act in a 5-4 decision. The government's interest in preserving the flag as a symbol did not outweigh an individual's First Amendment right to desecrate the flag in protest.[26]

Abe developed a reputation as a liberal—some said radical—among his students and some faculty members. Closet liberals who had been reticent to express their own views found their voices and announced their support in letters, telephone calls, and faculty meetings. George and Dorothy were among them. We had become fast friends with them, conversing long into the night at their home.

"George, this is Abe. We're lonely. Can we come over?"

"Sure, we're still up. We just got all the kids to bed," George said. "Bring some snacks, if you can."

"I'll whip up something. Marietta, we're going over to George and Dorothy's. Will you make some of those cream cheese and dried beef things?"

"Are we going over there now? It's 10:30."

"Yeah, I'm not sleepy, and neither are they."

"Okay, but I have an early class."

We frequently drove through the campus to arrive at their house in about 15 minutes. We spent an hour or two talking, eating, having a cocktail, and trashing the administration of the university.

Abe and I took a ride on the following Saturday to look at a piece of land we saw advertised in the local newspaper. After walking the property, we decided we could not pass up 15 acres of undeveloped ground surrounded on three sides by the Cherokee National Forest. We purchased it as an investment, or possibly as a site for a new home.

After we bought it, we took some friends to look over our purchase. We had been looking around for about 30 minutes when Abe jumped across a stream on one leg and hit a depression in the ground. When he landed, he had fractured one of his legs.

I rushed him to the emergency room in Johnson City, accompanied by two friends. The doctor on call who treated him had been drinking. He recognized Abe's name from his letter to the editor on the flag-burning bill. "Oh, yes, I recognize that name."

The doctor did not administer a painkiller. He said we had interrupted his golf game on a Sunday and hurriedly set

Abe's leg. It looked crooked, and I told the doctor to give him something for the pain and to reset the leg. The doctor cursed me and told the orderlies, "Get this hysterical woman out of here."

I refused to leave until the doc straightened the leg. The orderlies manhandled me out of the room while the doc was wrapping Abe's leg and putting on the cast.

Six weeks later, a different doctor X-rayed the leg. The leg had not mended correctly. The doc offered to remove the cast and reset it, but Abe decided to live with a crooked leg.

After the doc removed the cast, the broken leg was shorter than the other one. The recovery process proved painful, and Abe had difficulty with balance for nearly a year. We considered suing the doctor who had set his leg, but Abe was convinced he would lose the case, given the politics involved.

And then Abe got a letter from Ernest Seeman, the former head of the Duke University Press. Ernest had read all the press coverage and wanted to express his support. He and Abe exchanged a couple of letters, commiserating over the censorship issue in academia. We would hear from him and his wife Elizabeth again.

Many of Abe's students looked upon him as their hero. I knew many of his students and suspected he had a sexual relationship with one of them. She was Abe's ideal sex object. He confessed to me the ones he preferred: blondes with large breasts, long legs, and limited brainpower.

I certainly did not fit this description, and I did not consider myself a sex object. When I asked him about his student, he first denied having a relationship, then said there was nothing wrong with it. And then said it was over anyway.

His ego got the better of him. The publicity surrounding his new public status drew hangers-on. I thought it would pass. Avoidance decision making was one of my favorites.

Within the next couple of months, friend Dorothy revealed to me that Abe had touched her breast and tried to kiss her. She thought I should know. Not exactly his ideal sex object: black hair, Armenian, lanky, and smart. Their relationship lasted off and on for three years, though Abe claimed they were just close friends. She warned me!

Aquarius Rising

A student sitting next to me asked me one day, "What is your sign?"

"Taurus," I said.

"Your husband is an Aquarius," she said.

"Yes, he is Aquarius rising; that is, one of a kind."

Students were talking about astrological signs, and ages of becoming, what house the moon was in, and what Nostradamus had predicted in the 1600s.

I thought the moon was the Earth's satellite and was still orbiting the Earth, displaying its phases as regular as clockwork.

The popular culture was developing around the opening song "Aquarius" from *Hair: the American Tribal Love-Rock Musical.*

According to proponents of astrology, the Age of Aquarius would become an age of peace and harmony. To accomplish this, the world must stop making war, turn corporations over to the workers, and focus on creative individual and group behavior.

The Age of Aquarius would concentrate on innovation, progressive thinking, friendship, and empathy.

Power dynamics would change, and nation states would give up their penchant for wars. The value of material wealth would diminish.

Media covered "love-ins," peaceful public gatherings focused on expressing the values of the Age: meditation, love, music, sex, and/or use of recreational drugs.

Los Angeles radio comedian Peter Bergman coined the love-in term. Bergman also hosted the first love-in on Easter, March 26, 1967, in Elysian Park.[27]

Love-ins were peaceful gatherings, but many cities were also experiencing violence. Civil unrest arose in Detroit when police raided a welcome-home party for a returning Vietnam War veteran.

A series of violent confrontations between residents of predominantly Black neighborhoods and the city's police department began July 23, 1967, and lasted five days.[28]

The riot resulted in the deaths of 43 people, including 33 Black people and 10 White people. Many others suffered injuries; police arrested over 7,000 people. Rioters burned over 1,000 buildings during the uprising. The Black Power movement took root after the riots.[29]

I opposed the violence but empathized with the plight of the residents of Detroit. They did not own the property. Not by their own design, but the neighborhoods were rundown and dirty.

Police arrested thousands of people, leaders died, students took over campus buildings. Many times, I felt as though I was there, on the scene, watching the harm done to human beings, their homes, and to our justice system.

Despite the violence, there were moments of joy. *Hair: The American Tribal Love-Rock Musical* hit the New York stage in October 1967. The story centered on a group of multiracial hippies living in New York City searching for ways to oppose the war in Vietnam. Men celebrated their "elegant plumage" in the same way that birds were famous for theirs, using it to court potential mates.

Besides the anti-war theme, the music encouraged men to flaunt their beauty, especially their hair. I relied on my jeans-sewing skills learned from Abe's grandmother to make Abe a pair of gold velvet jeans. My tailoring job was superb.

He got many compliments on the jeans, especially when they asked if they could feel the fabric. He readily gave them permission.

The Nehru jacket I made him was a popular item of clothing for modish men of the period. The jacket was a hip-length article of clothing with a mandarin collar. Jawaharlal

Nehru, the first Prime Minister of India, wore the jacket, hence the name.

I also made many of my own clothes, mostly skirts to wear with turtle necks, a staple costume for me. I rarely owned store-bought clothes.

Many popular songs became anthems for the counterculture: "Respect," Aretha Franklin; "All Along the Watchtower," Jimi Hendrix; "Light My Fire," The Doors; anything by Bob Dylan; the Beatles; Peter, Paul, and Mary; and Pete Seeger. Such anti-war songs as Dylan's "Masters of War" and "I Ain't Marchin' Anymore" by Phil Ochs lit up gatherings of students.

The music sustained the euphoria that a sense of profound change was producing. Dance music always included Creedence Clearwater Revival. Their music brought out the air guitar players and pantomimists.

Janis Joplin and Big Brother and the Holding Company, or Janis and the Full Tilt Boogie Band, sent many to the dance floor.

Who Can Read and Write?

During my senior year, I won a teaching assistantship in the English department. I graduated in the spring of 1967 with a B.A. degree in English and a minor in French. All teaching assistants and some of the newer junior faculty taught introductory English Composition.

I started graduate school classes in the summer of 1967 and began teaching in the fall.

Every undergraduate had to pass the composition course with at least a "D." Students could take the course three times. Many of the freshmen I encountered were ill-prepared for a college English class. Several of my students could not find a noun in a sentence. They didn't know a clause from a phrase. Limited vocabularies reflected their limited experiences.

Athletic coaches pressured some teaching assistants to pass failing football players so they could retain their athletic scholarships and their places on the team.

I was one of those who experienced the pressure. I asked the other 10 teaching assistants if the coaches were pressuring them, and nearly every one said at least one coach had talked to them about two or three students. Some were afraid that if they didn't capitulate, they would lose their assistantships.

Several of us grad assistants agreed we would stick by our evaluations of students' papers and not give in. Some pleas the coaches made on behalf of their athletes:

> What difference does it make? Change the grade.

> Don't you want your alma mater to win its football games?

> What is the matter with you? Everybody knows English.

Why does everyone need to be a writer?

Football doesn't mean the same thing to girls that it means to us.

The coaches seemed unconcerned about asking us to cheat.

Football and Tennessee were like peanut butter and jelly. I recommended tutoring for several students, but I wondered if the coaches really cared about what happened to these young men. I thought they were depriving them of useful verbal skills if we passed the athletes who hadn't made the grade.

The teaching assistants were supposed to consult with each of our students once a week for 10 minutes. I had 64 students in the two classes I taught each quarter. If every student showed up for their consultation, I would have spent an additional 11 hours in my office with them each week.

One of my favorite professors—a Shakespearean scholar—told me to act with integrity and everything would be all right. She said she suspected most of the coaches could not read.

I stood on principle and refused to change grades, even though I had a lot to lose. I learned to find support from others if I shared my concerns and made my case.

The department took no action against me or the others. A victory!

Another Murder

In early 1968, Memphis sanitation workers, mostly Black men, lobbied the city council to improve working conditions, raise wages and recognize their union. The council rejected their demands. Then two workers took a break to get out of the rain by sitting in the rear of their truck. The compression device malfunctioned and crushed the two men to death.[30]

The image of the event was horrific.

These guys are doing their best in a job that many people would not do if their lives depended on it. And the equipment they operate killed them. What grisly irony.

Seven hundred workers staged a sit-in at the city council meeting room until the council approved their demands. The mayor negated the decision, saying he was the only one authorized to approve the formation of a union.[31]

Workers called a strike. The city's Black leaders, ministers, and civil rights groups supported the strike. Dr. Martin Luther King, Jr. arrived on March 18 to lead 5,000 striking workers through Memphis. He had been struggling with how to handle the flaws in the US economic system. After witnessing the plight of sanitation workers, he and the NAACP backed a massive strike.[32]

After weather delays, the strike began, but a few troublemakers started breaking windows and looting stores. Police moved in with tear gas and nightsticks, and the crowd dispersed. In response to the violence, the city council imposed a curfew and 3,800 National Guardsmen arrived to maintain order.[33]

On April 4, 1968, a gunman murdered Dr. King as he stood on the balcony of his motel in Memphis. It was the day after he gave his "I've Been to the Mountaintop" speech.

My friends and I were beside ourselves with grief and anger. We struggled, trying to understand what was happening to our country.

Conspiracy theories circulated widely. I heard conversations about how the FBI, the CIA, the Mafia, or the Ku Klux Klan took part in the murder. Rioting in approximately 100 cities across the United States lasted from April through most of May.[34]

Eyewitness reports, the rifle, and fingerprints implicated escaped prisoner James Earl Ray, an avowed segregationist enamored of George Wallace. Ray had escaped a Missouri prison where he was serving 20 years for repeated offenses.

Ray purchased a rifle under an alias two days before he went to Memphis. The FBI said Ray killed King with a single shot from the rifle. Several people identified Ray running from the rooming house opposite the motel. An abandoned package containing the rifle and some clothing had Ray's fingerprints on it.

Ray fled to Atlanta and on to Toronto, where he hid, but obtained a Canadian passport using the alias Ramon George Sneyd. He traveled to London, Portugal, and back to London.

As Ray tried to leave London for Brussels, an officer at London Heathrow noticed the alias on his passport. The

Royal Canadian Mounted Police had issued an alert, and the officer saw the alert, stopped Ray, and arrested him.[35]

Ray confessed to the crime to avoid the death penalty and escaped from prison a second time with several other inmates. Authorities captured them and returned them to prison. Ray unsuccessfully recanted his confession.

What does frequent violence do to the psyche of people, to a community? My friends and I did not know how to deal with the tragedy. We had lost civil rights workers, innocent bystanders, JFK, and now Dr. King. We wanted to do something.

Students and faculty participated in campus vigils, but our campus was silent. I don't recall having any Black students in the classes I took and only two in the classes I taught.

The people I knew expressed frustration and disgust toward segregationists, government officials, and the military.

Not only were there riots in response to the murder of Dr. King elsewhere in the country, but students in France staged a revolt involving millions of workers.

France came to a standstill. Students had called for educational reform, the release of arrested students, and the reopening of the University of Paris Nanterre campus. During much of May 1968, terrible rioting engulfed Paris.

I was particularly interested in the French situation because I had subscribed to the French versions of *Le Monde* and *Paris Match* as adjunct reading to my language classes.

The student revolt evolved into a protest that involved 40,000 people.[36]

A few friends and I wanted to support the students in France, but I deplored the violence. We wrote letters to the publications I had subscribed to, and *Le Monde* published one of them.

The ongoing war in Vietnam was a disaster. On January 30, 1968, the Viet Cong (VC) and North Vietnamese People's Army of Vietnam (PAVN) had launched an offensive (Tet) against the South Vietnamese Army of the Republic (ARVN), the United States Armed Forces and their allies.[37]

Reporting for the Associated Press in February 1968, Peter Arnett quoted an unidentified US Army major after the offensive, saying, "We had to destroy the village to save it." Arnett's coverage of the Vietnam War won the 1966 Pulitzer Prize in International Reporting for his Vietnam work from 1962 to 1965.[38]

Some members of Congress did not support the war, and I was waiting to see which ones would publicly declare their opposition and run for president.

The number of candidates for the US presidency grew. Eugene McCarthy had already signaled his candidacy before Lyndon Johnson dropped out. Hubert Humphrey, George McGovern, Channing E. Phillips, Lester Maddox, and Robert F. Kennedy were running or contemplating a run.

Lester Maddox, Democratic governor of Georgia, had come to prominence as a segregationist when he refused to serve Black people in his restaurant, the Pickrick. He withdrew and endorsed George Wallace, the governor of Alabama. Wallace ran on the American Independent Party ticket, advocating segregation as a national policy. Republicans Richard M. Nixon, Nelson Rockefeller, and Ronald Reagan announced their candidacies for the Republican ticket.

Bobby

Robert Kennedy was surging in the polls, with McCarthy and Humphrey running close behind. On June 6, 1968, a mere two months after the assassination of Dr. King, Bobby Kennedy was addressing a rally at the Ambassador Hotel in Los Angeles when a gunman opened fire and killed him. I was watching the live news coverage on television with a few friends when the murder happened. A somber cloud of dread enveloped the room, rendering everyone silent for a few moments. "Oh, no, no, no, it cannot be happening again," I heard myself say.

The world awoke to the tragedy, but words failed to express the sorrow and anger that permeated the country and the world.

A jury convicted Sirhan Sirhan of Kennedy's assassination. A Palestinian raised in Israel in an Arab Christian family, Sirhan opposed Robert Kennedy's support of Israel and his attempt to send bombers to Israel because they would harm Palestinians.[39]

People were killing each other because of the color of their skin, for their support of civil rights, for freedom of speech, and for demonstrating against the war.

The toxic atmosphere caused many, including me, to feel as though the country were on fire and coming apart at the seams. Students continued demonstrating against violence and the war. Opposition to the war in Vietnam was growing, as well as opposition to government attempts to stop the demonstrations.

Students were allegedly burning their draft cards. The Federal Bureau of Investigation (FBI) infiltrated progressive and radical organizations in the 1960s and 1970s, using informants to discredit members or the organization.[40]

Unfortunately, many citizens ridiculed soldiers returning to their homes after fighting in Vietnam. Students, frustrated by LBJ's refusal to end the war, unleashed their anger on US soldiers. News reports showed men and boys demonstrating and allegedly burning draft cards, meant as an act of courage because they faced draft-dodging charges.

Many of the demonstrators were women. The news stories frequently depicted women and girls as sluts burning their bras, demeaning themselves.

However, most participating women and girls carried signs and managed the food prep, attended to children, and took a backseat in public speaking opportunities.

Cameras did not focus on the quiet revolution occurring in women's groups, which gathered to find friendship and discuss how much they felt ignored, exploited, or abused.

Yippie

Abbie and Anita Hoffman, Jerry Rubin, Nancy Kurshan, and Paul Krassner had founded the Youth International Party (YIP) on December 31, 1967. The members called themselves Yippies.

Abbie Hoffman led a march on Wall Street and conducted many other political stunts, because they thought of themselves as a countercultural revolutionary offshoot of the free speech and anti-war movements.

For example, he, David Dellinger of the National Organization Committee to End the War in Vietnam, and others organized a march on the Pentagon. Hoffman claimed he was going to use psychic energy to levitate the Pentagon building and when it turned orange, the war would be over.[41] Poet and writer Allen Ginsberg led Tibetan chants to assist in the effort.[42]

I believed the intent of these stunts was to ridicule the system that was perpetuating the war and to highlight the absurdity of the conflict. I endorsed the stunts by pointing out their farcical nature. Not everyone appreciated the humor.

Hoffman later would belong to the Chicago Seven, a group of protesters at the 1968 Democratic Party Convention in Chicago. At first, seven protesters faced the court. Then the court added Bobby Seale to the roster of Hoffman, John Froines, David Dellinger, Tom Hayden, Rennie Davis, Jerry Rubin, and Lee Weiner.

I scrambled to see the news about the trial. I found the judge to be a racist and ignorant of trial procedure, even given my unschooled knowledge of the rules.

Bobby Seale called the judge a racist during the trial and demanded a separate hearing. He did not have a lawyer. The US federal government charged all of them with conspiracy, crossing state lines with intent to incite a riot, and other charges related to anti-Vietnam War and countercultural protests in Chicago.[43]

Judge Julius Hoffman ordered Bobby Seale to be bound, gagged, and chained to his chair in the courtroom. He appeared in court this way for several days without his lawyer present before the government declared the proceedings a mistrial. Seale did not face another trial because the government refused to indict him again.

The court found the remaining seven except Froines and Weiner guilty of crossing state lines to incite to riot. Each of them received fines of $5,000 for contempt and a five-year jail sentence. About two years after the trial ended, an appeals court overturned the contempt charges and the charges of inciting a riot. The appeals court cited the judge's "deprecatory and often antagonistic attitude toward the defense."[44]

The war in Vietnam raged on. President Johnson announced on March 31, 1968 he would not seek another term as president. Public opinion about the war was changing. People besides the protesters were calling for an end to the war. As we would soon see, Johnson's decision had major consequences for the Democratic Party.

8. CONVICTION COLLIDES WITH CONSEQUENCE

ETSU Students Stir the Pot

Near the end of my first year of teaching (Spring 1968), the editor of the campus newspaper *The Pirate Press* faced a threat to his college career. The university president called the editor in to his office after the newspaper's faculty sponsor censored a cartoon the editor had mocked up to publish.

The cartoon showed the student newspaper editor gesturing for attention because a muzzle labeled "Admin" covered his mouth and nose.

When word of the censorship reached the political science and sociology departments, several students published a broadsheet proving how the administration was validating the cartoon's message.

One of the campus ministers agreed to let students use the office mimeograph equipment to reproduce a hastily written and poorly edited flyer. After about 20 students distributed the piece, some of the same students produced a second one.

I distributed the second broadsheet. The two unedited broadsheets are in Appendix A.

After I had distributed about one hundred copies of the second piece, a man outside the administration building approached me.

"Are you a student at this university?"

"Who wants to know?"

"Let me see your ID."

"I'll show you mine. May I see yours?"

"I am the Dean of Students of this university. What are you doing here? Do you have permission to distribute that flyer, or are you here to cause trouble?"

"Here's what I am distributing. You can see for yourself."

He took a flyer and hurried inside the administration building, stopping no one else.

I saw two other people I thought were administrators stop several students, demanding to know who they were and what they were doing. The Dean of Women told Mike, one pamphleteer, "You are going to get yourself expelled, if you're not careful." The Dean of Men voiced a similar threat to Oscar, another student.

Much of the essay was a rant against the war in Vietnam, the censorship of the campus newspaper, and the silly rules for dormitory residents.

I talked to several students, and no one had heard anything about a university policy prohibiting the distribution of flyers. The university catalog showed no such rule.

Advertisers regularly stuffed their materials in boxes around campus, posted them on bulletin boards, and swamped dormitories with their materials. Credit card companies encouraged students to apply.

Apparently, attempting to influence students to go into debt was acceptable, but distributing materials about relevant issues of substance was not.

A few days later, the Dean of Students sent a letter to me and seven other students, four of whom I knew. The letter demanded we appear before the discipline committee of the university to answer charges of "distributing false, seditious and inflammatory material and attempting to incite to riot."

Sedition? You've got to be kidding! A hanging offense in Tennessee.

I reread the pamphlet to find the seditious parts. If I had intended to cause a riot, I could have done a better job.

I made an appointment to meet with the dean of the graduate school, Arthur DeRosier, to ask him if the undergraduate discipline committee could sanction me, a graduate student. He and I had met twice at university functions.

His office had the atmosphere of an educated man. Beautifully bound volumes and paperback books filled the mahogany shelves. Newspapers, monographs, and trade journals lay about on a small conference table and on the floor. Framed certificates and diplomas lined the walls. Born in Connecticut, he was a cheerful, witty man with a master's degree and a PhD from the University of South Carolina.

"What can I do for you today, Marietta? How are your classes?"

I showed him the letter I had received accusing me of "distributing false, seditious and inflammatory material and attempting to incite to riot."

"I heard about that," he said. "What do you think?"

"The undergraduate deans have ordered seven other students and me to appear before the discipline committee to answer these charges. Do I have to answer to the undergraduate deans or to you?"

"Oh, I don't think anything will come of it. See what they have to say. Let me know how things turn out."

I was wary of his decision, because he was ill at ease and would not look at me. Nevertheless, I agreed to attend the meeting.

On the day of the hearing, I was ready to confront the deans. I did not think I should apologize, and I didn't. The deans questioned me extensively about the content of the piece I had distributed.

The eight of us students conferred before the hearings. We agreed not to disclose the authorship of the broadsheet. I, for one, did not know who had written it. Authorship was irrelevant. Principles were at stake. One student took an attorney with him to the hearing.

The committee of seven deans held all the hearings in one day and questioned each of us. The deans were concerned about the form and content of the flyer. Dean Stout asked me if I was embarrassed to be associated with a document containing crude language, typos, and grammatical errors.

"The typos and grammatical errors bother me more than what you call crude language. Just to be clear, would you give me an example of crude language in this piece?"

"That isn't necessary. I know it when I see it, and so do you," he said.

"I support the First Amendment to the US Constitution," I said.

"Should a university allow a person responsible for verbal attacks on the president to teach at the university?" he asked.

"Yes, if the person is qualified to teach the subject matter," I said.

The dean of men said, "I am holding back 25 students who came to my office and told me they could take care of the radicals who were trying to incite people to take over the university."

"So, who is threatening violence? Are they, or am I? Perhaps you should protect us from the students who genuinely are threatening violence. We have threatened no one with violence," I said.

The committee did not receive my comments well. The dean of women stood up from the table and turned her back on me. I thought she was embarrassing herself rather than me.

Dean of Men Thomas sat in his chair, red-faced, trying to write notes with a shaking hand. At the end of the hearings, the committee suspended all eight of us.

We had not violated a university rule, but the committee decided we were trying to embarrass the university and incite other students to riot.

I wondered how the university could escape embarrassing itself by punishing eight students in excellent standing who had not violated a university rule nor caused any disruption.

Is it possible the university could not withstand mild satire and sarcasm? The committee did not present evidence of the "success" of our attempt to incite to riot.

I called Dean DeRosier's office. He dodged my calls for the duration of the time I was still on campus. I lost respect for this man I had earlier admired.

Disappointed with teachers, students, and the administration, I was both angry and sad.

Our group of eight consisted of seven males and me, aged 20-25. Three of us were married. The Columbia School of Law had accepted one of us to study there the following year. One was bound for divinity school. Another was an artist who had already begun making and selling handmade leather sandals. Another had earlier applied for acceptance to graduate school in Kentucky, two planned careers in politics, and one was a journalist. I wanted to finish graduate school. All plans, at least temporarily, went by the wayside.

The Johnson City *Press-Chronicle* reported the dismissals, and the letters poured in to the newspaper. I received a letter from Ernest Seeman congratulating me for taking a stand for the First Amendment, just as he had congratulated Abe, who had opposed the flag bill.

Ernest and Elizabeth asked if we knew Helen Lewis, a sociology professor at ETSU. They invited the three of us to their farm for a visit.

Helen, Abe, and I made a trip to Tumbling Creek to meet them. The treacherous road to their farm forced us to drive with care. Streams, valleys, foliage, and wildlife surrounded the farm.

Ernest and Elizabeth delighted us with their demeanor. Satirical but sweet, erudite but masters of conversation, the pair of pioneers told the kind of tale from which legends emerge.

Figure 26. Elizabeth and Ernest Seeman, friends who also tested university administration censorship. Abe and I met them after they established a farm in the backwoods of Tennessee, 1968.

After spending several years in the printing business with his father, Ernest had accepted a position as head of printing at Duke University. His tenure lasted from 1925 to 1934.

Ernest had cultivated a reputation as a radical on the Duke campus. He supported the students when they lampooned the University dean and president, and he participated in an uprising to support labor activism. The giant tobacco industry had a chokehold on Duke University, putting them in Ernest's line of fire. The administration fired him.

He moved to New York City, where he met Elizabeth; both disdained the city and moved to rural Tennessee to settle in a grand stretch of wilderness called Tumbling Creek in the Great Smoky Mountains.

In 1961 Elizabeth published *In the Arms of the Mountain: an Intimate Journal of the Great Smokies*, an account of their homesteading events. They built their cabin; they acquired goats, a dog, and a cat, chickens, ducks, bees, and hawks. A woodchuck found its way to the Seeman home.

Gifted with a satirical sense of humor, neither Ernest nor Elizabeth let the grim realities of the adventure deter them. Elizabeth honored me with a copy of her book.

Ernest wanted to write a novel, and he told me his working title was *Tobacco Town*. He published the novel, called *American Gold,* shortly before his death in 1979.

The Appalachian Movement Press published Ernest's lengthy essay, *What's Next?*, in 1970. He asked Abe to write an introduction to the essay, which delineates the problem of our society: capitalism. Abe wrote, in part, "Even in the face of all its power, capitalism has at last created problems with which it cannot cope."

The essay foreshadows the end of capitalism and perhaps the United States itself, but as Ernest wryly concludes, "that will not be the end of the world."[1]

The Seemans encouraged Abe and me to keep the faith, and we returned to our Johnson City home, renewed in spirit. Both of us harbored the notion that out-of-control capitalism and immoral uses of power result in injustice.

I continued to correspond with Ernest, his dry wit a welcome friend amid war, institutional racism, violence, and censorship.

Taking the University to Court

The "East Tennessee Eight" (ETE) appealed our suspensions to the president of the university, but he denied restitution. We all agreed to appeal to the courts, which involved suing the university, the deans, and the president. The US District Court in Nashville would hold the hearing.

I called an attorney in Kingsport, Tennessee, reputed to be a lawyer for the American Civil Liberties Union (ACLU). Bruce Shine agreed to take the case, and we met at our home in Johnson City. After he returned to his law firm, he withdrew from the case. His law firm ordered him not to continue. He had just passed the bar, and although he was excited to take the case, his bosses were not.

Many years later, he developed a well-respected labor law practice in Kingsport, Tennessee, and practiced all over the United States.

Delayed by the failed attempt for support, I contacted the ACLU in Nashville, and they agreed to take the case. We conducted our business over the telephone and by letter. Our attorney, Karen Ennis, instructed each of us to write a summary of the discipline committee hearing and send it to her, and we did.

The US District Court in Nashville heard *Norton v. Discipline Committee of East Tennessee State University* on June 26, 1968.[2]

Abe accompanied me and the other six students to Nashville for the hearing. The quarter had ended; one student had already returned home to Pennsylvania and did not attend the hearing. Attorney Ennis strategized that I should be the first to testify, and the other students agreed.

Two Southern Student Organizing Committee (student organizing group like the SDS) representatives contacted me to see if they could do anything to help. I thought any public action should wait until after the court had rendered a decision. The two SSOC members planned to attend the hearing, issue a news release, and report the results in the organization's newsletter.

The ETE wanted to make a favorable impression on the court, so we shaped up our clothing choices. I bought a conservative, sleeveless, gray and black cotton dress to wear.

Because I was teaching, I usually wore dresses or skirts and sweaters, as well as heels.

The men dressed in suits and ties or slacks, shirts, and ties. We met our attorney Karen Ennis for the first time in person at the courthouse shortly before time for the hearing. She wore a hot pink minidress with a flared skirt and a patterned suit jacket, stylish and professional.

Having been concerned about my own attire, I wondered about the length of her skirt, but she confidently presented herself, and my anxiety dissipated. She would shortly prove her amazing trial skills.

I entered the courtroom to the smell of old leather, dusty floors, and tobacco smoke. Spittoons dotted the courtroom. Someone shouted, "Go back to Russia," interrupting the sounds of shuffling feet.

Spectators numbered about 50. All seven members of the ETSU discipline committee and the president sat at the defendants' table. I commented to Karen that all the agitators must have left the campus if all the deans were available for the hearing. Karen said, "Don't get me started laughing."

The bailiff called the court to order and introduced the judge, William Ernest Miller. I testified first. The hearing lasted about three hours. Each student testified briefly, and so did several administrators.

Ms. Ennis questioned me to elicit several points:

1. Protections of the First Amendment to the US Constitution.

2. Lack of due process in very short notice of the hearing and prohibition of an attorney.

3. No university rule prohibited distribution.

4. Students had no intent to cause a riot, and no riots had occurred. In short, the university had subjected us to an arbitrary exercise of power.

I thought the administration should protect us from the 25 student vigilantes the dean of men was "holding back." They would be the ones inciting to riot and initiating violence. I asserted this point when Ms. Ennis questioned me about my disciplinary hearing.

Ms. Ennis asked me if I thought the committee focused on the content, rather than a university rule. I agreed they were demonstrating by example their penchant for censoring student publications because they had caused the issue to become an issue.

Had we tried to embarrass the university? I expressed surprise that a student pamphlet with narrow circulation would embarrass the university. Most students were unaware of the events. Plus, the action of the committee and the president escalated the problem by drawing attention to the pamphlet.

The university argued that college students are not adults, and the university was acting in loco parentis. They further asserted the material was calculated to cause a disturbance and disrupt school activities, as well as to ridicule and show contempt for school authorities.

During the questioning, ETSU's attorney, Mr. Fox, repeated his questions several times before the judge seemed to get the gist of what had happened on the campus. I thought the administrators embarrassed themselves because they sounded so petty, whining about minor typos or the use of the word "shit" in one pamphlet.

They continued to assert that we eight students had created this mob of 25 who wanted to "take us out." They argued that we students had disrupted university functions because the deans had to spend a whole day just to hold the hearings.

"And whose fault is that?" I asked Karen.

Judge Miller took the case under advisement for about 10 minutes and delivered an oral opinion. He ruled the university was correct. They had the responsibility to protect the rest of the students from the possibility of riots, disruption of final exams, and profanity, no matter how mild.[3]

The defendants asserted the potential for violence existed, but the only "evidence" was the 25 students the dean of men was "holding back." Their other chief complaint was that we had challenged their authority and tried to embarrass the university.

I could not believe the judge delivered such a hasty oral decision against us. We lost.

As Gloria Steinem had once remarked, "The truth will set you free, but first, it will piss you off." The truth was that administrative censorship was acceptable, and yes, it pissed us off. We were free to take further action or find another university.

Southern Student Organizing Committee representatives considered organizing a demonstration, but the ETE postponed any activity until we consulted with Karen.

Ennis suggested we appeal the case to the circuit court in Cincinnati. All of us agreed to do so, but first she suggested we return to the committee to see if they had changed anything about their rulings.

I appeared before the collection of statues, the discipline committee, in the same meeting room. I found the seven deans all seated around the same table in the same chairs they had occupied a few weeks before. The dean of the graduate school was not in attendance and was allegedly out of town.

The committee decided, "You may return to school if you promise never to do such a thing again."

"What does that mean?" I asked.

Silence.

No one gave an explanation.

"I came before the committee because I thought you might have changed your minds about censorship," I said.

My comment brought the meeting to a close. They did not want to admit any wrongdoing or find a compromise, and I would not give up my First Amendment protection.

Some of the other students found graduate schools or jobs after their second interview with the committee. None of them returned to ETSU. The graduate school dean never returned my calls.

In the meantime, I applied for admission to five graduate schools. I had a 4.0 average with the classes I had taken during summer school in 1967 and a full year of classes, plus a full year of teaching English composition. None of the five admitted me.

The University of Virginia in Charlottesville turned me down, saying they were not accepting any more outside agitators.

Abe was a tenured professor and wanted to stay at ETSU to maintain his tenure, which would not follow him to a different university. Unless I left the geographical region, I would have to wait to finish my advanced degree.

Student organizations in the five-state area contacted me to discuss the court case and the pending appeal. I honored several of these requests by traveling to the campus, talking with students, and showing them a copy of the transcript of the hearing.

Abe had two concerns: I would be gone too much, and he was better qualified to talk about constitutional law.

"Students are interested in organizing other students to address injustices on their campuses. I have experience with what they want to discuss," I said. "Two groups want to start a newsletter of student opinion, and we discussed possible ways to achieve that."

During the middle of the disciplinary hearings, Abe had changed his doctoral dissertation subject, pending from the University of Massachusetts, from political theory to constitutional law.

His action required establishing a new committee and a new chairman for his dissertation. The new chairperson,

Loren Beth, discouraged him from changing his subject because he had already done a great deal of work in political theory (review of literature, master's thesis, language requirements, orals).

Abe rejected Professor Beth's suggestion. If he followed through with his desire to continue with constitutional law, he would have extensive additional work to do.

"But I could give expert advice both in organizing students and in interpreting constitutional law. You would not have to travel around living out of a suitcase," he said.

"I see. You have found a reason to leave home. Are you sure you want to travel around living out of a suitcase?"

"I have classes to teach, so I would organize my time to be gone on weekends."

"I guess I'll stay home and wonder my life away. Will the appeals court hear the case? Will I ever get to finish my degree? Will you expect me to do your laundry when you return home from your speaking engagements?"

He walked away from this discussion. Further utterances on my part would have been addressed to a blank wall. So, we addressed each request individually, splitting them based on our availability.

In the summer of 1968, while visiting a few campuses, I began a waiting game with the Court of Appeals.

Would they hear the case or deny it?

Politics Forever

Politicking, the eternal force, carried on. The Democratic Party had scheduled their national convention to nominate the next president.

Events at the Democratic Party national convention in Chicago, August 26-29, 1968, demonstrated the public's stunning opposition to police and Mayor Richard J. Daley's violent tendencies. In the past decade, the Chicago police and government officials vehemently opposed protests in a manner unprecedented in the city's history.[4]

The protesters showed up by the thousands. Outside the convention arena, they were throwing rocks, taunting police, and trying to crowd into the arena. In Grant Park, barbed-wire-laced jeeps evoked images of Russian tanks rolling through Prague where students had demanded sweeping governmental reforms.

Activist US students were acutely aware of how their peers in other countries were responding to government violence and oppression.

Russia had invaded Czechoslovakia on August 20, 1968. Czech students had advocated strong reforms, and Russia had responded by invading the country. Alexander Dubcek had replaced conservative Antonin Novotny in early 1968 and had ended censorship. The new freedom had sparked demands for further reform.[5]

Student activists in the United States, including me, sympathized with the students in Czechoslovakia as we had with the French students who had advocated reform.

The protests in Chicago were more than just another antiwar protest, and the events constituted more than a riot. The social conflicts of the sixties were on display, invading every aspect of life. Eventually 6,000 federal troops and 18,000 Illinois National Guardsmen were outside the convention.[6]

I wanted to go to Chicago, but Abe and others persuaded me it was too dangerous to go by myself. No one else was willing to go. A group of friends watched on television at our house instead.

Outside the convention hall, police raised their nightsticks and cracked heads. They fogged the crowds with tear gas, mainly in Grant Park. Armored police lines stalked the demonstrators to push them away from the arena.

Figure 27. Protesters and Chicago police officers in Grant Park, Democratic Party National Convention, 1968.

Many other protesters stormed the convention arena. I cringed at the violence and voiced my opposition from afar to the police actions.

Too agitated to sit still, I paced the room and yelled at the police while shaking my head in disbelief.

This cannot be happening in America.

The fast-paced events created a chaotic atmosphere. Eugene McCarthy, Hubert Humphrey, and George McGovern had entered the race and were holding a debate.

Vice President Humphrey tried to distance himself from the policies of LBJ, particularly of the war, by focusing on unifying the party. He hoped for a peaceful settlement in Vietnam. I thought his speech received mild acceptance.

Senators McGovern and McCarthy received standing ovations after each of their speeches because of their consistent stances opposing the war and for criticizing the Johnson/Humphrey administration.

Until Humphrey became Vice President and caved in to LBJ and the war, I respected his accomplishments. At the 1948 Democratic National Convention, as a senator from Minnesota, he successfully advocated to include a proposal to end racial segregation in the party platform. [7]

Humphrey was a major leader in the rise of liberalism and of the civil rights legislation of 1964, as well as a proponent of the Peace Corps. But he had become a major apologist for the war, and I viewed him as LBJ's stand-in.

His repositioning felt like a betrayal of his integrity. He thought the protesters had gone too far, much like the labor leaders who had endorsed him believed.

Other leaders in the Democratic party opposed Humphrey for his backing of LBJ. Abe, our friends, and I gathered in our living room to watch as Senator Abraham Ribicoff of Connecticut nominated George M. McGovern for president, declaring, "With George McGovern as President of the United States, we wouldn't have to have Gestapo tactics in the streets of Chicago."[8]

The convention erupted in thunderous applause, and television cameras focused on Mayor Richard Daley, seated in the front row. Daley's stance and his raised fists threatened Senator Ribicoff, but the senator stared him down from the podium and Daley backed off.[9]

I whooped and hollered in praise of Ribicoff, and the people in our living room stood and clapped, drowning out the speaker. I regretted not having had the courage to join the protesters at this weighty historical moment.

Ted Warshafsky, a delegate from Wisconsin, nominated Julian Bond, a Georgia state legislator, for the vice presidency. Bond was a co-founder of SNCC and of the Southern Poverty Law Center and opposed the Vietnam War.

When Bond was elected to the Georgia legislature, they refused to seat him by a vote of 184-12 because he supported SNCC's stance on the war.[10]

The US District Court in Northern Georgia ruled 2-1 against Bond, but the US Supreme Court overturned the decision 9-0 in *Bond v. Floyd, U.S.116 (1966)*.[11]

Bond was the first Black person to have his name entered into nomination as a major-party candidate for Vice President of the United States. He withdrew his name. He was only 28 years old and did not meet the constitutional age requirement of 35 years.[12]

After all the wrangling, shouting, and threatening behavior of Mayor Daley, Hubert Humphrey won the nomination for president on the first ballot, defeating McCarthy and McGovern. Humphrey did not enter 13 state primary elections, but 80% of the primary voters had voted for antiwar candidates.[13] Despite the electorate's strong opposition to the war, Humphrey won the nomination in Chicago.

Humphrey selected Senator Edmund Muskie from Maine as his running mate. He believed Muskie would appeal to liberals and would not offend the establishment members of the party.

For the Democratic party, however, Chicago 1968 was one more factor that doomed the candidacy of Hubert Humphrey.

Out of spite (for the Democrats, I suppose), I swore I would vote for Eldridge Cleaver, a Black Panther. He had been involved in a shootout with the police that left one Panther dead and two officers wounded. Cleaver jumped bail, left for Cuba, and went on into Algeria.

He spent seven years in exile in Cuba, Algeria, and France. He returned to the US in 1975 and became involved in various unconventional religious organizations. After deciding he was a conservative Republican, he ran for the Berkeley city council and lost. Addiction to drugs badly affected his health, and he died in 1998.

I really know how to pick 'em, don't I?

Humphrey had disappointed me badly, but hoping he could reunite the Democrats after he distanced himself from Johnson, I voted for him. There was no question in my mind he and Muskie would be far superior to Nixon and Agnew.

Republicans Richard M. Nixon and Spiro T. Agnew won the election for President and Vice President, beating the Democrats.

The ticket of George Wallace for President and General Curtis LeMay for Vice President of the American Independent Party (AIP) carried five Southern states: Alabama, Arkansas, Georgia, Louisiana, and Mississippi. The AIP won 45 electoral votes and came close to receiving enough votes to throw the election to the House of Representatives.[14]

I believed the public at large would condemn the authorities' violent response to the protesters at the convention and in cities and towns. I thought the government would respond by enforcing civil rights justice and bring an end to the Vietnam War.

But the war did not end, resulting in young men escaping the draft by fleeing to Canada and other parts unknown.

Congress had not provided an official declaration of war in Vietnam. Article One, Section Eight of the US Constitution states that Congress shall have the power to declare war. Nevertheless, in March 1969, Nixon approved secret bombings of suspected communist camps in Cambodia, a neutral country, and the war raged on.

And the Suit Goes On

I didn't know whether I should take to the streets or sit around feeling sorry for myself. Reber Boult, an attorney from the new Southern Poverty Law Center, let me know the Center could defend the ETSU Eight pro bono if we all signed pauper's oaths. Everyone signed. No one could afford to continue without financial help.

The attorneys preparing the case were an exemplary lot. They included Karen D. Ennis, Nashville, Tennessee; Charles Morgan, Jr., Reber F. Boult, Jr., Atlanta, Georgia, on brief; Melvin L. Wulf, Eleanor Holmes Norton, New York City, of counsel, for appellants.

The Sixth Circuit Court of Appeals issued a decision on November 28, 1969: *419 F.2d 195—Norton v. Discipline Committee of East Tennessee State University No. 10197.*

The panel, made up of three justices, upheld the district court in Nashville in a split decision. Justice Anthony Celebrezze dissented, supporting us.[15]

Events happened quickly, and the next step was to appeal to the Supreme Court of the United States to grant certiorari, a writ, or order by which a higher court reviews a decision of a lower court.

All eight of us agreed to appeal the case.

ACLU attorneys firmed up their plea. I believed five of the sitting justices would exonerate us: Justices William O. Douglas, William Joseph Brennan, Thurgood Marshall, Abe Fortas, and Hugo Black. We thought Justices John Marshall Harlan, Potter Stewart, and Byron White would oppose our complaint.

We plaintiffs had no idea when the court would issue a decision to grant or deny certiorari. Life on campus and off moved on, at least temporarily.

Write While You Wait

A new publication called *The Frigate*, a play on words of ETSU's *The Pirate Press*, appeared on campus. Although I was not a student, I wrote for and distributed the broadsheet, mimeographed at the same campus religious organization that had published the "seditious" pieces.

The newsletter contained articles about campus events and opinion pieces about national and international affairs. To my knowledge, no one from the university administration ever confiscated this publication. Several students working on *The Frigate* left the campus when they graduated. I continued to publish *The Frigate* for several months.

Residents of the region wrote letters to the editor of the *Johnson City Press-Chronicle* criticizing the publication for its radical ideas. In one issue of *The Frigate*, I made the radical suggestion that the administration should eliminate the rules for girls living in dormitories. Rules included a curfew of 8:30 p.m. during the week, no television after 11 p.m., and girls must wear shoes in the lobbies of the dorms.

A columnist for the *Press-Chronicle* in his regular feature, *Squibbling*, condemned *The Frigate*, stating that writers at the student paper apparently supported girls walking barefoot in the dorm's lobby and watching television after 11:00 p.m.

He further condemned "them hifalutin' words . . . I took it the writer is angry at our form of government and might lead a revolution to topple it."[16]

I wrote a response to the *Squibbling* columnist, stating in part,

> The hifalutin' words (he took offense to) originated from two sources. 'That all power is inherent in the people. . .' and 'That government being instituted for the common benefit. . .. Good and happiness of mankind' are direct quotations from Article I, Sections 1 and 2, of the Tennessee State Constitution. The second quotation, beginning, 'This country. . .' is taken from Abraham Lincoln's inaugural address. I suggest if Mr. Squibb does not want to behave as the Tennessee Constitution demands, or does not want to recognize the value of the words of one of America's great presidents, he should leave the country (credit for this kind of analysis

and solution must go to the Boy Scouts), i.e., 'Love It or Leave It.'[17]

Students in political science, sociology, philosophy, and English contributed to the Frigate and to other broadsheets that had sprung up on campus.

Protests were a main event, but a monumental accomplishment was about to take center stage. In July, people gathered in front of their television sets to watch the United States land a spaceship on the moon. Just as President Kennedy promised.

Some people said this event would bring opposing factions together to support this scientific triumph. Students would stop demonstrating against the war, and police would stop creating chaos in the Black communities.

The moon landing, a dream of slain John F. Kennedy, was a scientific success unmatched by any other country. Some lone voices decried the enormous amount of money spent when people in the US were starving. Some denied it happened, but most people celebrated the triumph.

I still imagined a day when all the troops would come home, justice for Black people would prevail, and women would lead our own lives without fear of reprisal.

My lawsuit loomed large.

Although I was nervous about the outcome of our suit, I never felt the pressure draftable young men felt. Some of our group of eight were certain the FBI had tapped our phones to look for draft dodgers. After all, officials had accused us of distributing seditious literature and attempting to incite to riot, and we had roared our opposition to the war.

Abe and I thought someone was listening in on phone calls because we often heard snapping noises on the phone as we answered it, like bugging devices turning on.

When I answered the phone and heard the clicking and tapping noises, I often would begin a fantastical story about the invasion of Earth by Martians. Another of my favorites was to talk about how cute J. Edgar Hoover looked in his garter belt and fishnet stockings. Not very smart, but it felt good to say it. It was one way to express how ridiculous I believed the government had shown itself to be.

Curiosity prompted me to request my FBI file several years later, just to see if one truly existed. The Freedom of Information Act allowed this to happen. All I had to do was write to the FBI and ask for the file. I found transcription notes recorded from telephone conversations about:

- the stories I made up about J. Edgar,
- speculation about how they could arrest me,
- my comments I had reported to the police about threats I had received,
- comments about my unpaid federal telephone taxes.

The FBI was apparently trying to catch me in further "attempts to incite to riot."

Several of us students went to the campus to take pictures of the administrators' cars, which were parked outside the building. We were clearly visible from several offices. We called this absurdity our mini-Yippee period: Do something farcical to disarm your opponents.

The East Tennessee Eight were still waiting for news of the lawsuit. Pending before the Supreme Court was a similar case: *Tinker v. Des Moines, 393 US 503 (1969).*

In December 1965, Mary Beth Tinker, a 13-year-old student, wore a black armband to school to protest the war in Vietnam.

The school board heard about the protest and passed a preemptive ban on Dec. 14. When Mary Beth arrived at school on December 16 wearing an armband, the administration suspended her and four other students, including Chris Eckhardt and her brother John Tinker. The administration told the students they could not return to school until they agreed to remove their armbands.

After the Christmas break, students returned without armbands. In protest, they wore black clothing for the remainder of the school year—and filed a First Amendment lawsuit. [18]

The ACLU represented them, and the students and their families embarked on a four-year court battle that culminated in a landmark Supreme Court decision. On February 24, 1969, the court ruled 7-2 that students do not "shed their constitutional rights to freedom of speech or expression at the schoolhouse gate."[19]

The court found that the First Amendment applied to public schools, and school officials could not censor student speech unless it disrupted the educational process. Because wearing a black armband was not disruptive, the Court held that the First Amendment protected the right of students to wear them.

This decision sounded like a victory for our lawsuit, because we had not disrupted the educational process. By the time our case came before the circuit court, the US Supreme Court had already decided the *Tinker* case.

Justice Abe Fortas had written the opinion. In 1965, President Johnson appointed Fortas to the court when Arthur Goldberg resigned to become ambassador to the United Nations. Goldberg replaced the late Adlai Stevenson at the UN.

The ACLU thought our case and *Tinker* had many similarities. The three-person Sixth Circuit majority applied the *Tinker* decision to *Norton v ETSU* but found East Tennessee school officials had forecast substantial disruption of school activities. They "had the right to nip such action in the bud and prevent it in its inception."[20]

Justice Anthony Celebrezze dissented from the opinion because he wanted to hear the case in full. The District Court in Nashville had said that college students are likely to create disturbances and must be held in loco parentis. However, high school students like those in *Tinker* are responsible persons and less apt to create disturbances than college students are.

Does this make sense?

When Chief Justice Earl Warren announced his own retirement in June 1969, a cloud descended over the Norton household. The East Tennessee Eight worried about his replacement, because we believed Warren would have wanted to hear the case.

Before Warren resigned, President Johnson tried to elevate Justice Fortas to Chief Justice, knowing Warren would be resigning.

The events that followed created an environment of instability and uncertainty, adding to my anxiety about the case and my future career.

Conservative members of the US Senate, angered by the past decisions of the Warren Court, started a campaign to discredit Fortas. He faced hostile questioning about his close relationship with President Johnson.

Members of the US Senate criticized him for having accepted $15,000 from private business (about $139,000 in 2025 dollars) for nine speaking engagements at American University's Washington College of Law.[21]

Senator Strom Thurmond of South Carolina (Democrat until 1964, when he became a Republican) raised the idea that cases involving these companies might come to the Court, and Fortas might not be objective.[22]

Fortas recused himself from an SEC case against financier Louis Wolfson when it came before the Court.[23] He resigned from the court in May 1969, and as a result, the court had eight sitting members. Warren resigned in June 1969, leaving the court with only seven members.

Every day I wondered what would happen to the justice system, to the law of the land, and not least of all, to my lawsuit, reputation, and career.

How could they possibly decide a case with only seven members? Nixon will have two more appointees, and who knows who else might retire?

Unless Hugo Black, a staunch libertarian, still thought the First Amendment was absolute, we might not get a favorable decision from him, either.

Uncertainty in the court's direction contributed to my feelings of futility with the whole damn bunch. Fortunately, the ACLU and the Southern Poverty Law Center sustained their petition to the US Supreme Court.

President Nixon nominated Warren Burger as Chief Justice, and the US Senate confirmed him. As a result, the Court consisted of eight members.

The graduating senior in our group went on to law school after waiting a year. The US Army drafted one student. Another moved home to North Carolina and found a job at a newspaper. One moved to California. The others found jobs in other states and finished their undergraduate or graduate work. All agreed to appeal to the Supreme Court.

I was stuck in Johnson City, Tennessee. Abe had earned academic tenure as an assistant professor of political science.

Abe's students who supported the suit hung out at our house to find out the latest information about "Abe's case." They bragged that their professor had taken a case all the way to the Supreme Court.

Abe held court at our home on the history of First Amendment cases, the players, and the decisions. I wondered why they referred to *Norton* as "Abe's case" when students were the plaintiffs in the suit and my first and last name was the first plaintiff listed on the documents.

I heard a female student talking as I came out of the bathroom to join a conversation in our living room. "Be careful about how you talk about this. Is Marietta here?" she asked.

"Why is she claiming credit for the lawsuit?" asked another female voice. No one said anything.

"She knows the case evolved through the Socratic method I use with all of you. She is still understandably ticked off about the action of the discipline committee," Abe said.

I walked into the room and said, "I heard part of what you were saying. No one can claim all the credit for what has happened. But eight students have had a life-altering experience and were instrumental in bringing the case forward. I worked with the attorneys to develop the arguments. The consequences have fallen on us students. The university has not reinstated me."

Now, I suppose I'll become known as the bitchy wife of their esteemed professor because I wanted to "claim credit" for the lawsuit.

Eye-rolling ensued at my high-minded comment, but I did not think it was funny.

Holding Mock Court

Abe and I had talked often about his teaching methods, and I had taken a political philosophy class from him when I was an undergraduate. It was excellent. He was brilliant. Students hung on his every word. He often held forth in any group gathering, and he fell prey to his own magnetic personality to attract women.

Parties with students and faculty were venues for testing his flirtation quotient. Friends and students tolerated his flirtations, many of which current law would consider sexual harassment.

I observed much of this and confronted him from time to time. He said they meant nothing. The flirtations became commonplace, but sometimes he followed through to have full-blown affairs, usually brief.

Sometimes I believed he deserved to behave in this way, because he was the Golden Boy, the superb debater, the magical teacher, the philosopher king.

I was the hip wife who went along with his misbehavior so others would see me as a "tolerant woman," loyal for not complaining. Discussing his behavior with anyone else would have revealed my irrational jealousy.

In my more rational moments, I was furious and became angrier and sadder as time went on.

I admired Gloria Steinem, Robin Morgan, Angela Davis, Betty Friedan, Susan Brownmiller, and other women of the feminist movement, but men and boys claimed leadership in the civil rights movement. They expected women to support the guys by cooking, cleaning, and looking after children. Men and institutions ridiculed and ignored women who asserted their right to speak, lead, or organize.

I read *The Feminine Mystique* by Betty Friedan (1963), parts of *A Bunny's Tale* by Gloria Steinem (completed in 1970), the report of the *United States President's Commission on the Status of Women* (1963), and *off our backs*, an underground publication. Gloria Steinem founded *Ms. Magazine* in 1971. These publications included examples of other women's frustration with male dominance, experiences like mine, I thought.

I stopped shaving the hair on my body and stopped wearing a bra. These behaviors did nothing to curtail Abe's questionable behavior, but freeing myself from convention felt good.

Things Keep Changing

When friends gathered, usually at our home, people played songs from popular albums of the time: the Beatles' *Magical Mystery Tour*, anything by Bob Dylan, Janis Joplin, The Doors, The Grateful Dead, and Creedence Clearwater Revival. People knew the words to the songs; we danced; some got high. All were reveling in the freedom of the times. Music was a lead character in counterculture and mainstream dramas.

Abe did not like to dance, but I did. When the music played, I danced and Abe flirted, just not with each other.

I felt we were growing farther apart, that our experiences were different, and that sometimes we did not share the same views on current affairs. We often viewed the same event differently, especially if we discussed who was at fault. I stopped apologizing for women's public behavior that Abe found distasteful: bra burning, wild dancing, hollering into bullhorns at demonstrations.

While I waited for the next step in the judicial process, Abe and I became friends with more students and professors who supported the lawsuit. All this time, I never had a close female friend other than the public figures I adopted. Most of the students who came to the house were male.

If they brought girlfriends, some of them were content to talk about how cool Abe was.

Abe suggested I intimidated other women because I was too aggressive.

From Tennessee to Virginia

In the spring of 1969, the ETSU sociology department failed to renew the contracts of Professors Helen Lewis and Ed Knipe.

Students from many academic departments protested on campus, distributed leaflets, and wrote letters to regional newspapers. A new openness had invaded the campus, in part because of the East Tennessee Eight, and the wave of cultural change in the world.

I joined sociology and political science students to protest on campus and flood local media with letters.

Newspaper reporters were out in force to get the inside story on another campus uprising in conservative East Tennessee.

When students held a funeral for the sociology department, the campus came alive. Students left their classes to watch the funeral. Several students delivered eulogies for the loss of the department.

Reporters from Johnson City, Kingsport, Knoxville, Nashville, Atlanta, and independent papers like the *Great Speckled Bird* attended.

Despite the supportive press coverage for Lewis and Knipe, the ETSU administration did not reinstate them.

Helen had ties to Clinch Valley College, a branch of the University of Virginia (UVA) in Wise. Helen's husband Judd was a professor of philosophy at the college.

In the middle of coal mining country in the southern Appalachian Mountains, Clinch Valley College conformed to the same standards as the University of Virginia in Charlottesville. The college entered the University of Virginia system in 1999 and changed its name to the University of Virginia at Wise.

Helen began talking with Abe about leaving ETSU to take a position at Clinch Valley College. The administration had offered Ed and Helen positions in the fledging sociology department. Ed and his wife Ilse had relocated to Wise.

Then everything happened at once. Abe accepted a position at Clinch Valley, and we made plans to look for a place to live. This branch of the University of Virginia did not offer graduate school, so I would need to find a job.

A small enclave of Clinch Valley College professors and their friends had built or found houses in an area of Wise called Laurel Hills.

Abundant mountain laurel, rhododendron, and mature trees created a lush, dense park. The remaining available lot contained a private lake. We bought the property with dreams of a new house.

We led a frugal lifestyle, having saved money we could have spent on travel, restaurants, movies, or other entertainment.

Sometimes couples agree right away on the house they want. Abe and I did not. He wanted to plant a mobile home on the property because of the short time frame we had before school started. His parents lived in a mobile home, and he thought one in Laurel Hills would be perfect.

I wanted to find a stylish prefabricated structure that a contractor could build within the time limit and that would satisfy my sense of aesthetics. He thought I was demeaning his parents because I declared I did not want to live in a trailer. I convinced him I could find something that both of us would like.

When we purchased the property in Wise, we sold the 15 acres of woodland we had purchased in Tennessee for a nice profit. The improvements we made to the Johnson City house had increased its value. FHA approved it for a loan to someone else, and it sold quickly. We applied the proceeds to our new home project.

I had read about Buckminster Fuller, an architect and futurist who advanced "design science." Natural sciences explain things as they are, and design sciences are concerned with things as they should be. He created the geodesic dome, the only structure that a builder can set on the ground as a finished product.

Someone had already set a purple geodesic dome the locals called the purple pumpkin on a plot in Laurel Hills.

I researched prefabricated houses and building methods and discovered a company in North Carolina called Rondesics. The completed structures became octagons or hexagons, mimicking "round" houses.

Soon our dream house would join a traditional colonial structure, a bungalow, an A-frame, and the purple pumpkin.

Rondesics constructed individual panels complete with exterior redwood siding, fiberglass insulation, windows, and interior studs. The owner decided on the number of completed pieces she wanted. The company made up all the pieces and shipped the house components to the site.

Helen helped me find Bill Wampler, a local contractor. After looking over the preliminary plans, he agreed to complete our house in six months if I would be available to work with him.

We ordered the pieces, and Rondesics brought the house in one trip.

I had selected two pods. An octagon and a hexagon. A concrete block foundation would support the octagon, the main part of the house. It would contain our bedroom and bath, a living room, and a kitchen with access to the garage via a wrought-iron circular staircase.

A hallway would join the octagon to the hexagon that would contain two bedrooms and a bath. Steel poles would support the bedroom wing of the house.

The contractor did minimal excavation to the property to keep as much of the foliage and trees as possible.

The washer, dryer, and hot water tank sat on a concrete pad in the basement/garage. A section of the foundation wall held the electrical panel and outlets for the appliances. The Tennessee Valley Authority fueled the electric baseboard heating system we installed.

The hexagon, perched on steel poles, was level with the main part of the house. I left the rock and foliage under this part of the house, and it proved to be a good hiding place for Snoopy Beagle.

Plans for the entry did not come with the kit for the house. Thanks to my hard-won high school mechanical drawing skills, I drafted plans for the entry-porch addition and the deck facing the lake. The contractor agreed to build them.

I located the main entry on the side away from the lake. Bill cleared a pathway to the steps leading up to the landing of the porch. The front door opened onto a foyer which led to the deck, the living room, and the extra bedrooms.

I thought the deck looked like the perfect refuge to contemplate life, love, and justice. All I would have to do to enjoy the tranquil setting was to slide open a door, pull up a chair, and sit.

I was right, retreating many times to the deck, frustrated with the state of the world and my uneven relationship with Abe.

The contractor secured the panels to the foundation and to each other, inserted a cable into the top of each panel, and tightly ratcheted the cable to hold the roof and sides together.

The result was a finished structure, complete with windows, insulation, electrical outlets, and exterior redwood siding. Sliding the roof panels into each other and securing them into the sides completed the construction.

Inside, we finished the walls with oak paneling and vinyl tile floors resembling gray slate. I selected a lively durable blue and white patterned carpeting intended to withstand the abuse of muddy feet and wayward food. I painted the woodwork blue, not white.

We still lived in Johnson City, Tennessee, 45 miles away. The drive took me about one hour and 15 minutes on a two-lane highway through the mountains. I drove to Wise several days a week to meet with the contractor.

Will this be the house I think it will? Will the courts rule in our favor? Will I find a job?

Figure 28. Our two-pod Rondesic house sits at the edge of a pond in Wise, Virginia, 1969.

Each time I prepared to return to Wise, I got ready to become mildly carsick on the two-lane highway through the mountains. The density of the foliage blocked my vision around curves and provided hiding places for spirits, snake-handling churches, and forest dwellers.

Abe was finishing the semester at ETSU and preparing to move to Wise. Each day after I met with the contractor in Wise, I returned to Johnson City to help pack our things.

Frequent fog made the trip longer than the usual hour and fifteen minutes and added to the overall creepiness of the experience.

Helen had told me a witch lived in the nearby town of Norton. She grew herbs to treat physical, mental, and spiritual maladies.

In addition, a snake-handling church was near our new home-to-be. I felt the positive energy of the herbalist and the unnerving aura of the churches.

I knew I was getting close when the air stopped moving. The energy I felt bewildered me. *Was my imagination on high alert or will something of substance fly out of the woods?*

During the house design process, I learned someone was tearing down a one-room schoolhouse. They were giving away salvageable items. I secured a slab of chalkboard to mount on the wall over the sink in the main bathroom. The chalkboard inspired comments from guests ranging from gross to funny, including:

> There once was a farmer named Hollis
>
> Had possums and snakes for his solace,
>
> His children ate snails,
>
> Had prehensile tails,
>
> And voted for Governor Wallace.

When Abe completed his contract with ETSU, he took time to get acquainted with Clinch Valley College professors, course requirements, and students.

Neighbors were eager to see the house, and when students heard about "the cool house the Nortons had built," they showed up to hang out. We installed a free-standing fireplace. I painted the asbestos pad that protected the wall and the floor with the rainbow colors similar to many music albums: orange, hot pink, electric blue, and acid green.

Our furnishings had never been in an Ethan Allen showroom. Blow-up couches, beanbag chairs, and a big floppy purple thing filled our living room.

A full-sized mattress, lots of upholstery foam, and purple velour made up "Big Purple," a couch Abe and I made. It held four to six people.

Figure 29. Abe and I look down the circular staircase of our new house in Wise, 1969.

An ETSU student contributed a Styrofoam T-Rex dinosaur as an art installation. We called it Dean, in mock tribute to the ETSU disciplinary committee. It overlooked the lake from the living room and had its picture taken many times.

Figure 30. T-Rex and I show each other our teeth, 1980.

The kitchen would soon get a workout. Abe assumed the role of chef when we had small dinner parties. Guests for these special dinners were usually faculty members. He enjoyed putting on a show and always cooked something he thought our guests may not have eaten. He received many compliments for his excellent cooking and flair for presentation.

Students and faculty who dropped in frequently stayed for dinner. Spontaneous food preparation fell to me. Often, I made spaghetti, soup, sandwiches, or omelets for 20 people at a time. People came and went, always finding something to eat.

Abe conducted mini-seminars in the living room. Between performing my tasks as short-order cook and clean-up artist, I occasionally played with musicians who brought their guitars or banjos. Lively music, dancing, singing, and loud conversation—sometimes arguing—filled the house.

Ralph, our neurotic cat, favored his perch atop the open partition between the living room and kitchen. Some students declared Ralph a CIA operative, perfectly positioned to spy on everyone.

Snoopy, our sweet New Hampshire beagle, earned a place on Big Purple and accepted all the pats and rubs she could get from guests.

Once our reputations as radicals permeated the Appalachian student and university underground, we got requests to give asylum to people being hunted by the FBI.

Two people hid at our house for several days because the FBI had a warrant for their arrest for allegedly inciting a riot. They informed us they would get a call about their next safe house and would leave during the night.

On another occasion, we housed a man who had lost his job for protesting the war. He escaped to Canada. Three other students needing asylum stopped for a few days on their way to Canada.

As further means of protesting the war, I stopped paying the federal taxes on utility bills, as I had done in Johnson City.

We were convinced the FBI had wiretapped our phone in Wise as they had in Johnson City. We kept hearing strange noises coming from it, sometimes when it wasn't in use.

I thought if they could hear the conversations taking place in the house, they would get a good laugh.

I dubbed the deck a sanctuary during the building process. It had become a peaceful place to enjoy the outdoors and wind down. Birds sailed back and forth overhead, and I heard the flopping of a fish now and then coming from the lake.

The next day, I found a bat hanging in a bedroom closet. It is amazing how much birds and bats resemble each other when they are on the wing.

Abe and I shooed the bat out by pointing a fan at it and directing it with light toward the open door to the deck. The bat found its way out, but must have told a cohort how much fun it was to hang around in such a cool house. Another bat found its way in a week later. We removed a window and shooed the bat out into the night air.

"I wonder if the witch in Norton knows her bats are loose," I said. "This could be an opportunity to meet her. We can talk about how batty we are." Abe gave me one of those "she's lost it now" looks.

Having heard nothing from SCOTUS, I resigned myself to the fact we might not win. My graduate school career had ended, and I started looking for a job.

An opportunity for a job opened when two faculty members opened a retail store carrying items appealing to high school and college students. Merchandise included record albums, record players, adjunct books for college classes, popular novels, posters, and jewelry ("love beads").

This kind of retail store popped up throughout the country. Some were called "head shops," because they sold marijuana paraphernalia.

This store did not plan to sell those items, but would focus on symbols of the cultural change young people were experiencing, like peace symbols, anti-war posters, books about civil rights, and hair and body ornamentation.

The owners approached me about working in the store, and I agreed to manage and staff it.

Underground newspapers, as well as regional pamphlets about Appalachian life and coal mining, and comix by Robert Crumb made their way into the store.

I sold scores of anti-war posters. Popular posters bore Yin/Yang symbols and photos of rock and folk groups, including the Grateful Dead, Jimi Hendrix, and the Doors. Another popular poster promoted *Hair, The Tribal Love-Rock Musical*. The poster *War Is Not Healthy for Children and Other Living Things* was a best-seller. Love and peace figured prominently on many posters.

The two-room basement of a house became the store. It had an entrance accessible from the street. One side of the store had fully stocked bookshelves, boxes of posters, and racks of jewelry. The other side had LPs, record players, the cash register, candles, and free newsletters brought in by customers.

Scores of young people swamped the store, and many went away with pieces of jewelry, posters, albums, and books, mostly paid for. Despite the initial flurry of profitable activity, the love beads and some other small items were disappearing.

I told the owners we were losing merchandise. A location closer to the campus with more merchandise and square footage might have helped, but the owners sold out the merchandise and closed the store after a few months.

I began looking for a proper job. The Appalachian Regional Commission, part of LBJ's War on Poverty, created several agencies in the southern Appalachians to enrich community educational and economic development.

I soon found a job as an assistant librarian with DILENOWISCO. Dickinson, Lee, Scott, and Wise counties, and the town of Norton, Virginia, made up the membership of the agency, creating the acronym.

The director of the program had previously created and aired an original language arts program on public television. My function as assistant librarian was to research and order nonbook resources designed to enrich learning in southwest Virginia.

DILENOWISCO staff distributed the resources directly to schools, community centers, churches, coal camps, and private homes. The library we were building was open to everyone. Materials included still and video cameras, educational games, and instructions for building projects.

Two employees delivered and demonstrated the materials to the school, coal camp, family reunion, or community center. Part of my job was to explain to the staff how I thought people could use the new materials. I occasionally traveled to schools or camps when demand was too great for dedicated staff to fill all the requests.

Before one of the educational staff assumed his new job, he asked me to cut his beautiful light brown hair, which reached the middle of his back. When two local barbers told him they did not serve "scroungy hippies," he decided to have someone else cut it.

Although I cut my hair, as well as Abe's, I balked at this request to cut what this young man had prized. I eventually gave in, agreeing he probably would not get the job he wanted.

Everything went smoothly, and his hair looked okay, but I trimmed it again before his interview. He thought it looked just fine. His girlfriend helped by hovering close by and flinching every few minutes. He got the job.

Occasionally, Abe and I sneaked in a bit of entertainment away from the house. I treasured seeing live stage performances, so a trip to the Barter Theatre in Abingdon, Virginia, was a special treat.

The Barter opened as The State Theatre of Virginia in 1933. "With vegetables you cannot sell, you can buy a good laugh."[24] If you brought food, you gained entry to the theater. Actors swapped their talents for food.

Arthur Miller's *The Crucible* was playing and was perfect for its timeliness. The 1953 play is a fictionalized version of the Salem, Massachusetts, witch trials. Critics also say it is an allegory for McCarthyism, which accused so many people of being Communists.

Famous actors took the roles, and the play was a gigantic success. Afterward, friends gathered at our house to discuss the production. The similarities between current examples of red-baiting and disinformation and guilt by association were obvious to me.

I told my story about the ETSU English teacher who accused New Englanders and government employees of being Communists. Others shared stories about teachers, friends, and family who criticized them for being too left-wing and hanging out with hippies and traitors.

Cultural Detours: Lore, Liquor, and Local Flavor

During my time at ETSU and for years afterward, two English professors—Dr. Thomas R. Burton and Ambrose Manning—wrote a column for the local newspaper featuring Appalachian folktales, songs, and myths. The column motivated me to learn more about the culture and compare dialects between Massachusetts and East Tennessee.

Dr. Burton became an expert in the culture of the Southern Appalachian Mountains, including the culture of snake handlers.[25]

I wanted to see snake handlers perform their rituals. To observe the event, I would have to attend a church where snake-handlers were present. I had asked Dr. Burton if that might be possible.

There was a Pentecostal church not far from the campus where leaders regularly handled snakes. Dr. Burton warned me that congregants would easily recognize me as an outsider and would delay the service until I left. They preferred to share the service with people they knew who would willingly participate to test their faith in God and Jesus.

Figure 31. Snake handlings at the Church of God with Signs Following at Lajunior in Harlan County, Kentucky, September 15, 1946.

Knowledge of local lore proved helpful when I began graduate school and started teaching. I needed to understand the regional language and dialects and the local customs and religious practices to relate to my students.

That would be true for southwest Virginia, even though there were many differences between east Tennessee and southwest Virginia.

Helen said the snake handlers and their congregation probably would be demonstrably emphatic about pushing me out of the church, which was a short distance from our house.

———————

A friend told me that a cultural phenomenon I would not want to miss was a trip to Ray's in Big Stone Gap. Piquing my curiosity, I asked, "What is Ray's?"

Were they handling snakes, or was it a gathering of witches? I had become aware of an increase in references to witches floating in and out of conversations.

Not to worry, it was a restaurant. Mentioning a trip to Ray's Restaurant in Big Stone Gap was all it took to assemble some friends to go for dinner. Abe and I found several people who knew the location and how to get there. We decided on a date and picked out a leader who said she knew the way. The rest of us would follow.

Our caravan of five cars full of students and faculty snaked its way through the hills from Wise to Big Stone Gap. I hoped our rather scruffy bunch would be welcome there.

The evening drive unfolded on a winding two-lane blacktop road bordered by high banks of trees, kudzu, Virginia creeper, laurel, and rhododendron. Dense foliage darkened not only the roadside, but the sky. Eeriness has mass in Appalachia, just like clouds, fog, and the night sky. Scared the shit out of me.

We arrived at an unmarked building sitting in a poorly lighted gravel parking lot, so I was happy we were following someone.

Aging pickup trucks tricked out with gun racks filled the parking lot. Anxiety descended on our group when we came upon the scene. Tom said, "Oh, no, whose idea was this?"

Most of the men in our party wore jeans and denim shirts or T-shirts sporting the face of Jimi Hendrix, Abbie Hoffman, Malcolm X, or Jim Morrison. Headbands calmed their long hair. Five out of six wore beards and everyone wore a peace symbol. The women dressed in bell-bottom jeans or slacks and long-sleeved shirts or lightweight sweaters, dangling earrings, and sandals.

To get into the dining room, we had to walk through a dark, dingy barroom full of men drinking beer. Most of the men wore T-shirts, jeans, boots, or overalls to cover their beer bellies. They stood at the bar and sat in the booths.

Boot prints interrupted the blanket of dust on the floor. Remnants of mustard and beer spotted the high-backed booths. Black hats with Confederate flag insignias were plentiful. There were no women in the room.

One guy wearing a leather vest, jeans, and no shirt gave me the once-over, rose from his barstool, and made a step toward me. One of his cohorts intervened by touching his arm, which apparently dissuaded him because he sat down and resumed sipping his beer.

We made it into the back room, where some of our group had already sat down. Ray, our host and server, was a tall, lean Black man with closely cropped hair, long fingers, and a clean white apron.

Ray greeted us with a swooping gesture toward the vacant chairs and returned to the kitchen. Squeeze bottles of hot sauce and bowls of tartar sauce dotted the ten-foot-long table covered with a faded yellow and white oilcloth.

I could see the kitchen from where I sat. Two gray-haired Black women wearing clean white aprons came into the dining room briefly, smoothed their clothes, spoke to Ray, and returned to the cast iron wood-fired stove.

Giant black cast iron skillets were simmering with lard, waiting to begin. Their mission: fry mounds of potatoes, breaded catfish fillets, and hush puppies.

Ray returned to take our orders. Someone asked Ray if he had anything besides water to drink. He was "secretly" famous for serving wine, if customers brought their own.

Several of our crew produced bottles of Boone's Farm, Lambrusco, and Mateo rose. Ray assured us he could provide glasses—nothing fancy, mind you—and offered to pour the wine. He retired to an anteroom and returned with a large tray of plastic glasses full of wine.

Holding the tray high over his head, Ray served the ladies first. Moving on to the men, he stopped when everyone had a glass in hand. Someone asked Ray to join us. He hesitated, then poured himself a glass. We raised our glasses in a toast to Ray, and he bowed, holding a full glass of wine without spilling a drop.

As soon as he heard all of us had come to eat catfish, he disappeared. A short time later, he sailed in with heaping platters of food for each side of the table.

The fish was crunchy on the outside and tender inside. The chefs fried the potatoes in lard to a golden brown. Gritty cornmeal made the cornbread and hush puppies special because a local mill had ground the corn.

Soon, a second round of food platters made its way down each side of the dinner table. I could not eat another bite. The cooks joined Ray in the dining hall, and Ray introduced us to Missy and Mama Robinson.

Our group gave them a standing ovation, and they laughed and clapped hands. Mama danced around Ray right back into the kitchen, earning another round of applause.

Not much of a drinker, I drove Abe and me home. I did not like driving at night on roads that sucked up headlights before they hit the pavement, but I finally got us home.

I had enjoyed the evening of laughter and local food and suggested to Abe we repeat such an event whenever we could.

The sole legal source of liquor in Virginia was the package store (aside from the moonshine whiskey), where licensed merchants secured all the liquor behind a high-walled steel cage. One store we visited had a thick book perched on a podium in front of the cashier's counter. The book contained laminated pages listing the spirits. Adjacent to the cage behind the counter stood a shotgun.

Shoppers thumbed through the menu of choices and ordered from the cashier at the counter. The cashier selected customers' choices and brought them to the counter.

Legend had it that highway patrol officers from neighboring dry states lay in wait behind trees and signs to catch people with out-of-state car tags. When they spotted one, they stopped the car and searched it, fining the driver and confiscating the liquor.

One could easily buy moonshine, if one dared. Not only was it illegal, but improper distillation could make it poisonous. The fight against legal liquor saw moonshiners, preachers, and law enforcement on the same side. They all had a stake in keeping their states dry, albeit for strikingly different reasons.

Reality Returns

As much fun as I had at Ray's, I felt sure it wouldn't last. "Jesus, Abe, they're going after more Black people," I said while reading the newspaper. In December 1969, a tactical unit of the Cook County, Illinois, State's Attorney's office drugged, shot, and killed Fred Hampton in his bed. Fred was a progressive Black man who had founded the first Rainbow Coalition.

The Rainbow Coalition included the Black Panthers, the Young Patriots, and the Young Lords, appealing to Black,

White, and Brown people. The coalition included major Chicago street gangs that helped end infighting and worked for social change.[26]

The Chicago Police Department and the FBI led the attack. Law enforcement sprayed over 90 gunshots throughout the apartment, killing Black Panther Party leaders Mark Clark and Fred Hampton, and maiming several others. The occupants fired once in response.

Police failed to seal the apartment, and filmmakers suspicious of the findings went into the apartment to take pictures. The raid took place at the time filmmakers were working on a documentary about the Black Panthers and later used the pictures in the production of *The Murder of Fred Hampton*, a documentary.[27]

My friends and I showed our support for the coalition by sharing our opinions at folk festivals, picnics, and small gatherings.

In January 1970, the Cook County Coroner held an inquest. A jury concluded that Hampton's and Clark's deaths were justifiable homicides.[28]

How could this happen in America?!

Home provided temporary respite to the violence rampant in the country and the world. In the daytime, I usually went home to a house or yard full of students. On the occasion when no one was there, I knew Abe and friends were at school or at the "Flop House," where several students lived together. *I can retreat to the deck.* Many of the students were studying the culture, music, and coal economy of the Southern Appalachian Mountains in classes Helen Lewis led.

Figure 32. Abe is in the front row, third from the left, with inhabitants of the Flop House, 1970.

King Coal

Helen was one of the few women who had journeyed into a deep coal mine. Women were bad luck, according to the miners and their wives. The inhumane living conditions suffered by miners and superstitions surrounding the work were new to me.

Conglomerates that included other energy companies owned most of the deep mines. They employed local men and provided meager homes for the workers. Some miners received pay in scrip, "money" good only at the company store.

Some mine operators liked to call strip mining "surface mining," a euphemism implying they took only the topsoil. They took the topsoil and everything else until they found coal. Strip miners dumped what they removed into streams and rivers, or left a slag heap beside the mine.

I asked people in our circle of friends if this kind of mining was illegal or at least subject to cleanup and restoration after the mine closed. No one enforced the scant regulations, apparently.

I should have known discrimination existed in the coal camps. The owners enforced segregation, separating Black people from Whites. I abhorred the squalor Black coal miners existed in: standing water, mud, swarms of mosquitoes, peeling shingles, and broken windows. I could not believe an employer of people in a dangerous profession could get away with housing them in what appeared to be the slave quarters of a plantation, or worse.

Still burning in the miners' memories, a series of explosions rocked the No. 9 coal mine of Consolidation Coal in Farmington, West Virginia, on November 20, 1968. Ninety-nine men worked the graveyard shift that day. Seventy-eight died in the explosion that sent flames and smoke 150 feet into the air.

Rescuers got 21 miners out, but on day nine of the rescue, they pulled back.

Ten days later, rescuers sealed the mine with concrete. The remains of nineteen miners rest in the mine to this day. No one asked the miners' families about how they wanted to deal with the remains of their loved ones.

Tony Boyle, President of the United Mine Workers, said, "As long as we mine coal, there is always this inherent danger. This is one of the better companies, as far as cooperation with our union and safety is concerned."[29]

The injustice of the hazardous workplace, the poor compensation, and the violence toward union organizers made a deep impression on me. I wanted to do something, but I wasn't sure what that might be.

While I was meeting with the building contractor for our house during the summer of 1969, my attention shifted toward the injustices of coal mining. I attended a conference in Huntington, West Virginia focused on coal mining, union organizing, and poverty in Appalachia.

At the conference, I met Jeanne Rasmussen, a freelance journalist and photographer, whose essays I had seen in several regional publications.

I saw her outside before we entered the building. Curly black hair cascaded to her slight shoulders, and her cotton dress fluttered in the breeze. At first reserved and subdued, Jeanne's presence transformed when she rose to speak, dispelling any pale characterization of her.

She was eloquent without bombast, quiet yet effective. Her skill as a journalist took her to mine disasters, camp events, organizing activities, political candidates, and the United Mine Workers.

Born in Lubbock, Texas, she attended Baylor University. At various times in her career, she had worked for *The Washington Post, Business Week, Time*, and *Fortune*.

Her goal was to encourage people to write about their experiences in Appalachia, to focus on the poverty of the unemployed as well as employed miners. Her husband Donald Rasmussen, a pulmonologist, had become a leading advocate for compensation to miners with black lung disease.

I told Jeanne I was interested in accompanying her to some rallies and speeches she might be covering. We discussed my situation with ETSU and she indicated her wholehearted support for the suit, as she, too, had narrowly eluded censorship many times.

Despite the dangers involved, mines continued to operate, and miners continued to organize laborers. Many miners who were afraid of losing their jobs stayed out of the fray or turned against union organizers.

Some coal operators paid miners to oppose the unions, and Boyle had, in the opinion of scores of miners, become too cozy with the coal operators.

The union had a bank in Washington, D.C., outside of the Appalachian region. Rank and file members said they suspected Boyle of using it as his own bank account. In early March 1971, a federal district court indicted Boyle for embezzling $49,250 in union funds (about $800,000 of buying power in 2025 dollars). He used the money to make illegal campaign contributions in the 1968 presidential race.[30]

The court convicted Boyle in December 1973 to a three-year sentence and imprisoned him at the federal penitentiary in Springfield, Missouri.[31]

Joseph "Jock" Yablonski, an officer of the union, had voiced opposition to the corrupt practices of Boyle and other UMWA officials. In May 1969, he ran against Boyle for the presidency of the union, as a reformer, not a radical. He recommended many changes to benefit workers, rather than the union officials.[32]

The union's inaction on black lung disease disgusted Yablonski, as it became clear the disease impaired the miners' health. Boyle appointed him director of Labor's Nonpartisan League, the political arm of the union, to placate him on the black lung subject. The League had very little clout.[33]

Yablonski set about to get the support of 50 union leaders to get his name on the ballot for the presidency of the United Mine Workers of America. He thought he would get that support from the 68 leaders in the southern area of Pennsylvania. Yablonski asked Ralph Nader to help add to his support, but Nader diddled around until it was too late. Yablonski said, "He never did deliver."[34]

Boyle stripped Yablonski of his position with the League. When Yablonski fought to keep his position, the International Elective Board voted him down. Boyle met with Albert Pass, secretary-treasurer for District 19 in east Tennessee and Kentucky, to discuss how to deal with Yablonski.

"We're in a fight. Yablonski ought to be killed or done away with," Boyle said. Albert Pass agreed. They devised a money-laundering scheme to take $20,000 from union funds and transfer it to the nonexistent Research and Information Committee. Then they transferred the money to retired miners who kicked it back to Pass. Pass contacted another retired miner, Silous Huddleston, who contacted his son-in-law Paul Gilly. Gilly would round up a murder squad.[35]

At a rally in early summer in Springfield, Illinois, an unknown assailant attacked Yablonski, knocking him out. Yablonski thought he was paralyzed, because when he awoke, he could not move his arms. The Boyle goons, to whom Yablonski attributed the attack, had convinced him the electioneering would get even uglier. Yablonski still wanted all the marbles.[36]

The FBI opened an investigation into the beating that Boyle's supporters allegedly gave Yablonski.

No one filed charges.[37]

Local Wise County, Virginia, union officials invited Yablonski to hold a rally in Wise, but his advisors told him the threat of violence was too great.

Yablonski agreed to hold a rally in Grundy, in Buchanan County, Virginia, if the union and the campaign would provide plenty of security.

Many of the Clinch Valley College students studying Appalachian culture planned to attend.

Jeanne Rasmussen was traveling with the Yablonski campaign, and we agreed to meet at the rally in Grundy.

Jeanne's husband, Dr. Donald Rasmussen, proved that breathing coal dust particles caused black lung disease. His presentations usually included X-Rays of coal miners' lungs.

Jeanne and I met to strategize the development of our interviews featuring Yablonski and Dr. Rasmussen.

In coal country, the sky is often gray and overcast, mimicking the look of winter even on warm days. On that July day, the air was warm, and the sky was a dreamlike blue.

The rousing strains of "Solidarity Forever" wafted above the crowd in anticipation of hearing Jock Yablonski address the crowd.

Children were tagging each other, laughing, and hiding behind cars. Men dressed in their best jeans or work pants and women in cotton dresses or jeans and T-shirts strolled toward the podium to hear the speaker.

The Peoples Appalachian Research Collective, a group funded by the Institute for Policy Studies, distributed *People's Appalachia*, a monthly publication. The newsletter analyzed the effects of the coal industry on people and the environment.

I spoke with the writer who shared a study the collective had published on "interlocking directorates" of White men who sat on boards of directors of several energy companies.

For example, a director of Consolidation Coal was also on the board of Anaconda Copper, and a member of an electric company was also a member of Consolidation, Kennecott, and Anaconda boards. A few corporate CEOs controlled the major suppliers of raw materials for massive amounts of power creation.

"It looks like the same 12 men control most of the energy production in the US. An individual coal miner must destroy his land or risk his life so that millionaires can get even richer." I said.

Jeanne showed me some of her husband's X-Rays of lungs infected with pneumoconiosis and silicosis. They were fraught with black smears, swelling nodules, and scar tissue. If I had not believed the dangers of coal dust were real, I did after seeing the X-rays.

Coal mining was hazardous. I thought the law should hold operators accountable, and the union should work harder on behalf of the deep miners. Surely proof of the dangers would spark movement toward justice for miners.

Or were the corporate miners making too damn much money to be concerned about the people doing the work? So what if some of them got sick or died? They could always hire miners. Jobs were hard to come by.

After considering the intense hazards and extreme risks of coal mining, I felt an undercurrent of negative energy, a menacing, a vulnerability of impending danger to the profound truths on display.

In Grundy, local miners had constructed a stage for Yablonski. Two steps on each end of the stage allowed access. A podium stood in the middle of the stage. Four people sat on each side of the podium, and Yablonski stood on the ground behind the stage. Another set of steps led from the ground to the stage for the speaker.

Yablonski started up the steps to speak.

Jeanne and I reached the stage just as a shadowy figure appeared. He had a white beard and wore a trench coat and glasses.

Moving silently, he crept up the rear steps of the stage. Suddenly, he lunged toward Yablonski with his arm raised.

Yablonski dodged his attacker.

Missing his target, the assailant ran down the steps and disappeared.

This can't be happening again. Those goons tried to kill him in Springfield, and they are trying it again.

Two of the security officers in the crowd raced after the attacker, but he had disappeared, never to be found. A few days later, someone found the beard, trench coat, and glasses stuffed in a trash can.

One man on the stage rose and seemed to cue a woman in the front row. The haunting strains of "Which Side Are You On," rang out.

Yablonski walked to the microphone, shaking his head. The crowd erupted, and Jock began his speech as the noise subsided.

> You know this reign of tyranny that they're putting on. . . trying to scare people from going to meetings; trying to scare pensioners; trying to

scare a fellow from standing up and expressing himself? Who the hell do they think they are? Do they think this is Gestapo Germany? No! This is the United States of America! And let me say this to you. . . hundreds of thousands of dollars that are being spent—taken out of the union treasury. It belongs to coal miners! And this campaign is being investigated right now by the Federal Bureau of Investigation and the Justice Department.[38]

After the rally quieted, security and campaign staff questioned people in the crowd. Many were reluctant to share their observations or speculations for fear of reprisal from Tony Boyle's thugs. The Sheriff of Buchanan County did a mock interview of Jeanne and me about what we saw, but he sloughed off the incident as just another union problem.

"They've been fightin' each other fer a long time. Those unions from back east should leave us alone down here, and we'd get along okay," the sheriff said.

He blamed Yablonski's supporters for stirring up trouble. The FBI did not open a case because the local authorities would not request one.

Jeanne, union officials, and I pressed the sheriff to invite the FBI. He refused, claiming it would only stir up more trouble, and that Yablonski seemed to be all right. "He's a big guy. He can handle it."

Jeanne and I wrote a piece covering the entire incident, including the sheriff's comments. We submitted it to wire services, but never saw the story in print.

Yablonski's lawyers filed a complaint with local authorities, but they did not find the perpetrator. Yablonski continued to campaign, but he lost the election.

On New Year's Eve, 1969, hired gunmen entered the home of Jock Yablonski and murdered him, his daughter, and his wife. His son found the bodies a few days later. Someone had cut the home phone lines and slashed the tires on the cars in the driveway.[39]

Yablonski supporters, shocked by the murders, harbored suspicions of foul play in the election of Tony Boyle and demanded the US Department of Labor open an investigation. A later investigation discovered Boyle had 100,000 extra ballots printed in District 19, Harlan County, Kentucky.[40]

The Labor Department overturned the election results in 1972, three years after Yablonski was murdered. In the new election, a reform candidate defeated Boyle.

A jury convicted seven persons of murder and conspiracy to commit the murder of Yablonski. The judge handed down death sentences to two of the assassins on charges of first-degree murder.

In 1973, a Pennsylvania jury indicted Boyle for the three Yablonski murders and convicted him in 1974. He received three life sentences and died in prison in Pennsylvania of heart failure.[41]

In 1973, miners struck the Brookside Mine in Harlan County, Kentucky, against Duke Power Company. Barbara Kopple filmed the events.

Her 1976 documentary, *Harlan County USA*, included a segment on Yablonski's murder and its aftermath. Hazel Dickens sings "Cold Blooded Murder" (also known as "The Yablonski Murder"). Kopple won an Academy Award for Best Documentary at the 49th (1977) Academy Awards.[42]

Coal mining continued to grind and shovel away. Some landowners operated their own surface mines, which included strip mining, open-pit mining, and mountaintop removal mining.

In other cases, corporations wheedled the minerals out from under poor landowners to operate the mine themselves, with little or no regard for the consequences.

The impact of surface mining can be devastating: water contamination, habitat destruction, landscape wreckage, ecological disruption, and lead contamination.

Between the towns of Wise and Norton stood a row of operational beehive coke ovens. Steel producers heated coke mixed with iron to produce steel. At one time, workers used ponies and carts to haul coal to the sites. They hand-shoveled coal into the ovens, open in the front. Sometimes they ran across the tops of the ovens to smother a fire that had broken through the tops of the ovens.

The burning ovens between Wise and Norton created a quarter-mile long wall of smoke that hovered over the ovens until a gust of wind blew particulate into the surrounding fields and towns.

Stories about men falling from the ovens or through a burn hole in the oven's top were part of the local lore. Airborne ash and sulfur from the fires stuck to buildings and streets, and people inhaled and swallowed it.

Protesting these ovens proved difficult because the roadway was narrow. Massive trucks loaded with tons of coal rolled by slowly to a trans loader or railroad. Standing by the ovens was dangerous because they were on fire, and a truck could easily nick a protestor, especially one with long hair.

Besides letters to the editor, some protesters found other means of expression. A few students and union organizers visited coal company offices to see the lists of miners hired for the day. One list contained the names of those chosen to work and a second list had the names of miners blacklisted for their union activity.

If a worker's name appeared on the blacklist, the coal company offices would not hire him, and the posting made it clear to all who saw the list. Union sympathizers suffered violent lessons from the hands of company thugs.

The postings usually took one of two forms, depending on the mine office location. A blackboard outside the office showed the names of notorious union organizers and sympathizers written in chalk.

Sometimes, a coal operator tacked the names to a corkboard inside the office. Many of the office buildings looked like someone had slapped them together with tobacco barn wood.

When office staff were not looking, union supporters seized the lists off the board and destroyed them, after they saved the names of those blacklisted.

I participated in two of these raids, with fear and trembling. Once, a friend and I heard a shotgun blast, and she jammed down the gas pedal to speed away from security officers.

After the raids, we contacted the blacklisted union organizers, many of whom she knew, to provide moral support and assistance.

Some miners joined the folk festivals, coloring the hollers with old-timey music. Performers sang union protest songs in addition to the traditional songs. Florence Reece, wife of a union organizer in Harlan County, wrote *Which Side Are You On* in 1931. Pete Seeger's *Greatest Hits of 1967* album released his recording of it.[43]

Protest songs told the stories of people who had fallen prey to corporate greed, experienced layoffs of breadwinners, and faced the dangers of union organizing. War protesters, students, coal miners, and local folk artists became cohorts through music.

I was still learning many of the traditional songs. Many of the latest folk songs were based on older melodies. I played when I had time. My favorites were the older blues tunes, like those sung by Mississippi John Hurt, Blind "Lemon" Jefferson, Lead Belly, and Ma Rainey.

Political activists had learned many of the indigenous folk songs from local people who were happy to share tunes and the stories imbedded in the music.

One of many folk musicians we met and housed was Earl Gilmore, a Black Christian musician from Clinchco, Virginia. Helen Lewis had brought him from his home to experience the music festival brewing.

Earl was a slight, tall man with long fingers and a mass of slicked-back black hair. He demonstrated his powerful fear of Mother Nature when he chastened me for standing close to the windows during a thunderstorm.

"You should be afraid," he said, "come away from the windows. Mother Nature can be violent."

After feeling the eeriness and potent energy of the mountains, I stopped to take stock of his words and backed away from the windows.

Jack Wright, a friend and a student at Clinch Valley College, organized the musical event on High Knob, a peak in the Blue Ridge Mountains in Virginia. The event attracted people from the hollows, the coal camps, and many cities to experience this remarkable event.

In an interview with Marianne Worthington in *Still: The Journal*, Jack tells how he became involved in Appalachian culture and its music.[44]

Jack's father had worked for Peerless Coal Company as a bookkeeper in Glamorgan, Virginia, and they lived in the coal camp owned by Peerless.

A veteran of the Vietnam War, Jack developed a career in music, storytelling, film production, and cultural history.

Women who did not perform on stage handled the food. I usually cooked and served pots of chili. Occasionally, a woman took the stage to introduce a performer. I could play the guitar in my living room, but I wasn't good enough to perform for a crowd. Local storytellers, dancers, and musicians headlined the programs.

Female performers included Jean Ritchie on three-string acoustic dulcimer or Hazel Dickens, bluegrass singer-songwriter, double bassist, and guitar player.

Ralph Stanley, renowned for his distinctive singing and banjo style, along with Carter family style music filled the hills and valleys. Dock Boggs, Mike Seeger, and many local singers grew up with the traditional songs and embraced the protest songs.

Musicians brought their banjos, guitars, dulcimers, autoharps, mandolins, fiddles, and spoons. A wooden platform on stage amplified the rhythmic tapping, clogging, and dancing.

As uplifting as much of the music could be, the words also told the story of pain, death, and injustice.

Not much dancing surrounded the organizing of coal workers. Violence or the fear of it was a mainstay throughout the history of the labor movement.

I was never sure where Abe was during the festivals when he wasn't teaching. He did not participate in coal mining protests or in planning the festivals. We frequently went our separate ways, did our own things, worked our jobs, and were often reading different publications.

In 1970, a collective of feminists began publishing *off our backs*, a radical periodical that lasted until 2008.[45] I agreed with the editorial statement of the first edition which said, "*off our backs* is a paper for all women who are fighting for the liberation of their lives, and we hope it will grow and expand to meet the needs of women from all backgrounds and classes."[46]

Many alternative publications (some called them "underground" pieces) showed up at music festivals. One could find *The Great Speckled Bird*, established in 1968, *off our backs*, *Mountain Life and Work*, and other publications addressing poverty and union issues.

At first glance, I found these publications to be at odds with each other, but later discovered they had one thing in common: dissatisfaction with capitalistic exploitation.

I wanted to learn more about *The Great Speckled Bird*, so one Friday I left my job early, packed a bedroll and a few items of clothing and drove to Atlanta to find the *Bird*.

After I got to Atlanta in the general area of Peachtree Street where hippies hung out, I asked a young woman sitting in a chair on a corner, "How do I find the *Bird*?"

"Follow the marijuana smoke," she suggested.

There are many Peachtree streets in Atlanta, but I quickly found the office. The staff welcomed me with an invitation to stay overnight if I did not want to rent a hotel room.

I learned everyone participated in editorial decisions and voted on the pieces to run in the next issue. A staff member told me the *Bird* was the largest paid newspaper in Georgia, with a circulation of well over 20,000.

I stayed overnight and watched and listened as they completed the next edition. They asked about my lawsuit and expressed their disgust with the justice system. We had fun publishing news about the counterculture, leftist events, and musical performances.

The next day, I grabbed a stack of printed copies and found a corner to stand on to sell them. Staff relied on volunteers to sell the papers on street corners and on college and high school campuses.

Many salespeople suffered harassment at the hands of police and business owners, mainly because of their "hippie" costumes and the content of the paper. Some had been arrested on charges of distributing pornography, but authorities trumped up this charge to get the paper off the street.

No one harassed me, and I sold my stack of papers. I left the next day and arrived back in Wise with an interesting experience to add to my growing list.

A Few More Obstacles

Not long after I started working at DILENWISCO, the librarian, wife of a Protestant minister, approached me and Abe about becoming foster parents to a teenage girl. The girl was living with my coworker and her husband.

Abe and I discussed this at length. I wanted to try, if Abe did.

We discussed what expectations we had for her stay. We would expect her to live with us, keeping her private space clean. She should keep us informed about where she went. We wanted to meet her friends. She would have a curfew and could have friends over to the house if we met them and talked with them. We expected her to go to school and do her homework. We would help her with her studies.

We also talked about her background and whether we thought we could care for a girl who came from an abusive situation in which she had relied on illegal drugs to cope.

She had an ongoing relationship with the minister and his wife and with a psychologist. I thought with their help we might try to bring Nancy into our home. I thought Abe and I agreed on everything we discussed.

Abe concluded it was something we "ought" to do and agreed to accept her into our household. This should have been a clue that he was uncertain about his willingness to help raise a teenager, but that it would look good if we did.

We were novices. In over our heads. Unpaid. Not sanctioned by an organization. No insurance.

We embarked on this important lifestyle change with some reservations. Nancy came to live with us carrying a background of childhood sexual trauma and drug issues.

She had bounced from school to school and had difficulty acclimating to new surroundings. During the first week she came to live with us, the high school principal called me. Having reacted to a potent drug, for which she did not have a prescription, she was recovering in the high school infirmary. She experienced strong heart palpitations, which frightened her, and she panicked.

I left work to pick her up at the infirmary. She said she had asked the student next to her for an aspirin, and he gave her a pill he said would help get rid of her headache. She panicked when she had heart palpitations and ran to the infirmary, crying.

One evening while Abe and I were visiting a neighbor, she had a party, against our instructions not to have anyone over. She had homework to finish. We came home to an empty house and a dishwasher that had overflowed and flooded the kitchen.

She dropped her clothes wherever she took them off. Sometimes, we didn't know where she was. She came home past curfew. She did not tell us where she was going. I was worried most of the time about this very troubled teenager.

I talked about hopes we had for her and attempted to get her to talk about her goals in life and how she hoped to achieve them. She lacked conversational skills for this kind of discussions. So, I listened intently for clues to what she thought. She seemed lost.

Knowing we were trying to establish a home for Nancy, students rarely stopped by just to hang out. I felt relief, because our guests often "found" something to smoke. Abe began to stay away from home more frequently than before Nancy moved in.

The final straw fell one evening when all three of us were sitting on the big, floppy purple couch watching television news. Nancy started talking during one news story about how much she liked living with us. Abe shouted for her to shut up, told her she was not to talk during the news, and said he had had enough.

Abe wanted me to contact my coworker, who had originally approached us about fostering her. He was ready to send her back to live with the minister and his wife. Well, not him personally.

He said it was my responsibility since I was the one who originally suggested the plan. I took care of it, but the entire episode embarrassed and saddened me. Nancy was a very troubled girl, and I am sorry I failed to help find justice for her.

Visit Sparks a Decision

In the spring of 1970, I rode to Kansas with Aunt Charlene and Uncle Bob, who lived in Kingsport, Tennessee. Charlene's miniature poodle, Gigi, was a drama queen. She was apricot-colored and spoiled rotten. Charlene and I fanned that dog most of the way to Kansas to keep her from getting overheated. Bob stopped the car to see why we had started an unstoppable laughing fit.

My brother Mike had just undergone a severe flare-up of Crohn's disease. A talented musician with a degree in business from Bethany College in Lindsborg, Kansas, he had been working in a music store and singing in local nightclubs. He was on the mend.

Mike liked folk music and hoped a move to Virginia would give him a chance to rest and discover more about local and regional styles.

We would be ready to leave for Virginia after Mike and I made sure his 1953 Chevy Bel Air was running well.

Everything but the windshield wipers worked. Dad cautioned us not to drive over 55 miles an hour. The car was running but might not make a long trip if we drove it as if it were a new car. We started our trek back to Virginia with Mike's guitars, amplifying system, and our clothes loaded in the back seat and trunk.

We were about 60 miles west of Little Rock, Arkansas, when we saw a young man by the side of the road. Many young adults hitchhiked when they did not have cars or rides. It was an inexpensive and usually safe way to travel.

I pulled over to see if he needed a ride. He carried a backpack, had shoulder length red hair and a mustache. His T-shirt, branded with the face of Jimi Hendrix, topped his bell-bottomed jeans.

John introduced himself and said he was going to New Orleans to a folk festival. We said we could take him as far as Memphis. He agreed and got into the front seat, because the back was full of musical equipment. He and Mike had a lively discussion about their favorite artists, and I continued as chauffeur. After traveling for an hour or so, our guest asked if we would like to stop and have some smoke.

I knew I was going to be driving, and that I did not tolerate marijuana or hashish well, so I only took in secondhand smoke. It was enough to impress upon me the need to stop for a while.

"I'm getting off at the rest stop," I said. "We can take a break and go to the bathroom."

My two passengers were feeling no pain and were laughing and talking about the images they were experiencing when I encouraged them back into the car.

I turned back onto the road when the sky turned black and a torrent of rain hit the windshield. A two-lane highway is a difficult road to drive—especially when the windshield wipers are not working.

Eighteen-wheelers screamed around us, the lone little '53 Chevy Bel Air going at a top speed of 55 miles an hour. I found a safe place to pull over so that we could wait out the storm, which took about an hour.

When we approached Memphis, our rider reminded us he wanted to catch a ride going south to New Orleans, and although Mike and I were tempted to turn that little Chevy south, we said goodbye and good luck. Mike and I slept in the car at a truck stop in Memphis and were on our way very early the next morning.

The next day was a long one; we traveled from Memphis to Wise, approximately 550 miles, about an 8-hour drive in 2025, but two hours longer at 55 miles per hour. As we approached Wise, I felt a sense of relief, but also a sense of foreboding.

The mountains felt menacing, the foliage alive, and the wind whispered the secrets of the forest dwellers. I reminded myself how easily the blacktop roads sucked up headlights and cut them off right before the never-ending curves.

The 1953 Chevy made it over the 1000 miles without falling apart. I wasn't so sure about the passengers.

To my surprise, an MG Midget was sitting in our driveway. I entered the house, curious to know who was the owner of the new car. Abe and Frank, a friend, were sitting in the kitchen having a beer and laughing about speeding around the curves in the mountains.

I was never sure if Frank was a student or if he had a job in the area. He seemed to have plenty of drugs for his own use and to share.

With disheveled brown hair and clothes in need of a wash, he possessed a wicked sense of humor, often revolving around jokes mocking women's bodies. I was not one of his fans.

Abe had bought a car while I was gone, accompanied by the likely cohort Frank, without telling me. We had never made a major purchase without talking it over together.

I was furious. Abe and Frank just laughed and started teasing me about how I wasn't in charge of everything, just because I was a liberated woman (punctuated with air quotes).

I had made the mistake of telling Abe when Frank was there on another occasion that one of our friends told me I must be liberated because I didn't shave my armpits or legs.

"Since when do we make major purchases without consulting each other?" I asked.

"You weren't here," Abe said.

"Let's talk about it after Frank is gone."

"Whoa, I can take a hint," Frank said, laughing all the way to his car.

Abe and I had a loud discussion about quite a few things. "Why have you made this decision without consulting me?" I asked.

"I don't ask your permission for everything I do," he said.

"I can certainly attest to that. You don't ask my permission for all your extramarital liaisons."

"Whoa, 'extramarital liaisons.' The English major has a few new words."

"Don't change the subject. Why did you do this?"

"I'm not taking it back. You have a car and I have a car, and that's that."

"You kept the station wagon, which is the car you drive to work, and traded in the one I use."

"Yes, I did." He walked outside and got into the car to leave.

I'm glad Mike had gone outside to wander around the house and the neighborhood, because I did not want him to hear this nonsense. I let the car discussion go, because I couldn't do anything about it. Abe talked to Mike for a few minutes and left the house, saying he had an errand.

In any case, we had made it back safely and Mike fit in well with the community of musicians who frequented our home.

Earth Day

April 22 was a beautiful day in Wise, Virginia. The morning air was crisp as I sat on the deck drinking coffee. I felt lucky to live in a house I loved and to have interesting acquaintances. The deck proved to be my peaceful haven, as few people ever used it besides me.

In 1969, the UNESCO Conference in San Francisco accepted peace activist John McConnell's proposal to honor the planet Earth and the concept of peace. They selected March 21, 1970, the first day of spring in the northern hemisphere. UN Secretary General U Thant sanctioned the day and signed a proclamation honoring McConnell.[47]

A month later, US Senator Gaylord Nelson (D-Wisconsin) proposed holding a nation-wide environmental teach-in on April 22, 1970. He hired Denis Hayes, a young activist, to be the National Coordinator. Nelson and Hayes renamed the event "Earth Day." Approximately 20 million people in the United States participated in the first Earth Day.[48]

The Cuyahoga River in Ohio had caught fire several times because industrial oils and chemicals leaked into the river. An oil rig off the coast of Santa Barbara leaked, the population of the bald eagle species was plummeting from the effects of DDT, and whales were hunted to near extinction.[49]

I wondered whether Earth Day would cause a distraction to the fight for civil rights, violence toward demonstrators, and the Vietnam War. Would Earth Day become a diversion from other important social issues?

Abe and I attended the celebration on campus planned by Clinch Valley College students and faculty. Clinch Valley's president gave a brief message about conserving our natural surroundings. Students praised the environmentalists and lamented the slow pace of effecting change.

A professor of chemistry explained that the ozone layer was deteriorating and that the consequences would be dire. The earth's temperature would rise, as would the oceans. The glaciers would melt, and the ecology of the planet would deteriorate.

Someone suggested methods that could stem the tide of global warming. The concrete but difficult solutions included cleaning up potential contaminants in rivers and streams. Eliminating the use of coal and other fossil fuels would have to occur. Corporate interests would not allow this to happen.

Despite the dire warnings, spectators were willing to start immediately working on solutions. I sensed a spirit of hope permeating the crowd. Some of the weariness left me when I helped to organize volunteers to do a roadside cleanup between Wise and Norton.

The serious clean-up of energy production methods looked far into the future.

Later that day, I sat on the deck watching the birds flying over the pond, swooping and racing each other across the pale blue sky. *What's next?*

I lurched back to reality on May 4, as another crushing blow to human rights fell at Kent State University. President Nixon had sent the Ohio National Guard to the university because students were protesting his expansion of the war into Cambodia.

The Guard fatally shot four unarmed students and wounded nine others, marking a tragic event in history.[96]

Across the country, over four million students walked out of class in immediate protest.

Groups of friends gathered once again on the campus to lament the violence caused by the authorities in response to protesters' opposition to the war.

Everyone knew someone who had perished in the war, been involved in a demonstration, evaded the draft by moving to Canada, or engaged in civil rights or union marches.

Earth Day dissolved in a cloud of gunshot smoke.

Waiting for SCOTUS

I awaited the Supreme Court decision in *Norton v. Discipline Committee* while students from various colleges reached out to me. They invited me to speak to their campus organizations about what had happened at ETSU. I accepted invitations from Emory University and Appalachian State University. Students and some faculty members were keen on organizing around issues of free speech, women's rights, and voting.

I conducted teach-ins to explain how to attract indifferent students to the issues.

"Find the injustices on your campus, write and talk about them, contact the ACLU, and explore filing lawsuits on behalf of those wronged," I said. "Confront the college administration by starting your own newspaper. There are ministers and faculty who will help you. Whatever the US Supreme Court says about our case will be important to freedom of speech."

In Denial

President Nixon nominated Warren Burger as Chief Justice of the Supreme Court. The Senate confirmed conservative Burger in June 1969.

ETSU students distributed the two pamphlets in early June 1968. The US District Court heard the case and delivered an opinion while we sat in the courtroom on June 20, 1968. The

Sixth Circuit Court of Appeals delivered an opinion with one dissent without hearing the case in November 1969.

On June 22, 1970, one month after I turned 27 years old, the eight-person Supreme Court denied certiorari. Denial meant the Court refused to hear the case, and that the original judgment in June 1968 in the District Court in Nashville would stand.

Supreme Court Justices Thurgood Marshall, William O. Douglas, and William J. Brennan agreed to hear the case, but certiorari required four justices. President Richard Nixon did not nominate a ninth justice until 1971, when he appointed William Rehnquist. After much debate, the Senate confirmed Rehnquist in 1972.

Justice Marshall wrote a dissent from the denial. Appendix B contains the full quotation. Marshall summarized the reasons for our suspensions, noting the publication and distribution of "false, seditious, and inflammatory materials and attempting to incite to riot."

Marshall said no charges were brought against us as to the propriety of time, place, or manner of distribution. The administration focused solely on the content of the pamphlet.

Further, he stated that there was no evidence that the pamphlets caused a disturbance or any danger that they would. He compared the pamphlets to historical broadsides, which were far cruder and intended to incite violence, concluding our broadsides paled in comparison.

Colleges should be able to distinguish rioting and fires from peaceful protest, as should the public at large. Marshall concluded, "Our system promises to college students as to everyone else that they may have their say, and when it breaks that promise it gives aid and comfort to those who say that it is a sham."[50]

The Law Is an Ass

There was no other legal recourse for us. We had exhausted all avenues of justice. I believed common sense would win the day, but I was wrong. Numb to the core, I reread the transcript of the District Court proceedings, looking for mistakes in the testimony. Nothing. What do we do now? We did not cause a riot. No one got hurt. *What do you do when the US Supreme Court makes a mistake?*

Was it a mistake? Or did I just become a citizen with all the rights accorded to other citizens, now that I was no longer a student?

Many activist groups invited me to talk about organizational strategies, First Amendment battles, or human rights. I was free to fill these requests in the evenings and on weekends, and I was ready.

But Abe filled several of the requests. He asserted that his status as a professor of political science qualified him. He asserted the case had evolved from his classes and his stance on the flag-burning issue.

He said he would use the information he exchanged with audiences to enhance his dissertation on constitutional law. He must have been working on it at the Flop House, because I had not seen him working on it at home.

My energy was waning under the weight of my job, taking part in folk gatherings, cooking for students, agonizing over my court appearance, and fighting emotional battles with Abe.

Frustrated students and faculty continued to drop by the house to complain about world affairs, play music, or get high. They did not come because they thought they would find free drugs, but because they thought they could hang out in a safe atmosphere.

One evening, someone brought something that looked like marijuana, and I agreed to try it, as did Abe.

I was sitting on our big, floppy purple couch. Abe and a student were laughing, pointing at each other, and wandering around the house. They joined me on the big floppy. I did not know her. In fact, I'd never seen her before. She had long dark hair and was wearing a T-shirt and jeans. Abe did not introduce us.

Some folks were watching television. I wasn't particularly a fan of *Dark Shadows*, a program about vampires, but someone had turned it on without the sound. People wandered about the house and grounds, singing or talking.

Someone handed me a joint. I took a mini-toke and gave it to Abe. After a few puffs, Abe and his student started to kiss and caress each other. I was still sitting next to Abe.

Then the joint kicked in. The room was closing in on me. Black clouds approached me from both sides. This experience was more unpleasant than the other two times I had tried what I thought was marijuana. I felt frightened and reached out to Abe. He climbed off the couch with his student and walked into our bedroom.

"What are you doing?"

They ignored me.

Can I stand up?

I slowly rose from the couch by moving to my knees. Someone offered a hand and helped me pull myself up. I walked through the house to reorient myself.

I felt agitated and jumpy. Someone wrapped me in their arms and kissed me. I lumbered into the other section of the house, sat on the bed, and in a few minutes, I felt much better.

Eventually, people drifted outside and went away. I did not see Abe's student leave the house, but he was still at home.

"Did you have sex with whatever her name is in our bedroom?"

"Her name is Connie, and yes, I did."

"You mean the woman Mike was dating? That is despicable. You betrayed both of us. What is the matter with you? Does our marriage or your friendship with Mike mean nothing to you?"

"It has nothing to do with our marriage or with Mike. And I changed the sheets."

"I thought we made promises to be faithful to each other."

"I am not your property. You cannot control my behavior."

"Nor am I yours, to be treated with contempt, humiliated, and betrayed. Do you think this kind of shit has no impact on me? What would you do if I behaved this way?"

"I wouldn't like it. I think if you had sex with someone else, it would mean more to you than it does to me."

"Jesus, Abe. Are you going to keep seeing Connie?"

"Next weekend we are going to Appalachian State so she can check out the graduate school program. Richter Moore (former chairman of political science at ETSU) is the chairperson, and he told me we could stay with him."

"Are you going to sleep together?"

"More than likely, yes."

"You really are disgusting. I don't understand why you do this."

"I guess I am entitled. No one ever objects but you."

Betrayed and sad, I couldn't bring myself to say anything. I stood frozen.

Why don't I pack a bag and leave? I really don't care anymore.

I felt trapped.

When Abe and Connie returned from their trip, I wanted to talk to him about it. He said he didn't want to talk about the weekend other than to say that some things went well and others did not.

I never saw this student again, and we never discussed her again. I suspected she had rejected him. Served him right.

9. CHANGING PATHS

What Now?

Students and faculty continued to hang out at our house. Many conversations revolved around academia. Abe liked to talk about the "publish or perish" dilemma circulating in some universities.

"There's little respect for teaching. Administrators expect staff to publish every year. Is this a reflection of the real world or the ivory tower?" He asked.

Because I thought he was still working on his dissertation, these comments surprised me. I continued encouraging him to finish his degree program.

"What about your dissertation?" I asked.

"Haven't you heard my comments about the artificiality of academia?"

"Yes, many teachers want only to teach and not have to publish. Wouldn't you feel a sense of accomplishment if you finished your PhD?"

"I don't think that is the solution for me. Out of the ivory tower and into the forum, where intellectuals of all kinds can gather to discuss issues, is where I want to be."

"Ah, yes, the philosopher kings' forum," I said.

He wanted to establish a salon—an assemblage of notable literary figures, artists, or statesmen, held by custom at the home of a prominent person.[1]

We already had a salon of sorts at our home. But he had frequently talked about the grand life of the philosopher kings. Plato first introduced the idea of philosopher kings in his book, *The Republic*, where he asserted philosophers should lead the ideal government.

In Plato's community, philosopher kings created government through salons. Abe saw himself as a potential philosopher king.

"So, you don your toga and all you need then is a group of women to wait on you and obey your orders?"

"That would be nice."

I laughed it off. I thought he was kidding.

When my parents visited us in Wise, Abe must have voiced his disillusionment with academia, because Dad started talking to us about an opportunity in Kansas that would constitute a big change.

A small town in western Kansas had lost its grocery store. Dad was excited about the prospect of someone in our family owning a grocery store, but also hoped we would all move back to Kansas.

I still enjoyed working at the educational cooperative, but was very unhappy with my relationship with Abe. Gatherings at our home consisted of card playing with faculty members, eating, drinking, and feeding students who came and went at will.

Abe epitomized the words to a song by Steven Stills: "If you can't be with the one you love, love the one you're with."

One thing was wrong with that philosophy. He was supposedly with the one he loved—me.

One afternoon, friends invited us to their home to meet a niece who was visiting. They had a bidet installed in their bathroom and insisted everyone try it out.

Abe was Johnny-on-the-spot, so to speak, to use the bidet. After his bathroom experience, I recall seeing him follow the niece downstairs, presumably to see her living quarters. When they came upstairs, she looked awkward, even sheepish.

Sometime later, Abe revealed to me that Helen's niece had given him a blowjob that day.

"What in the world were you thinking?" I asked.

"I don't know."

I surmised the bidet aroused him. The two of them had met for the first time that day.

What kind of person does this?

About three weeks after the bidet incident, we went to a faculty member's home nearby to drink and play cards. We drove because it was snowing. When I was ready to go home, I looked around for Abe and finally found him, lying head to toe with another woman I knew well. They were clothed, eyes shut, but Abe was stroking her nipple.

"Abe, for chrissake, what the hell? I'm going home. Find your own way."

I left without him and was sitting at the kitchen table when he came in.

"Jesus, Abe, what is the matter with you?"

"We were tired of the card game and found a place to relax."

"And with someone who is my very good friend."

"It was nothing."

The tension in our home thickened. Maybe it was time to walk away.

How can this be accomplished? Most of our friends will sympathize with Abe. What options do I have for housing until I work things out? Abe won't leave the house because he doesn't think he is at fault. He will have no incentive to move. I could go to Kansas to work on opening the grocery store. Staying in Virginia to find a graduate school is not an option. Leaving Appalachia will undoubtedly make me feel better. Bad associations haunt me here, as well as the spirits and witches.

———————

I began talking to Dad and Mike about opening a store. Abe was debating with himself about his role, but finally decided he would finish the semester at Clinch Valley and learn meat cutting by working at the Piggly Wiggly grocery in nearby Norton.

I quit my job and was hanging on, but barely.

Mike and I returned to Kansas and, with Dad's help, we mapped out a plan. We shopped for equipment, visited with bankers, and contacted grocery distributors. Mike, Dad, and I did the financial, infrastructure, supplier, and equipment work.

Abe finished his last semester of teaching. With the help of local students, he found a meat market where he learned how to break down a side of beef. He sold our house for a nice profit, and with the aid of some students, he moved to Kansas.

The store will eventually become Abe's, I thought. Mike and I named the store "Abe's AG," despite his limited role in setting up the store for the opening. Associated Grocers (AG), with a warehouse in Wichita, agreed to supply groceries, meat, produce, and expertise to the store.

Maybe I should file for divorce now. But we are so far into this; I'm going to hang in here to see how things shape up. Cursed with optimism again, but feeling very much separated from Abe.

I was solving problems, having some success with plans for the store, and spending time with Mike and Dad. We found much to laugh about as we discovered how much we did not know.

Change activates possibilities. Sometimes, one change is the catalyst for a world of adjustments. On the advice of a physician, I stopped taking the birth control pills I had been taking for nearly 12 years.

After I had returned to Kansas, Abe's physician called to secure my consent for Abe to undergo a vasectomy.

We had discussed the procedure before I left Virginia, but I did not think we had decided. However, I thought if he didn't want children and I was pretty sure I did not, it would be senseless for me to insist he should have consulted me. Now I had to decide whether I wanted to return to pills or just wait and see how our relationship evolved.

Children should enter the world to a peaceful family situation where parents are not at odds with each other.

Onward into the Abyss

The stark contrast between Virginia and western Kansas was stunning. The lush greenery stayed in Virginia with the snake handlers, witches, and coal mines.

I could see the horizon.

I found myself back in the land of tumbleweeds, flat land, waving wheat, and wide-open spaces. And yes, the rolling hills, grazing cattle, hail, and tornadoes. I wasn't ready for tornadoes, but everything else was pleasantly familiar.

What about a whirlwind of new people invading the town of Ransom, Kansas? Could the new grocers win over the people of this small town? Would they accept an academic, a leftist, and a musician as their new grocers?

The former store owner had vacated his building and wanted us to buy it. It was a cavernous, dirty structure. Mike, Dad, the banker, and I looked at the building, but as soon as I stepped inside, I wished I hadn't. Rundown fixtures, broken shelving, and uneven, grimy wood floors turned my stomach.

Sixteen-foot-high ceilings, chipped paint and plaster, and broken sheetrock greeted us. I could see the electricity and heating bills skyrocketing. The building would cost too much to renovate. We asked the banker about alternative sites.

The local bank had built a new building, and the old bank building stood vacant. The building looked small for a grocery store, but on the advice of the banker and the consultant from Associated Grocers, Mike and I decided the bank building was the best option.

We could start small, get a foothold, and expand when the store succeeded. Abe's AG started fresh in a small building with clean fixtures, fresh paint, and enthusiastic owners.

The vault of the former bank became the meat cooler after we insulated the interior with wipeable Styrofoam panels. Fred, a local carpenter, built a check stand and created a meat cutting station closed off to customers. Dad found a large butcher block table, and we installed it in the center of the cutting area close to the walk-in cooler.

Mike and Dad found a used service meat case to display chicken, beef, ham, pork, and deli items. I found a produce display case with sliding glass doors.

Fred also built a display rack for potatoes, onions, and bananas, and we purchased shelving for dry groceries from Associated Grocers. Soon we would be open for business.

So, here we are in Ransom, Kansas, population 450, four or five churches, 24 dogs, one Co-op service station and grain elevator, and one police officer. Residents were eager to see the new store and its owners in action.

Insurance salesmen magically appeared from Ransom, Ness City, and McCracken to convince us they had the best coverage for the store and a residence, if we could find one. The owner of the insurance agency in Ransom found us a house—no mean feat in a town of this size.

Mike and I rented a small house until Abe arrived. Then we bought the two-bedroom place the local insurance salesman found. Mike, Abe, and I shared this house until Mike married a local girl and moved into a mobile home in town.

Abe's AG had a soft opening to check everything out, and then a grand opening two weeks later.

Associated Grocers supplied décor paraphernalia for the meat case and produce cases and hung balloons outside the store. Dad convinced Ray, the Keebler salesman, to have drop shipments sent to the store. Mike became a fantastic cookie salesman, claiming he had placed a bag of cookies in the hands of every person who entered the store.

Abe and Mike prepared the service meat case, which involved breaking down a side of beef to create roasts, tenderloin steaks, hamburger, and other cuts. They made pork chops, pork cutlets, and ham steaks. They cut up chickens for display and on demand.

Lunch meats such as ham, bologna, liver loaf, turkey, and scrapple were favorites among customers. I declined to try the scrapple, also known as head cheese, because the product contained parts of the animal head. We added Longhorn, Swiss, and pimento cheeses, pickled pigs' feet, beef jerky and pickled eggs.

Mike also stocked shelves, bagged potatoes, and arranged onions and bananas.

I oversaw ordering everything, processing wet produce, and cashiering. Associated Grocers called me once a week and I placed an order, which they delivered a few days later. When the truck came in, the townspeople gathered to watch the unloading. I hired local high school students to help unload the truck.

One student was Nolan Cromwell, whose father worked at the Ransom Co-op. Nolan was a star high school athlete with a gentle demeanor. When he spoke, his high-pitched voice stood in contradiction to his well-toned, athletic body. I tried to make him laugh a time or two, but he was very timid.

After graduation, Cromwell went on to Kansas University and earned the honor of All-American for his athletic prowess in football. The Los Angeles Rams drafted him, where he played for 10 years.

I continued to order groceries and produce, prep produce, and serve as cashier. It didn't take long before I could hoist a 100-pound bag of potatoes onto my shoulder and carry it to the display rack. I bagged them in fives and tens and left the remainder in the open gunny sack for those who wanted fewer than five or ten pounds.

The store operated smoothly, and townspeople liked our new, clean store, despite the limited number of brand choices.

———————

The Ransom High School principal's wife was a frequent shopper. I told her I had been working toward an advanced degree in English. Not long after that conversation, she and her husband asked me if I would direct a high school play.

I thought about it for about a week and decided it might be fun. I would have to rehearse in the evenings after working all day. It was a challenge—first to select a play that would work. I picked Kurt Vonnegut's *Welcome to the Monkey House*.

In 1970, Christopher Sergel adapted 25 Vonnegut short stories to create the play, complete with satire and messages on human nature, with Vonnegut's edge. I was pretty sure I had lost my mind.

Once I had selected the cast and blocked the play, I had my doubts about whether every cast member was up to the challenge. I stopped rehearsals frequently to explain the text. After several rehearsals, however, I was pleasantly surprised that cast members had been studying and were getting into the swing of things.

One evening, I became very frustrated when the cast didn't want to pay attention. Word of the tirade I performed, complete with curse words, didn't take long to get back to the principal. And then to me. I apologized to the cast, and they agreed we all needed a break from rehearsing.

I found some volleyballs in the gym, and after tossing them around and acting silly, everyone settled down. After the next rehearsal, everyone decided we were ready for the big time.

On opening night, the cast performed well and got four curtain calls, giving me a renewed feeling of accomplishment and pride for the students.

New Faces, Strange Places

We had opened the store in the summer of 1972. The presidential election of 1972 revealed a right-wing streak in the Ransom citizenry. Customers felt free to express their own opinions in the store, but I felt uneasy about initiating discussions about politics. I was not looking for another fight.

I had disclosed my preferences to the wife of the high school principal on one occasion in the store, and she fiercely defended President Richard Nixon. I got on my high horse and told her that her position would come back to haunt her.

One might guess that between George McGovern and Richard Nixon, most Ransom residents would favor Nixon. After the election, I found that Mike, Abe, two others, and I were the only ones in the county to have voted for McGovern.

The Capitol Hill police had already arrested five men for breaking into the headquarters of the Democratic committee in Washington, D.C., at the Watergate complex.

Nixon won a second term, even though the press had expressed suspicion about the involvement of two former White House aides in the break-in. The Nixon administration denied any involvement.[2] Less than two years later, Nixon resigned under threat of impeachment after the US Supreme

Court ordered Nixon to turn over White House tapes of conversations relevant to the break-in.[3]

The high school principal's wife Vera was in the store one day, and I approached her. "I wonder how Pat Nixon feels now that her husband has been disgraced," I said.

"I'm sure she is as embarrassed as I am by his behavior. He let the possession of power overtake his better judgment. Haldeman and Ehrlichman gave him rotten advice."

The outcome did not surprise Abe and me. Some Ransom residents believed Nixon was set up, but I found a few who thought he was a crook.

One of them was a woman who had studied to become a reflexologist. She charged $20 an hour for a treatment. I scheduled an appointment as often as I could. Some of my aches and pains diminished, and I enjoyed her earthy humor.

"You should stop lifting 100-pound bags of potatoes and get into bed more often. You'll never get pregnant otherwise," Grace said. She nagged me about having a child and said she was working on Abe, too. I did not want to discuss my sex life or family planning issues and did not respond to these comments.

I found it easy in those days to ignore many things that bothered me. Grace was the least of my problems, and I let her comments go in one ear and out the other.

One day, a local man named Marvin blew into the store, his hair flying and his clothes unkempt. He packed a cart full of groceries, produce, and meat and put everything on the counter for me to check out. I checked and bagged everything and gave him the receipt.

"I don't have any money. I'll have to pay you later. The guy who owned the other store used to let us charge groceries, and then collect at the end of the month."

"It's hard to pay for food after it is gone. You can't see what you bought. We said when we started this business, we would not be charging groceries. We're just getting started here."

No one else ever asked for credit, but I helped someone who really needed help. When the wiring in an older couple's home started a fire, I took them groceries while they were having repairs made on their home.

Fern, a single woman who was a regular customer, came into the store while I was checking out another customer. She looked up at the ceiling, threw up her hands and said she needed to see me.

"There are a lot of vampires trying to get into my house," she said.

"Would you like some help?" I asked.

"Yes, come with me."

We walked to her house and went inside. She pointed to the back window of the mobile home. "There are only five there now. There were a lot more."

"You have scared them away by getting help," I said.

"Now they are trying to get in."

I knew I was not qualified to help her, so I called the local physician, who was her brother. He said she likely was having delusions brought on by diabetes and asked me to stay with her until he could get there.

We three grocers were cultivating new ventures.

Mike had been dating a local girl, and they were planning a wedding. He left the grocery business to work on his wife's family farm. His in-laws were wheat farmers, as were the extended family members.

Mike and Abe came upon a scheme to invest in a car leasing business. It required a $5,000 investment (about $37,000 in 2025 dollars) and a commitment to lease a quota of cars each quarter.

I thought the difficulty of leasing even one car in a small town in western Kansas would be off the charts. Despite my opposition, they both invested anyway. The deal fell through, and we lost our investment. I was very unhappy and full of recriminations toward Abe.

Within a year, Mike and his wife moved to Hays, where he earned a real estate broker's license and began selling real estate in Ellis County.

The leasing con job eventually resulted in a lawsuit against the company. Mike traveled to Chicago to testify about the nefarious dealings of the imaginary leasing company, but the original investment was not recovered.

What interested me was that a local farmer had built a prototype of a lawnmower with a zero turning radius. He and other local men raised money to support the manufacture of the Marty J mower. I invested $500 in the venture.

The principals leased a building to manufacture the product and created an assembly process. They hired local people to replicate and assemble the parts.

Many local people, as well as some of our relatives, invested in the company. The company held its own for several years.

The original inventor also created an industrial mower. The company hired a professional sales rep, and he sold several industrial mowers to the US Navy. This new model was the most successful piece of equipment, mainly because competition in the small mower market was fierce and well established.

Eighteen years later, two employees of the company bought the stock and inventory and dissolved the company. I invested $500 and got back $5,000.

After Mike left the store, we needed to hire another person to complete dressing the meat case every day. Lulu had worked at the previous store and agreed to come to work for us. Her experience cutting meat and her acquaintance with vendors were invaluable to the operation of the store. Customers liked her, and she had a warm sense of humor.

Lulu put her hands in mine and said, "Here, feel this."

I complied. "Your hands are so soft," I said.

"Years of handling raw meat, especially pork, did that for me. I'm happy to go back to work."

If You Can't Stand the Heat

In 1974, after Abe's AG experienced two years of successful sales in the grocery business, a fire destroyed the town's only restaurant. Abe, the bank, and I decided to build a new store building and a new restaurant building, staff both, and manage both. We selected metal buildings and a local contractor.

We planned to open our own Alice's Restaurant, in homage to Arlo Guthrie and the song he wrote and sang in 1967. The thought of Alice's brightened my spirits until the construction of the restaurant began.

I still have nightmares about the restaurant building process. I opposed several of the decisions about interior building materials for both buildings, even though I understood that cost was a big factor.

We blew cellulose insulation onto the ceilings and walls of both buildings. It absorbed the sound well, but I thought it looked creepy. Others involved in the decision thought it was acceptable because it was different and a conversation starter. A large AG store in Wichita had installed the same insulation, and it allegedly raked in the dough.

Paul, our Associated Grocers representative, visited Ransom often during the planning process. I wanted to add something exciting that would distinguish us from the AG store in Ness City, 15 miles away. After brainstorming, we decided on what Paul called a bake-off.

The bake-off concept was a modified version of a full bakery. The process involved proofing dough before baking, shortening the turnaround time for the final product. One person could operate the bakery part time, and the aroma of baked bread would greet customers as they walked into the store.

I was so excited I drove to Hays and bought a new camera to create a record of our accomplishment. Finally, a replacement for the one the policeman took from me in 1965, nine years earlier!

Figure 33. Nine years after the police confiscated my camera in Selma, Alabama, I replaced it with a 35mm Canon, 1974.

The bakery would be the only one in the region. The store build went well. Customers complimented the variety of selections, display capacity, and the electronic cash registers. Business increased.

We agreed I would manage the store and, when possible, help in the restaurant on Sundays.

The same contractor who built the grocery store also tackled the restaurant. He and his crew assembled the steel structure and blew in the insulation. Salina Coffee House laid out a kitchen to our specifications.

Two days after the contractor poured the concrete floor, Abe was ready for the tile flooring to be installed.

I took a break from the store to see how things were going. When I walked into the restaurant, the workers had finished sticking down the tile, but it was buckling. I called the contractor, who was not to be found. Abe was upset that I had "taken over" his restaurant project.

A few residents had warned us about hiring this contractor because he had a drinking problem. At the time we hired him, he assured us he was sober and had been for a long time.

"I thought we agreed to take a chance on him. I'll take care of it," Abe said.

"Okay, go find him. This floor is awful."

"Let's wait until tomorrow. It might settle down. We have advertised a Sunday dinner special, and I want to follow through."

"Surely, you won't open."

"I have everybody lined up."

"It's all yours," I said. I returned to the store, went up into the loft and sat at my desk, shaking my head.

Abe found the contractor drunk at his home.

Alice's Restaurant opened, wavy flooring greeting customers. The tile had developed pockets of moist air because the concrete had not cured long enough. I was embarrassed to tears. Servers tried to wait on people while walking on a wavy floor; I vowed we would not open again until we fixed the floor.

I asked the contractor to distribute color chips on the concrete after it dried completely and then to seal the floor. It took another two weeks to complete the project.

The coffee drinkers loved coming to Alice's restaurant. They lined up outside the restaurant door in their overalls, feed company caps, work boots, and tan work shirts and jeans.

Some of them ate breakfast and left to go to work. Most paid for a cup of coffee and stayed for free seconds and thirds on coffee and gossip. They rarely ate anything until the grocery store bakery sent over cinnamon rolls.

At first, their constant demands for service bothered me, even though the restaurant industry is a service business. However, the employees enjoyed working there, and I didn't have to.

I took pride in the store. Each day I prepped the produce and arranged it for display—iceberg lettuce, tomatoes, celery, carrots, lemons, apples, potatoes, turnips, parsley, onions. Seasonal fruits completed the display.

I stocked shelves and managed one of the cash registers. We installed two cash register stands and hired a recent high school graduate to stock shelves and act as cashier.

Figure 34. The new grocery store building in Ransom, 1974.

"I want you to learn to prep and display the produce, too," I said.

"Aw, that's women's work," Randy said.

"If you work here, you will learn as much about the business as you can."

He soon realized the work took stamina, and took pride in his work.

I had laid out the store so that the bakery sat next to the meat market in the rear of the store. A part-time employee could handle the bakery. I planned to sell the bread, rolls, buns, and other specialties in the store and to the restaurant.

I hired Lisa, a woman who had worked at the drugstore, to staff the bakery. She started early in the evening to set up. The next morning, she baked the proofed bread, cinnamon rolls, dinner rolls, breadsticks, and hamburger buns. Every week or so, she baked whole wheat and cheese bread. She wrapped each variety and arranged them in the display case.

Is there an aroma more enticing than freshly baked bread?

Lisa was an amiable person with a quick smile and personal experience baking for her family. She enjoyed the bakery but wanted to move to the restaurant and work as a server.

Another local woman, Candy, expressed an interest in managing the bakery. She, too, had worked in the drugstore. I knew she was personable and capable, so I hired her.

The bakery and meat market departments sat side by side. Most of the staples people purchased were displayed on racks around the perimeter of the store. The two perimeter stops made a handsome display, smelled good, and always looked appetizing and clean.

When I wasn't working produce or waiting on customers, I handled administrative tasks in the store's loft. I could see the entire store.

Abe broke down sides of beef, made hamburger, cut chops and roasts, displayed whole and cutup chickens, and dressed the meat case. Candy took to the bakery job well, and she and Abe laughed and entertained customers who were waiting for their orders. Everyone enjoyed the camaraderie and showmanship and complimented us on the features of the new store.

Everything was working well, and I felt more optimistic about life than I had in quite some time. At the end of a day, I was tired but gratified.

As time went on, Abe and Candy often disappeared from their posts into the back room, which was out of sight of shoppers. I could not see them from the office loft, so I walked to the back room to talk to them.

"Hey, you guys. I've had customers ask if we had lost our bakery and meat market workers," I said.

"I don't think we need to be out there all the time. We have things to do in the back room, " Abe said.

"I'll get one of those bells to set on the meat case for customers to ring to let you know they are here," I said.

After I placed the bell on the display case, another customer complained. Abe finally admitted he had been listening to Candy's stories about how unhappy she was in her marriage.

"Oh, gee, are you 'counseling' her? Or are you having a little 'thing' with her?"

"Uh, you could say that."

Should I fire both of them? They were both at fault.

I stewed about it for a couple of weeks until a customer told me she had waited for several minutes for them to emerge from the back room. I had been busy in the office with a vendor and missed the event.

I reluctantly fired Candy, even though it went against my principles, since I should have fired both. She was furious.

I felt terrible. Abe was more than likely the instigator, and I wasn't ready to dismiss him. Holding two conflicting values was uncomfortable, to say the least.

Three women applied for the bakery job. An acquaintance from Ness City was the best applicant. She was smart and capable of handling the work. And she needed the job. She was pregnant and unmarried. She expressed her gratitude and did her job better than Candy had. In later years, she graduated from law school and moved to Wichita to practice.

Abe and I diverted our attention from work and personal issues by cooking dinner for friends or going to the American Legion when it was open to everyone. I made a dress to attend a New Year's Eve party. I found a remnant of fabric I thought would make a long, fancy dress. Purple flowers with green leaves peppered the silver background. I did not have a pattern, but I had a sewing machine.

I lay down on butcher paper and had Abe trace around my 118-pound shape to create a pattern.

I pinned the pattern to the fabric, cut out two pieces, and sewed the whole thing up. We had a good laugh, something we had not done in a long time.

It worked. It felt good on my body, and it was cheap!

Abe donned a suit for the occasion. He and I walked into the American Legion arm in arm. Two people were dancing on the well-polished oak floor, strewn with corn meal. Other folks, mostly men, were standing at the bar or sitting at tables.

Three or four women wandered in from another room to check out the new arrivals.

We attracted some attention, mainly because no one had seen us dressed in anything but jeans, casual tops, and aprons.

Abe and I cruised the room, facetiously introducing ourselves, as though we were newcomers. In fact, we were newcomers to the American Legion. Our silliness broke the ice as people got a chuckle out of our performance.

A young single man, Patrick, asked me to dance. He surprised me, but I smiled and took his hand. Abe did not like to dance. A sense of guilt crept up on me.

Then it hit me. Why should I feel guilty? I was having a good time and wasn't embarrassing myself or anyone else. When Abe was ready to go home, I balked. I wasn't ready to leave.

"You can find a ride home, if you want to stay," he said.

I decided to go home with him.

"Did you have a good time tonight?" I asked.

"Not particularly, but I got to talk to Martha, Patrick's girlfriend."

"She seems nice."

"She is, but she was a little put out because you were dancing with Patrick."

"I doubt that. You know she has nothing to worry about."

"Good."

We rarely left town; mostly we worked, went home, ate dinner, and went to bed. Hays had the nearest movie theater, 50 miles away.

If we wanted entertainment, we had to create it. The son of one of our employees, two or three years out of high school, asked us at some point if we wanted to get high. Abe was willing, thinking it might relieve some of the stress in his life. We discovered there were several other people in Ransom who smoked weed.

Occasionally, Dad came out to the store to visit. He enjoyed the customers and usually had excellent suggestions for improvement in the store. His congenial interaction with customers lifted my spirits as well as theirs.

One of his visits coincided with my bowling team's night. Dad had run out of cigarettes and was debating about getting some or quitting. I had four cigarettes, but usually smoked about two packs a day.

We decided to split the cigarettes, and when they were gone, we would stop smoking altogether. Dad proposed a bet. Whoever restarted first would owe the other one $50 if a startup occurred in the first week. Cigarettes cost $.35 a pack, compared to about $8.00 today.

After the first week, the cost to smoke again would be $.70 a day from the day we quit. Neither one of us wanted to give in to the other one. The bet worked. We both quit. I felt a good deal healthier; Abe declined the challenge.

My start-up contributions to the store and restaurant gave me a sense of accomplishment, but I found day-to-day operations boring. I wanted a creative challenge, but I wasn't sure what that would entail. I contemplated graduate school, moving to a larger city, and looking for different employment.

About a month later, Abe and I had a party at our house. Those attending were Mike's sister-in-law and her husband, the insurance salesperson and his wife, a couple of single friends, and two other couples.

Patrick lingered after others had gone home. He was the man who had asked me to dance at the New Year's party. A handsome young man with long black hair and a blue-collar hippie vibe, he gently took my arm and pulled me close. "I saw your husband make passes at two women tonight. One of them was my girlfriend," he said.

"Yeah, I know. He's done it before. He claims it's just teasing. Tell him you disapprove and tell your girlfriend to make it clear he's out of line."

Good grief, I had apologized for Abe once again. The man left the house and I went to bed. When I went to bed, Abe accused me of making out with Patrick. I told him how ridiculous the accusation was and confronted him about what the young man had told me. He didn't comment on the accusation.

"I know you were making love to him. I heard you."

"What a crock. You're transferring your own behavior to me, and I don't like it."

Tension grew and took its toll. My body ached. I felt weak and sad but recovered my ability to go to work, thanks to the Anderson work ethic.

I was fed up. The next day, I told Abe I was taking some time off. I left Ransom. A friend helped me find a temporary place to stay away from Ransom. I scrounged a few pieces of furniture and accepted a job with my friend's husband Bobby, a CPA.

———————

Accounting was a bit like German to me: a foreign language. Bobby wanted me to enter numbers in ledgers and add columns. I didn't know how to use his mechanical adding machine very well because I had become used to our electronic cash registers. I was better at doing arithmetic in my head. It didn't take long for me to confirm that bookkeeping would never be my dream job.

After about a month, Abe contacted me to say he wanted to get together. We convened in Russell to talk.

When we met, I explained my feelings of betrayal, of being gaslighted, and my ambivalence toward the store and restaurant.

"I want to do something creative and intellectual. Everything is up and running, but I am bored by day-to-day maintenance. And I'm tired of your acts of betrayal."

I did not feel appreciated by the customers who constantly demanded service after hours or threatened to take their business elsewhere. There were two people I could consider friends.

I wanted to sell the store and restaurant and move to a larger city. He wanted to keep everything the same, but said he would try to be "good."

We were sitting in his car. I opened the door to get out. Abe gasped for air, crying, and convulsing with what I took to be grief. I couldn't take it. I gave in and returned with him to the store and restaurant.

"I don't want to lose you. We have worked so hard to get two businesses up and running. Let's not give up everything," he said.

I believed he was ashamed and would try to work things out. I returned to our home. We talked about having children. I suggested that having children was a horrible reason for two people to stay together. But he had a physician reverse his vasectomy.

I was 32 years old. The doctor evaluated Abe's sperm. It was viable, but low in number. Despite the challenges, we kept trying to make everything work.

Even with my frequent headaches and general malaise, we had some of the same people to the house for dinner. After dinner, people were milling around the house, getting drinks, playing games, and listening to music.

One woman pulled me aside to tell me that Abe had made a pass at her. She had also told her husband, who was a burly man with a big temper.

The husband approached me, looking for Abe.

"Where is that sonofabitch husband of yours? I need to talk to him. He has violated my wife."

"How did he do that? Have you talked to him?"

"No, but I am going to hurt him for what he did."

"Let's go outside. Maybe he is out in the yard."

"I am going to whip his ass."

"Wow, how would that look if you beat up someone half your size? Go home or go blow off some steam where you won't hurt someone."

"Why don't you come with me? I could really make you happy."

"You're as bad as Abe. Go home."

Everyone finally left our house, and Abe came back inside.

"Where were you? I saved your ass one more time. Kyle was ready to take you out."

"I was outside talking to Lisa."

"Kyle told me you made a pass at Gwen."

"Yeah, I kissed her. She had no objections."

"Why do you do this?"

"I don't know. She was willing."

"How do you think that makes me feel?"

"I can't control your feelings. Only you can do that."

Pounding headaches interfered with my work. I checked out groceries but forgot to bag them. I added columns of numbers incorrectly and forgot to lock the store one day after I closed.

Figure 35. Abe and I share a ridiculous moment when I tell him I will take my tambourine to the streets to earn money so I can leave Ransom, Kansas, 1975.

Finally, I visited the local doc. I told him I was experiencing terrible headaches and disorientation. He prescribed a powerful drug, whose name I don't remember. It made me feel worse. I felt as though I were a shadow living outside my body, like I thought a zombie might feel—suspended in a nowhere state of being.

One Sunday, I was still in bed when both Abe and Lisa, restaurant employee and friend, came into the bedroom. Both sat on the bed to tell me they were afraid their relationship was becoming too close. They wanted to tell me they recognized potential problems with their feelings and wanted to let me know they would do nothing about it out of respect for me.

Demeaning? Patronizing? Condescending? How about eat shit and die!

Seething with anger, I said, "Well, gee, thanks so much for telling me. What in the hell is the matter with you people?"

They looked at each other and shook their heads in disbelief at my reaction.

My God, We Left Town!

One Friday morning, when we were both working in the store, the phone rang.

"Harold is on the phone," Abe said.

"Harold who?" I asked.

"Our old debate coach, and his wife Kitty."

I got on the other phone.

"What in the hell are you doing in Ransom, Kansas?" Harold asked.

"Selling groceries, what do you think?" Abe said.

"Come to Topeka. Kitty is here. Stay overnight at least."

We both thought it would be interesting to visit our old debate coach and his wife, so we turned the store and restaurant over to employees.

When we reached their home, we learned they were in the middle of a divorce. Both showed up so that we could all visit together. Tension was very much the order of the day, as we all revealed our unhappiness with our current situations.

Harold had not been faithful to Kitty. I knew that. I thought it might be an opportunity to talk to her about how she was handling her divorce. Abe cornered Kitty, whom he had always had a fondness for, leaving me stranded to fend for myself. Harold had joined Kitty and Abe for a while, and then he stayed in the den to drink.

A pounding headache forced me to calm it with the drug the Ransom doc had given me, but I felt disoriented and on the verge of hyperventilating.

I lay down on the bed and closed my eyes. A few minutes later, I opened them to gray haze. I wasn't sure where I was. My head felt as though it would rise above my body if I didn't hold it on.

My body was somewhere else. I pleaded with Abe to take me to the doctor or the hospital, but he thought I was faking it to keep him from being with Kitty. Anger and panic overwhelmed me. I slept intermittently, not knowing where Abe was.

We left the next day. I continued to feel as though my head might explode. A week passed and I still felt terrible. I scheduled appointments with a gynecologist and a neurologist in Wichita to conduct testing.

After checking into Wesley Hospital, I underwent a successful laparoscopy to address blockages in my Fallopian tubes caused by taking the birth control pill Enovid for 12 years. The doctor suspected a hormone imbalance, and the lab would test the material the tubal insufflation produced.

Next, I met with the neurologist. During our initial consultation, I showed him the drug the Ransom doctor had prescribed and told him how it made me feel. "I feel as though my body is here, but my mind is over there somewhere. This is a very disorienting, scary feeling."

The neurologist told me the drug was used to treat epilepsy.

For God's sake!

The neurologist performed a spinal tap, did an electroencephalogram, and gave me the Minnesota Multiphasic Personality Inventory (MMPI), used to diagnose mental health disorders. The questions were ridiculous. For example, "Do you prefer having sex with a doorknob or cleaning out chicken coops with your bare hands?"

After all this probing, gouging, and sticking, the obstetrician-gynecologist and the neurologist presented their findings to me. They both gave me big hugs and told me I would be fine if I got out of my present surroundings and stopped taking the anti-epilepsy drug.

No more panic attacks, severe headaches, or ill-prescribed drugs. I had already concluded I would leave the marriage, and I was mulling over the logistics. I wanted a divorce. The neurologist prescribed Valium for me, and I believe it was a lifesaver.

Abe had not called to find out the results of the testing, and I wanted to leave the hospital and get on with my life. I was experiencing a massive headache from the spinal tap and didn't have a car.

I called a cousin, who came to pick me up and let me stay at her house for a day or two. Abe joined us a couple of days later. He didn't ask about the results of the testing.

I initiated a conversation about my future. "The store, the restaurant, the town—I want out. It is time for me to create a different life that connects me to interesting people, theater, music, and books."

We spent the next day discussing the divorce. Though we shared a bed that night, the next morning he joined my cousin in her bedroom, where they had sex. Last straw? This wasn't the last straw; it was a whole bale of hay.

Why did I wait so long? I wanted him to change.

We returned to Ransom.

"I want to go to law school or finish my master's degree."

"We don't have any money for you to do that."

"We had money for you to diddle away your PhD."

"That was different. I had a fellowship."

"And I had a job."

"So, what do we do now?"

"There is no more 'we.' I am leaving without you."

It is hard to leave the one you love unless your own well-being is at stake. I had endured enough rejection for a lifetime, and though my heart hurt, I had to leave.

I took a car and left, established residence in Russell, and contacted a lawyer. In the divorce settlement, I asked Abe to pay for the divorce ($400). I wanted the MG Midget. I asked for no furniture and for some of our precious red Dansk bowls.

If Abe sold the store and restaurant, I would receive some of the profit. He agreed, though was reluctant to share the red bowls.

Never had I felt so good. Free of tedium, free of manipulation, free of betrayal. For me, this painful break from a 14-year relationship resulted in my improved health, and at age 32, I was free to choose a career path that challenged my communication skills. Three months later, the divorce was final.

I began to change my frame of reference, to peel off the sticky baggage of disappointment and recapture the inner strength and curiosity to explore the world that characterized my early life.

After working for two years, I enrolled in graduate school and earned a Master of Arts in Communication from Wichita State University 10 years after ETSU suspended us eight students.

As a klutzy child, I experienced cuts and scrapes, learned to distinguish between right and wrong, and defended the marginalized. I learned how to act when I felt something strongly and was not afraid to stand by my belief that everyone has intrinsic worth.

The battles of my youth shaped the woman I became. As a child, I stood up to bullies, defended my friends against racial bias, and as a teen, faced sexual discrimination. I led organizations with creativity and argued my way to victory as a debater. I was happy.

As an adult, I faced a red-baiting teacher, joined a dangerous protest march to support voting rights in Selma, braved the dangers of the coal industry to stand with coal miners, and protested an unjust war by distributing leaflets until the university suspended me from school. I fought this case all the way to the Supreme Court. Even though we lost the case, when I walked into the courtroom, the voices of the silenced walked with me.

10. A Final Word

Each confrontation, each hard-won stand, taught me that silence is too often the accomplice of injustice. Speaking out isn't just a right—it's a responsibility. The fight for justice didn't end with my lawsuit, or even with my generation. It continues—in classrooms, on street corners, in voting booths, and around kitchen tables. And if there's one thing I know, it's this:

Words matter. Use them wisely. Don't lie. Listen.

Authentic communication can ignite action, bringing the disenfranchised and marginalized back into the fold—and sometimes even reaching those hardened by hate. Don't assume you know what your friends, family, or communities think about the issues, your relationships, or the future. Be curious. Ask questions. Listen.

Common ground is forged through truth-telling. Share what you value and ask others what they hold sacred. Then persuade them to act—because the planet, and our future, are on the line.

We must dethrone the demagogues. Restore sanity and science to our frames of reference. These are the most daunting challenges of our time—but not beyond our reach. Together, we can survive. Together, we can bury the ruin sown by greed.

If I could stand up at age 25 with nothing but a voice and a stubborn belief in justice, so can you. So must you. Don't wait for permission. The world is burning, and silence will not save us.

Gather your friends, colleagues, and family. Don the mantle of truth. Sprint joyfully into the wind.

APPENDIX A.

Students Are People Too is the title of two separate pamphlets East Tennessee State University students wrote, published, and distributed in June 1968. Find the text of the pamphlets here, under the subtitles First Piece and Second Piece, which the courts assigned to the pamphlets. The court assigned numbers to paragraphs for the sake of reference during discussions.

STUDENTS ARE PEOPLE TOO (First Piece)
47

It's been a long quarter, hasn't it? And an interesting one too. Too interesting in fact. This has been a quarter wherein the administration spent $94,000 to buy a lousy half-acre of land (rumored to belong to a near relative of a prominent Dean); a quarter wherein the administration has refused an opportunity to advance the school's athletic status (and God knows, it needs it) by rejecting membership in the Southern Conference; a quarter wherein the administration has forbidden girls to wear the latest fashions (the threat of a riot overturned that ruling); a quarter wherein the administration fired some poor student from his job at the library because he grew a beard; a quarter wherein mandatory ROTC has continued unchallenged (the school gets paid so much money per head by the Army, so, son, like it or not there is a price on your head); a quarter wherein the bookstore monopoly has persisted in its blatant piracy (and blew a fortune putting out a propaganda sheet), a quarter wherein the cafeteria fare has progressively worsened; a quarter wherein the administration seriously threatened censorship of the school newspaper (all those filthy pictures); a quarter wherein women's social rules were maintained at a level of liberality that was old when Queen Victoria was young; a quarter wherein the campus law (rent-a-cop) was permitted to continue carrying guns (caution: your local copy is armed and may be dangerous); a quarter where the administration bureaucracy achieved new heights of rudeness, inefficiency, and intolerance. Yes — an interesting quarter.

48

And how has the ETSU student body reacted: Have they precipitated a revolution like French students? No. Have they brought about an entirely new and liberal administration like Polish students?-- No. Have they been the forerunners of a new democratic spirit like Czech students?-- No. Have they seized buildings and raised havoc until they got what they were entitled to like other American students?-- No. What then have the ETSU students done? They have sat upon their rears and let the administration crap upon their heads, thats what.

49

That's right folks, in case you'd not noticed, ETSU students are in the vast majority apathetic-- they open their mouths only to yawn, life their arms only to stretch, and like unto L'il Abner's Smoes, exist only to serve those who would take advantage of them.

50

Well, Smoes, what have you to look forward to next year? Maybe the administration will buy some Dean's turnip patch for ninety grand. Maybe all the girls will be required to wear chastity belts (the keys to be kept on reserve at the library-- check 'em out for an hour at a time). Maybe social hours will be made applicable to males as well as females. Maybe-- Maybe-- Maybe--

51

Maybe students will get some sense and learn that this should cease and that the only way to see that it does is to stand up and fight. Maybe students will learn that the Supreme Court has declared that young people do not sacrifice their citizenship and all rights and privileges therewith by enrolling in a university. Maybe students will learn that no matter what the despots who run this school say, students have the constitutional right to protest, demonstrate, and demand their rights; that women students may not constitutionally be campussed; that students may damned well wear what they want and say what they please. And maybe, just maybe, they will discover that there are student leaders, organizers to rally around so as to assault the bastions of administrative tyranny. Maybe students will learn that at least. And remember that when the time comes to fight for what you are justly entitled to, that if you refuse to come along then you have no justification whatsoever for ever complaining again. When you are called to protest and you sit back on your butt, then, baby, that means that whatever the administration does is OK with you. When we move against them, remember, like the man says, "Put up or shut up."

52

PLEASE SEAL AND STAMP ANY CORRESPONDENCE TO BOX 9527 ETSU

EXHIBIT A-I

53

"STUDENTS ARE PEOPLE TOO"(Second Piece)

54

"Congress must not interfere with freedom of religion, speech or press, assembly, and petition. Congress shall make no law respecting an establishment of religion or prohibiting the free exercise thereof; or abridging the freedom of speech, or of the press; or the people peaceably to assemble, and to petition the government for a redress of grievances." (first amendment, US constitution)

55

These aged words are a reality to most American people. "Students are people too, American people." These are young words that should be a reality. We find the administration at ETSU denying the reality of one group of these words by certain rules, regulations and policies. For our purposes we will put these unjust rules, regulations and policies into two broad categories. The first are those that restrict our personal freedom as "American people." The second being those that deny us the right to openly descent disagree with the first.

56

Even as we write this we are in danger with the school administration. Is this just, denying American people rights that are clearly stated in the first amendment of the constitution? By restricting our personal freedom and denying us the right of open descent about this, the administration of ETSU is saying that we are not "American people,", and to those principles shall this publication be devoted.

57

* * * THE PRESIDENTS DOOR IS ALWAYS OPEN BUT HIS MIND IS CLOSED

Appendix B.

The United States Supreme Court denied certiorari in the case of *Norton v. Discipline Committee of East Tennessee State University* in June 19670. Justice Thurgood Marshall wrote a dissent from the Court's decision. Justices Douglas and Brennan joined in the dissent. The text of the dissent follows.

Justice Thurgood Marshall Dissents

"The petition for a writ of certiorari is denied.

Mr. Justice MARSHALL, with whom Mr. Justice DOUGLAS and Mr. Justice BRENNAN join, dissenting.

Petitioners were suspended as students at East Tennessee State University for distributing leaflets critical of the university administration. They brought an action in federal district court under 42 U.S.C. 1983 seeking reinstatement and expungement of the records of their suspension, claiming that their rights to freedom of speech and procedural due process had been violated. The District Court denied the requested relief after holding a full evidentiary hearing, and the Court of Appeals affirmed, Judge Celebrezze dissenting. 419 F.2d 195 (C.A. 6th Cir. 1969). I would grant certiorari.

The pamphlets involved in this case were published and distributed by students angered by what they regarded as the backward policies of the university administration and the apathy of their fellow students toward these policies. They criticize, often in a crude and sarcastic tone, the positions of the administration on such matters as dress, social regulations, ROTC, campus police behavior, and censorship of the college newspaper. They go on to draw unfavorable comparisons between the response of students at East Tennessee and the response of other students in Czechoslovakia, France, and elsewhere in this country, and call upon students to 'stand up and fight' for their 'constitutional right to protest, demonstrate and demand their rights.'*

Page 399 US 906, 907

No charges were brought against these students that the time, place, or manner of distribution were in any way improper. The sole charge was based squarely on the content of the pamphlets-namely, that they were 'of a false, seditious and inflammatory nature.' There is no evidence that the pamphlets created any disturbance on campus, nor is there any concrete evidence from which one could infer any substantial danger that they would. Rather there is only the conclusory testimony of university officials that the pamphlets 'could conceivably' have caused an eruption, and reference to 'fears that we might have serious consequences.' The only support given to these assertions is the description of an incident in which some 25 students visited the Dean after the pamphlets were circulated and stated that they 'wanted to get rid of this group of agitators.'

It seems to me altogether too late in the constitutional history of this country to argue that individuals can properly be punished for pamphleteering in these circumstances. These pamphlets are similar in some ways to the broadsides circulated by popular writers in England and the Colonies, official suppression of which helped lead to adoption of the First Amendment; to the writings of Republican polemicists, against which the Sedition Act prosecutions were aimed- prosecutions this Court has said violated the First Amendment, New York Times Co. v. Sullivan, 376 US 254, 273-276 (1954); and to leaflets distributed by protesters during the First World War and the 1920's, which evoked the classic opinions of Holmes and Brandeis, since vindicated by history, upon which so much of our law of free speech and the press is based. Abrams v. United States, 250 US 616, 624 (1919) (Holmes, J., dissenting); Gitlow v. New York, 268 US 652, 672 (1925) (Holmes, J., dissenting); Page 399 US 906, 908cf. Whitney v. California, 274 US 357, 373 (1927) (Brandeis, J., concurring).

Indeed many of these older examples of the pamphleteering art were far cruder in tone and more inflammatory in content than the rather mild invocations of student protest before us here. Where such writings are suppressed, they are normally called "'seditious'" and "'inflammatory,'" and legal action against them is justified-as it was here-on the ground that they constitute an "'incitement'" to crime or other disturbance that the offended officials have a right or duty to prevent. But to accept that formula without close examination of the facts would be to submerge the First Amendment altogether, for as Mr. Justice Holmes said, in words that are often quoted but at least as often disregarded, "'[e]very idea is an incitement.'" Gitlow v. New York, supra, 268 US at 673, 45 S. Ct. at 632. On this record, there was nothing approaching incitement of the kind which could constitutionally be punished as extending beyond the realm of speech into that of action. In their own testimony, the university officials demonstrated no more than the sort of "'undifferentiated fear or apprehension of disturbance,'" which, as we held in Tinker v. Des Moines Independent Community School District, 393 US 503, 508 (1969), "'is not enough to overcome the right to freedom of expression'" even in the context of a classroom and as applied to high school rather than college students.

I cannot believe that this Court would hesitate one moment before striking down a criminal conviction based upon these pamphlets, or for that matter a civil judgment, or a prior restraint by injunction or administrative order against their distribution. This case differs in that the distribution took place upon a campus, the authors were college students, and the sanction was suspension from the university. As to the last point, it seems clear that suspension is punishment, and that punishment for speech is "abridgment" in the constitutional sense. Tinker v. Des Moines Independent Community School District, supra. As to the former two points, they do not change the case. "The first amendment applies with full vigor on the campus of a public university." Wright, The

Constitution on the Campus, 22 Vand.L.Rev. 1027, 1037 (1969). Officials of public universities wield the powers of the State, and in my view they are no more free than policemen or prosecutors to punish speech because it is rude or disrespectful, or because it causes in them vague apprehensions, or because for any other reason they do not like its content.

Student protestors are unpopular today, and the activities of some of them fall far outside any plausible construction of the constitutional guarantees of free expression. There is a tendency to lump together the burning of buildings and the peaceful but often unpleasantly sharp expression of discontent. It seems to me most important that the courts should distinguish between the two with particular care in these days, when officials under the pressure of events and public opinion are tempted to blur the distinction. Our system promises to college students as to everyone else that they may have their say, and when it breaks that promise it gives aid and comfort to those who say that it is a sham."[1]

MEDIA CREDITS

Notes

3. Finding Our Feet

1. Editors, "Rainbow Gets Girls Ready for Life," The International Order of the Rainbow for Girls, https://gorainbow.org.

2. Brown v. Board of Education of Topeka, 347 US 483 (1954), https://supreme.justia.com/cases/federal/us.

5. Crossing State Lines

1. *Today in Civil Liberties History*, "Fire Hoses and Police Dogs Attack Birmingham Civil Rights Demonstrators," May 3, 1963 , https://todayinclh.com.

2. Karen Grigsby Bates, "Trials & Transformation: Myrlie Evers' 30-Year Fight to Convict Medgar's Accused Killer," *Emerge 02 1994: 35. ProQuest*, May 27, 2017.

3. Editors, "NAACP Evers Biography," Archived from the original on October 4, 2013. Retrieved June 13, 2013, https://www.naacp.org/pages/naacp-history-medgar-evers.

4. "Six Dead After Church Bombing," *The Washington Post*, United Press International, September 16, 1963, Retrieved May 27, 2019.

5. *Warren Commission*, "The President's Commission on the Assassination of President Kennedy," September 24, 1964.

6. "Essay: Autopsy on the Warren Commission," *Time Magazine*, September 16, 1966, Archived from the original on November 4, 2012.

https://time.com/archive/6630223/essay-autopsy-on-the-warren-commission.

6. YANKEE GO HOME!

1. Dr. Martin Luther King, Jr., "Letter from Birmingham Jail," April 16, 1963.

7. THE FIGHT FOR JUSTICE

1. "Low-Income Families & Unrelated Individuals in the United States: 1963" (United States Census), June 18, 1965 Report Number P60-45.

2. "Lyndon B. Johnson, Inaugural Address, January 8, 1964," Cited in https://www.infoplease.com/primary-sources.

3. George C. Wallace, "The 1963 Inaugural Address of Governor George C. Wallace," Alabama Department of Archives and History. Retrieved January 2, 2009.

4. General Article: "Murder in Mississippi," *American Experience, PBS.* Retrieved November 14, 2016, https://www.pbs.org/wgbhamericanexperince/features/freedomsummer-murder/.

5. *Encyclopedia Britannica,* "Malcolm X, American Muslim Leader," by Lawrence A. Mamiya, updated July 28, 2025, https://www.britannica.com/biography/Malcolm-X.

6. Ibid.

7. Ibid.

8. Jonah Bromwell, Ashley Southall, and Troy Clausen, "56 Years Ago, He Shot Malcolm X. Now He Lives Quietly in Brooklyn." *The New York Times,* November 22, 2021.

9. Marable, Manning, *Malcolm X: A Life of Reinvention,* New York: Viking, 2011. *ISBN 978-0-670-02220-5.*

10. James Queally, "Watts Riots: Traffic Stop Was the Spark that Ignited Days of Destruction in Watts Riots," *Los Angeles Times,* July 29, 2015.   https://www.latimes.com/local/lanow/la-me-ln-watts-riots-explainer.

11. Jill A. Edy, editor, "Watts Riots of 1965," https://www.u-s-history.com.

12. Michael Syzmanski, "How Legacy of Watts Riot Consumed, Ruined Man's Life," *Orlando News-Sentinel*, August 5, 1990.

13. *World Atlas Online*, "How Many Died in the March on Selma? https://www.worldatlas.com/articles/how-many-died-in-the-march-on-selma.html.

14. Ibid.

15. "Civil Rights Martyr Viola Liuzzo," International Brotherhood of Teamsters, *Teamsters*, March 11, 2010, Retrieved March 28, 2012, https://teamster.org/2013/03/civil-rights-martyr-viola-liuzzo-0.

16. Sylvia Ellis, *Freedom's Pragmatist: Lyndon Johnson and Civil Rights*, (University Press of Florida), p. 203-204: "March 13,1965 Press Conference at the White House," The Miller Center, the University of Virginia, 2013.

17. President Lyndon Johnson's Speech to Congress on Voting Rights, March 15, 1965, *The Center for Legislative Archives*, https://www.archives.gov/legislative.

18. World Atlas, Ibid.

19. James M. Lindsay, "The Water's Edge Remembers: The First Combat Troops Arrive in Vietnam," Blog Post, March 8, 2015, *The Vietnam War in Forty Quotes*, Council on Foreign Relations, https://www.cfr.org.

20. Joshua Bloom and Waldo E. Martin Jr., *Black against Empire: The History and Politics of the Black Panther Party* (Berkeley: University of California Press, 2013), 313.

21. Editors, "Vietnam War: 1964-1975," *Stories of War*, https://aavmwny.org. (African American Veterans Monument).

22. Editors, "Black History and the Vietnam War, a Story," *African American Registry*, June 20, 1967, https://aaregistry.org/story/black-history-in-the-vietnam-war.

23. Warren W. Norton, letter to the editor *Johnson City Press-Chronicle*, May 16, 1967.

24., "Flag Desecration Act, H.R. 10480," and "Flag Protection Acts of 1968 and 1989," *The First Amendment Encyclopedia*, https://mtsu.edu, 2009.

25. Texas v. Johnson, 491 U.S. 397 (1989).

26. United States v. Eichman 496 U. S. 310 (1990).

27. "Elysian Park Love-in, March 26, 1967," *am on the radio*, Retrieved 7 December 2021.

28. Traqina Quarks Emeka, "Detroit Riots of 1967," *Encyclopedia Britannica*, last updated July, 2023, https://www.britannica.com/event-Detroit-Riot-of-1967.

29. Tabitha Wang, "Detroit Race Riot, (1967)," *Black Past*, July 3, 2008, https://www.blackpast.org/african-american-history/detroit.

30. Collette Coleman, "The 1968 Sanitation Workers' Strike that Drew Martin Luther King to Memphis," https://www.history,com/news/sanitation-workers-strike-memphis, (Sage Publications, updated May 18, 2023).

31. Livia Gershon, "How the Memphis Sanitation Strike Changed History," *JSTORDAILY* https://www.jstordaily.org, February 9, 2018.

32. Coleman, Ibid.

33. Coleman, Ibid.

34. Michael Eric Dyson, *April 4, 1968: Martin Luther King, Jr.'s Death and How It Changed America*, (New York: Basic Civitas Books, 2008).

35. "James Earl Ray, Suspect in Martin Luther King Assassination," *This Day in History*, June 8, 1968, https://www.history.com/this-day-in-history/june-8/king-assassination-suspect-arrested.

36. Richard Wolin, "Events of 1968: Significance and Facts," *Encyclopedia Britannica* https://britannica.com/events-of-May-1968.

37. Ang Cheng Guan, "Decision-making Leading to the Tet Offensive 1968: The Vietnamese Communist Perspective," *Journal of Contemporary History, 33 (3)*, Sage Publications, July 1998.

38. Editors, "The 1966 Pulitzer Prizes," *The Pulitzer Prizes*, https://www.pulitzer.org/prize-by-year/1966.

39. "Sirhan Felt Betrayed by Kennedy," *The New York Times, Associated Press.* February 20, 1989, from David Frost interview, Retrieved October 20, 2013.

40. Kathleen Cleaver and George Katsiaficas, "To Disrupt, Discredit and Destroy: The FBI's Secret War against the Black Panther Party," *Liberation, Imagination and the Black Panther Party,* 2001, 92-13, https://www.lib.berkeley.edu.

41. Paul Krassner, *Confessions of a Raving, Unconfined Nut: Misadventures in the Counter-culture,* (Simon & Shuster, p. 156, 1994).

42. "The Day the Pentagon Was Supposed to Lift Off into Space," *American Heritage,* Archived from the original on December 19, 2005, Retrieved April 10, 2017.

43. Bruce A. Ragsdale, "The Chicago Seven: 1960s Radicalism in the Federal Courts," *Federal Judicial Center, 2008,* https://www.fjc.gov/history/famous/cases.

44. Andrea Park, "The Trial of the Chicago 7: What Happened to the Real-Life Defendants?" *Marie Claire,* Aug. 19, 2021.

8. CONVICTION COLLIDES WITH CONSEQUENCE

1. Ernest Seeman, What's Next? Appalachian Movement Press, ca. 1970.

2. Norton v. Discipline Committee of East Tennessee State University, F.2d 195.

3. Ibid.

4. Dean Blobaum, Chicago 1968 Democratic National Convention, https://www.chicago68.comS, 1995.

5. *History,* "Soviets Invade Czechoslovakia," February 9, 2010, Updated August 19, 2019, https://www.history.com/this-day-in-history/soviets-invade-czechoslovakia.

6. "Warring Democrats Face Floor Fights On 3 Fronts," *The Evening Independent,* St. Petersburg, Florida, p.8, August 26, 1968.

7. Alonzo L. Hamby, "1948 Democratic Convention," *Smithsonian Magazine,* August 2008, Archived from the original on January 1, 2014, Retrieved April 25, 2013.

8. Abraham Ribicoff, "Gestapo Tactics at 1968 Chicago Convention," Excerpt of speech nominating George McGovern for President, *History Channel* (audio), August 28, 1968, https://www.history.com/speeches.

9. Peggy McCarthy, "Ribicoff and Daley Head to Head," *The New York Times,* August 26, 1996, Sec. CN, p. 13, https://www.nytimes.com.

10. "Julian Bond Only Candidate for Vacant Post," *Rome News-Tribune,* Associated Press, February 6, 1966.

11. Arlinda Smith Broady, "Bond Denied Seat in State House, Triumphs a Year Later," *Atlanta Journal-Constitution,* January 7, 2015.

12. Rick Campbell, "The Whole World Was Watching—Chicago 1968, Part 4," *The Houston Chronicle,* August 30, 2008. Retrieved August 16, 2008.

13. Lewis L. Gould, *1968: The Election That Changed America,* (Chicago: Ivan R. Dee Publishing), 1993, pp. 142-150.

14. *Encyclopedia Britannica,* "United States Presidential Election of 1968," November 5, 1968, https://www.britannica.com/event/United-States-presidential-election-of-1968.

15. Federal Reporter, Second Series, 491 F.2d.   419. F2d 195. https://www.justia.com.

16. Gerald Squibb, "Squibbling," *Johnson City Press-Chronicle,* April 20, 1969.

17. Marietta Norton, letter to the editor, *Johnson City Press-Chronicle,* April 20, 1969.

18. *United States Courts,* "Facts and Case Summary–Tinker v. Des Moines," February 24, 1969, https://uscourts.gov/topics/administrative-office-us-courts.

19. *United States Courts,* Tinker v. Des Moines Independent Community School District 399 US, 503 https://www.uscourts.gov.,1969.

20. US Court of Appeals for the Sixth Circuit, 419 F.2d 195 (6th Cir. November 28, 1969).

21. Marjorie Hunter, *The New York Times,* September 13, 1968, p. 17.

22. Laura Kalman, *Abe Fortas: A Biography,* (Yale University Press, 1992).

23. Kalman, *Ibid.*

24. Carrie O'Brien, "Barter Theatre," *Encyclopedia Virginia Online,* accessed October 20, 2023.

25. Bryan Handwerk, "Snake Handlers Hang on in Appalachian Churches," *National Geographic News,* April 7, 2003, http://news.nationalgeographic.com/news/2003/04/0407_030407snakehan dlers2.html.

26. Amy Sonnie and Tracy James, "Hillbilly Nationalists, Urban Race Rebels and Black Power," *Community Organizing in Radical Times,* (Melville House Publishing, 2011).

27. Mike Gray, *The Murder of Fred Hampton,* http://Mike-Gray.org, Retrieved September 25, 2005.

28. Dave Roos, "The 1969 Raid that Killed Black Panther Fred Hampton," *History,* https://www.history.com/news/black-panther-fred-hampton-killing, January 29, 2021.

29. Ken Hechler, "Tony Boyle," *The West Virginia Encyclopedia,* September 26, 2012, https://www.wvencyclopedia.org/entries/601.

30. "The Fall of Tony Boyle," *Time,* September 17, 1973.

31. Kenneth J. Yablonski and Joseph A. Yablonski v. United Mine Workers of America et al., 466 F.2d 424, August 3, 1972.

32. Ben A. Franklin, "Rank and File Rebellion Stirs in Mine Union, Posing Threat to Lewis Legacy," *The New York Times,* June 13, 1969.

33. "Yablonski of U.M.W. Slain with Wife and Daughter," *The New York Times,* January 6, 1970. Retrieved May 31, 2023, https://www.nytimes.com/1970/01/06/archives/yablonski.

34. Joe Dalton, "The Yablonski Legacy," Review of Trevor Armbrister, *Act of Vengeance: The Yablonsky Murders and Their Solution,* (E.P. Dutton,

January 1975), reported in *the Harvard Crimson*, March 20, 1976, https://www.thecrimson.com/article/1976/3/20.

35. Trevor Armbrister, *Act of Vengeance: The Yablonsky Murders and Their Solution*, (E.P. Dutton, January 1975).

36. "The Yablonski Contract," *Time*, May 15, 1972.

37. Ben A. Franklin, "UMW Candidate Charges Beating; FBI to Investigate Alleged Attack on Yablonski," *The New York Times*, July 3, 1969, p. 16.

38. Jock Yablonski, "The Spotlight of Truth," Speech given in Beckley, West Virginia, July 13, 1969 and Grundy, Virginia, July 20, 1969).

39. "Bodies of Family Killed by United Mine Workers Found," *History*, January 5, 1970, https://www.history.com/this-day-in-history/January-5/the-united-mine-workers-killings.

40. Vince Guerreri, "Fifty years Ago, the Murder of Jock Yablonski Shocked the Labor Movement," *Smithsonian Magazine*, December 31, 2019.

41. "Jury Indicts Boyle in Yablonski Case," *The New York Times*, December 18, 1973, p. 14.

42. Gary Arnold, "'Harlan County': Ardent, Absorbing," *The Washington Post*, March 23, 1977), Retrieved September 8, 2020.

43. Pete Seeger, *Talking Union and Other Union Songs*, originally recorded in 1955.

44. Marianne Worthington, "Interview with Jack Wright," *Still Journal*, Fall 2009, https://www.stilljournal.net/jack-wright-interview.php.

45. Susan Brownmiller, *In Our Time: Memoir of a Revolution*, (New York: Dial Press), 2000. *ISBN 978-0-385-31486-2*.

46. *off our backs*, "Editorial Statement," Personal copies of Marietta Anderson and "Roz Payne's Sixties Archive," https://rozsixtiesunl.edu/items/show/732.html.

47. Megan Mitchell, "Vagabond Youth Led Earth Day Founder to Life of Peace," *The Denver Post*, retrieved January 17, 2013.

48. Walter Cronkite, "CBS News Special Report: A Question of Survival, April 22, 1970, *CBS News,*
https://www.cbsnews.com/news/earth-day-history-founder-gaylord-nelson, From the Archives: Earth Day Report.

49. Ibid.

50. *Norton v. Discipline Committee of East Tennessee State University* 399 US 106 (1970).

9. CHANGING PATHS

1. *Merriam-Webster*, "'Salon' Definition and Meaning,"
https://www.merriam-webster.com/dictionary/salon.

2. Alfred E. Lewis, "5 Held in Plot to Bug Democrats' Office Here," *The Washington Post,* June 18, 1972", Archived from the original on June 22, 2011, Retrieved December 28, 2017.

3. Marisa Lati, "Inside the Supreme Court Ruling that Made Nixon Turn over His Watergate Tapes," *The Washington Post,* October 3, 2019, https://enewspaper.latimes.com.

APPENDIX B.

1. David L. Hudson, Jr., "Norton v. Discipline Committee of East Tennessee State University 399 US 106 (1970)," Free Speech Center, https://firstamendment.mtsu.edu/article/norton-v-discipline-committee-of-east-tennessee-state-university/.

SELECTED BIBLIOGRAPHY

Books

Armbrister, Trevor. *Act of Vengeance: The Yablonsky Murders and Their Solution*. New York: E. P. Dutton, 1975.

Bloom, Joshua, and Waldo E. Martin, Jr. *Black against Empire: The History and Politics of the Black Panther Party*. University of California Press, 2013.

Dyson, Michael Eric. *April 4, 1968: Martin Luther King, Jr.'s Death and How It Changed America*. New York: Basic Civitas Books, 2008.

Gould, Lewis L. *1968: The Election That Changed America*. Chicago: Ivan R. Dee Publishing, 1993.

Krassner, Paul. *Confessions of a Raving, Unconfined Nut: Misadventures in the Counter-culture*. New York: Simon & Schuster, 1994.

Marable, Manning. *Malcolm X: A Life of Reinvention*. New York: Viking, 2011.

Sonnie, Amy, and Tracy James. *Hillbilly Nationalists, Urban Race Rebels and Black Power: Community Organizing in Radical Times*. Melville House Publishing, 2011.

Newspapers and Magazines

Bates, Karen Grigsby. "Trials & Transformation: Myrlie Evers' 30-Year Fight to Convict Medgar's Accused Killer." *Emerge*, February 1994, 35. ProQuest.

Campbell, Rick. "The Whole World Was Watching—Chicago 1968, Part 4." *The Houston Chronicle*, August 30, 2008.

Editor, "Six Dead After Church Bombing." *The Washington Post*, United Press International, September 16, 1963.

Franklin, Ben A. "Rank and File Rebellion Stirs in Mine Union, Posing Threat to Lewis Legacy." *The New York Times*, June 13, 1969.

———. "UMW Candidate Charges Beating; FBI to Investigate Alleged Attack on Yablonski." *The New York Times*, July 3, 1969.

Smith Broady, Arlinda. "Bond Denied Seat in State House, Triumphs a Year Later." *Atlanta Journal-Constitution*, January 7, 2015.

Websites and Digital Sources

Blobaum, Dean. *Chicago 1968 Democratic National Convention*. https://www.chicago68.com

Cleaver, Kathleen, and George Katsiaficas. "To Disrupt, Discredit and Destroy: The FBI's Secret War against the Black Panther Party." In *Liberation, Imagination and the Black Panther Party*, 92–113. 2001. https://www.lib.berkeley.edu

Coleman, Collette. "The 1968 Sanitation Workers' Strike that Drew Martin Luther King to Memphis." *History.com*,

updated May 18, 2023.
https://www.history.com/news/sanitation-workers-
strike-memphis

Editors. "Black History and the Vietnam War, a Story."
African American Registry, June 20, 1967.
https://aaregistry.org/story/black-history-in-the-
vietnam-war

———. "Fire Hoses and Police Dogs Attack Birmingham Civil
Right Demonstrators." *Today in Civil Liberties History*,
May 3, 1963. https://todayinclh.com

Edy, Jill A., ed. "Watts Riots of 1965." https://www.u-s-
history.com

Federal Judicial Center. Ragsdale, Bruce A. "The Chicago
Seven: 1960s Radicalism in the Federal Courts." 2008.
https://www.fjc.gov/history/famous/cases

Handwerk, Bryan. "Snake Handlers Hang on in Appalachian
Churches." *National Geographic News*, April 7, 2003.
http://news.nationalgeographic.com/news/2003/04/04
07_030407snakehandlers2.html

History.com Editors. "Bodies of Family Killed by United
Mine Workers Found." https://www.history.com-this-
day-in-history

Hudson, David L., Jr. "*Norton v. Discipline Committee of East
Tennessee State University* 399 US 106 (1970)." *Free
Speech Center*.
https://firstamendment.mtsu.edu/article/norton-v-
discipline-committee-of-east-tennessee-state-
university

Ramos, Mitzi, and Legal Information Institute. "Flag Desecration Act, H.R. 10480." *The First Amendment Encyclopedia*, 2009. https://mtsu.edu

Worthington, Marianne. "Interview with Jack Wright." *Still Journal*, Fall 2009. https://www.stilljournal.net/jack-wright-interview.php

Court Cases and Legal Documents

Tinker v. Des Moines Independent Community School District, 393 U.S. 503, https://www.uscourts.gov.,1969.

Brown v. Board of Education of Topeka, 347 U.S. 483 (1954). https://supreme.justia.com/cases/federal/us

Norton v. Discipline Committee of East Tennessee State University, 399 U.S. 106 (1970).

United States v. Eichman, 496 U.S. 310 (1990).

Texas v. Johnson, 491 U.S. 397 (1989).

Speeches and Primary Writings

King, Martin Luther, Jr. "Letter from Birmingham Jail." April 16, 1963.

ACKNOWLEDGEMENTS

Anyone who thinks a writer completes a book alone lives in denial, or has never finished one. A memoir might flow easily from brain to page for the likes of Doris Kearns Goodwin or Anne Lamott. But I asked, yea, begged, friends to read and reread drafts of this memoir. They made it better.

Many thanks flow out to former high school classmates and friends Glenda Wright Jackson and Yvette Leerskov Ehrlich, to other best of friends for decades Anna Spradlin, Margalee Pilkington Wright, Keith Williamson, and Charli Frederick, to Jack Wright, friend and compatriot from Pound, Virginia, and to Nancy Robinson, book lover and critic extraordinaire.

To Clare Crawford, kindest and most relevant critic in my experience, and to Charlotte Crawford, who can cite chapter and verse of Amazon's requirements for selling a book and knows the Chicago Manual of Style cover to cover, I appreciate you.

To my public school English teachers and debate coaches, particularly Elizabeth Vinaroff and David Blackim, respectively, I thank you for encouraging me to immerse myself in the subjects I loved.

Before moving to the Appalachian region, I held some notions about the people, terrain, folklore, and history. Many resources were available to acquaint me with aspects of the culture and history. Here are some that still resonate with me:

Burton, Thomas G. *Serpent-Handling Believers*. Knoxville: University of Tennessee Press, 1993.

Caudill, Harry M. *Night Comes to the Cumberlands*. Boston: Little, Brown, and Company, January 1963.

Lewis, Helen M., and Monica Appleby. *Mountain Sisters: From Convent to Community in Appalachia*. Lexington: The University Press of Kentucky, 2003.

Rasmussen, Jeanne. *Collection*. East Tennessee State University: Archives of Appalachia. Identifier: AppMs-0355, 1949-2009.

Seeman, Elizabeth. *In the Arms of the Mountain*. New York City: Crown Publishers, March 22, 1961.

Any books or articles about East Tennessee and Southwest Virginia written prior to 1980 will be good resources for interested readers.

I am proud to be included in the galaxy of fine books Post Rock Press has published.

And, as always, to my entertaining brother Mike, I send special thanks for helping me maintain a sense of humor throughout the process.

The cheerleaders were many. Rah! Rah!

ABOUT THE AUTHOR

Marietta Anderson is a seasoned communicator whose career has spanned politics, education, sales, corporate communications, and entrepreneurship. Her journey has taken her from the heartland of Kansas to the liberal East Coast and the conservative South, immersing her in the social and political currents of the 1960s and 1970s. Along the way, she experienced civil rights marches, antiwar protests, shifting gender roles, and the quiet battles of everyday people. *Rebel Heart*, her debut book, draws on these turbulent years—and the personal betrayals that shaped her resilience. Marietta lives in Wichita, where she continues to reflect, write, and tell the stories that matter.